TABOO TUNES

A History of Banned

Bands & Censored Songs

by Peter Blecha

Published by Backbeat Books
600 Harrison Street, San Francisco, CA 94107
www.backbeatbooks.com
e-mail: books@musicplayer.com

An imprint of CMP Information
Publishers of *Guitar Player*, *Bass Player*, *Keyboard*, and *EQ* magazines

CMP
United Business Media

Distributed to the book trade in the US and Canada by
Publishers Group West, 1700 Fourth Street, Berkeley, CA 94710

Distributed to the music trade in the US and Canada by
Hal Leonard Publishing, P.O. Box 13819, Milwaukee, WI 53213

Cover design by Richard Leeds - BigWigDesign.com
Cover Illustration by David Michael Beck
Composition by Michael Cutter

Photo Credits
Getty Images: page 93
Corbis: pages 43, 75, and 148

Library of Congress Cataloging-in-Publication Data

Blecha, Peter.
    Taboo tunes : a history of banned bands and censored songs / by Peter Blecha.
    p. cm.
  Includes bibliographical references (p.) and index.
  ISBN 0-87930-792-7 (alk. paper)
  1. Music—Censorship—History. 2. Music—Social aspects. I. Title.

ML3916.B54 2004
303.3'76—dc22   2003024260
Printed in the United States of America

04 05 06 07 08   5 4 3 2 1

Contents

Foreword
Ring, Ring Goes the Bell...

by Krist Novoselic

I n the mid-'50s, rock 'n' roll hit the mainstream with the Bill Haley and His Comets single "Rock Around the Clock." Later on, Bob Dylan sang "the times they are a-changin'." Public Enemy told us "what time it is."

The beat of popular music sets the pulse of its time. At its most conscious, music is the alarm clock—or early warning system. The Powers That Be all too often respond to the sound of the bell rather than the brushfire triggering the alarm. (They habitually run to the firehouse thinking that turning off the bell will solve the problem.)

Censorship is founded in ignorance, denial, and opportunism. The ignorant fail to recognize the distress call. They believe killing the messenger will maintain their comfort, which is padded with denial. The opportunists kill the messenger to use the corpse as a pedestal. From such heights, they wax on about how they work to save our children from nothing less than certain doom.

Corruption, lack of democracy, and a pro-Establishment and subdued media plague our United States. This situation serves the ruling elite well. The scapegoat is one of the veils our corrupt elites hide behind. Complicit politicians, religious leaders, moral authorities—whoever—are all unmasked by the sound of the alarm bell. Just as music will forever change form into different styles and sounds, and as dependably as a clock's hand passes twelve, you can always count on the censors among us to divert attention from themselves, and the actual causes of our social ills, and point the finger of blame toward popular music. Fundamentally, we have to recognize that powerful music speaks to people in a way the censor can't—and having a history of controversial music like *Taboo Tunes* at hand makes this realization most clear.

Krist Novoselic is the founder of www.fixour.us and JAMPAC (Joint Artists and Music Promotions Political Actions Committee), and is the former bassist for Nirvana.

A Prefatory Note

At root, it is a story as old as Eve and the apple. In that ancient tale, humans are tempted by the "fruit of knowledge" forbidden them by the ultimate authority figure, God. In modern times that knowledge more likely comes in the form of a song, a book, a movie, or a public speech—and when it is placed off limits by powerful social and/or political authorities, that heavy-handed act is commonly known as censorship.

All censorship incidents are the result of cultural or political tensions, and they often serve as a means by which the powerful choose to impose their sensibilities upon those who lack power. *Taboo Tunes* traces how, in America and many places around the world, scapegoat-seeking authorities have periodically asserted that music is the *cause*—rather than a reflection—of social disorder. A key to understanding why music has so often been attacked by politicians is recognizing the intrinsic power that songs have to suggest new and different ideas to people. It is this factor—music's ability to transmit unauthorized and unregulated notions—that society's leaders have feared.

History teaches us when a citizenry's freedom to publicly express unapproved thoughts is curtailed—and/or their ability to access information is stymied—that limitation has had a deleterious impact, whether it is in some Third World dictatorship, or even the democratic United States of America. Because we are a diverse, pluralistic nation largely formed by immigrants of far-flung origins who arrived here with varied beliefs and cultural practices, the USA has *always* had a built-in dynamic of cultural tension. And part of that tension arises because our society, like others, is structured with not only an established body of written law, but unwritten social codes as well. Loosely meshed, these systems help govern the boundaries of acceptability—those elusive lines often referred to as community standards—for a majority of mainstream Americans.

Fortunately, the diverse racial, ethnic, religious, generational, and political subgroups within our society have generally found ways to coexist—by *agreeing to disagree* on some issues and maintaining a certain respect for each other based on a shared commitment to be fellow members of the same great democratic nation. On occasion, however, that generous spirit of inclusion has failed us, and opposing factions have engaged in cultural skirmishes. Music has often been a casualty on the front lines of those battles. History indicates that social conservatives have displayed a tendency to object to certain topics such as sexuality, the challenging of authority, intoxication, the supernatural, and others in songs, while social liberals have—albeit on *far* fewer occasions—challenged lyrics invoking violent, racist, and sexist imagery, along with other discriminatory stereotypes. So, here we have worldviews emanating from two polar opposites of the political spectrum—and each has had an impact on free musical expression.

Most censorship incidents have been sparked by the accidental exposure of the "wrong" idea to the "wrong" person at the "wrong" time. Lots of folks just seem to have forgotten where the Off button is on their radios and TVs—with the all-too-frequent result being that an offended party's discomfort over some song escalates to a ridiculous level. There is a critical point here—and one that the moral guardians of every stripe have consistently failed to grasp: in America literally *no one* is "in charge." In fact, any individual can easily find cause to disapprove of anyone else's ideas, opinions, beliefs, or lifestyles. The key opportunity for citizens who disagree with an idea is to counter it with an opposing, and potentially superior, one. If you are factually correct—and your opponents are committed to open-mindedness—your insights will, in the marketplace of ideas, trump the objectionable notion through logic and reason. Debate is about the only legal way of conquering a "wrong" idea. Granted, this social arrangement is not pleasant for everyone at all times, but, in fact, freedom of expression *is* protected by the law of the land. Indeed, the US Constitution's First Amendment was effectively designed to safeguard "bad" taste and "wrong" ideas—it exists to shield the minority from the tyranny of the majority. It is the concept that democracy cannot flourish without the free flow of ideas that is the real beauty and strength of our system.

For all the boilerplate blather we hear about the vaunted unity of the American people, the fact is, we *do* differ on matters of great substance. Opinions are in conflict. The nation is plainly divided on critical policy issues. To its great credit, our society allows for serious disagreement amongst its peoples. We have time-proven ways of registering where we differ on various matters. Some squabbles find adequate venting through beer-hall debates, letters to newspaper editors, or call-ins to talk radio shows. Other grievances merit more organized protest like the signing of petitions. Still others though—those which seek to address our most serious and stubborn social conflicts— result in street marches, boycotts, and picket lines.

It is when people take their personal objections about something to the *next* level—pressuring cops, congress, or the courts to restrict or suppress the offending item to the extent that other citizens no longer even have a choice of whether to access it or not—that we have a genuine problem at hand. A problem called censorship.

Taboo Tunes recounts the rich history surrounding controversial music and the various attempts to control it. It seeks to reveal the patterns of censorial behavior which have occurred and reoccurred throughout time. By surveying this historical landscape it is hoped that we can gain a more informed understanding of how crusades to ban music—usually in the guise of "protecting society"—have been woefully misguided, often destructive, occasionally comical, and remarkably unsuccessful.

Here my friends, is that story....

Peter Blecha

CHAPTER 1

Fear of Music

Their heads are fraught with all kinds of lascivious songs, filthy ballads, scirvy rhimes.

—Philip Stubbes, *Anatomie of Abuses*, 1583

The children have as their heroes banal, drug and sex-ridden guttersnipes who foment rebellion not only against parents but against all noble sentiments.

—Prof. Allan Bloom, University of Chicago, 1983

'Round and 'round we go. Like an old skipping record, the "this is the end of civilization as we know it" refrain has been sung over and over again by various societies' moral watchdogs. It seems as if some things *never* change—and so even early complaints like Mr. Stubbes's classic 16th-century rant ring a perfectly familiar note. And that is because even today various busybodies, bullies, and crusaders carry the torch as his modern-day counterparts. Then as now, it is often the arts that the censorious find to be a ripe target, and in so doing, they habitually trap themselves into making the ludicrous case that art (or songs, or dance steps) are the *cause* of other terrible social ills.

Mind you, it is not just prudes, philosophers, and fire and brimstone–spewing preachers who insist that overly permissive moral values among the young result in the "fraying of the national fabric." Even some of history's keenest thinkers have been susceptible to this fear. In the fourth century BC, the Greek sage Plato warned the politicians of his day that the government needed to be wary of poets who were corrupting the youth by teaching false ideas. And even though another of his contemporary sages, Socrates, contributed to defining what would later be called the "generation gap" by bemoaning the disrespectful younger generation, he was later charged with "corrupting the young" himself—a conviction that led to the forced drinking of poisonous hemlock.

While it is natural that parents keep their eyes peeled for early signs of defiance in their offspring, it is rather more disconcerting when politicians take up speechifying about some perceived increase in social disorder. This sort of hysterical hand-wringing by officials is often intended to mask a hidden agenda of forcing their narrow views on the world. And a key tool they often use is cultural censorship.

Censorship—the act or practice of supervising the manners or morality of others—is a seemingly irresistible impulse that drives the censors' attempts to control other people's behavior, expression of artistic concepts, or political ideas. And make no mistake, *ideas*—and the efforts by authorities to suppress them—are at the heart of the matter here. Authoritarians essentially resent the fact that new and different notions can be transmitted through art, and the pattern of attempting to control and contain such ideas—be they of a literary, musical, political, scientific, or other nature—is a long and rich one.

Authorities in the totalitarian Chinese Qin dynasty (221–206 BC) understood that to maintain firm control over the populace they needed to restrict the public's access to various forms of art and literature. Music was condemned as a "wasteful" pastime and nearly all musical instruments, songbooks, and manuscripts were ordered destroyed—a culturally tragic purge capped by the torching of the entire imperial archives. Ruining physical materials is but one part of the problem. The question of what to do with uppity songsters who resisted such taming was answered a full two centuries earlier, by leaders of the Roman Republic who created the position of the Censor, whose job description encompassed conducting the census and, presumably in his spare time, monitoring and regulating public morals. And thus, the mere singing of insulting or "evil" songs came to be designated as a disruption of the public order—infractions specifically noted (in the 450 BC legal code of the Twelve Tables) as meriting the punishment of death by clubbing. With such power being so harshly wielded, some Romans "saw the inherent danger of the office, and posed the very pertinent question: *Quis custodiet ipsos custodes?* (Who guards the custodians?)"—an inquiry that remains perfectly valid.

While musicians today rarely face such state-sanctioned murder as a disincentive to perform, there has long been a serious price to pay for crossing certain boundaries. Around the world artists who have dared to sing about such indiscreet topics as immoderate imbibing and joyful fornication, or who have had the temerity to challenge church doctrines, or espouse radical political rhetoric (or tweak ruling-class noses by ridiculing pompous politicians) have suffered severe punishment. In fact, even in recent years the death penalty has been applied to such musical transgressors in various lands.

The reason? Music is *powerful*.

History, myths, legends, and lore all back up that observation. Recall the old spiritual, "Joshua Fit de Battle of Jericho"—or the biblical story (Joshua 6:8–20) it retold? It was music (well, okay, actually the blowing of seven rams-horn trumpets) that brought the walls of the fortified city of Jericho tumbling down. In Greek mythology, the sea nymphs known as sirens sang in such a mesmerizing way that they lured sailing ships to crash upon rocky shores. In the 17th century the great English poet William Congreve said that "music hath charms to soothe the savage breast, to soften rocks, or bend a knotted oak."

Yes, music is a serious force to reckon with and, in fact, its harshest critics have been correct about one thing: music can be *dangerous*.

The revolutionary power of music was also recognized early on by Plato. Surveying the effects of music on a society, he, as an enthusiastic *advocate* of top-down censorship, cautioned in *The Republic* (circa 375 BC) that:

> Forms and rhythms in music are never altered without producing changes in the entire fabric of society and its most important political forms. It is here that we must be so careful, since these new forms creep in imperceptibly in the form of a seemingly harmless diversion. But little by little, this mischief becomes more and more familiar and spreads into our manners and pursuits. Then with gathering force it invades men's dealings with one another and goes on to attack the laws and the constitution with reckless impudence until it ends by overthrowing the whole structure of public and private life.

One of America's premier thinkers, Henry David Thoreau, was equally wary of music's potential impact on society, and pessimistically asserted in 1854 that like liquor, "even music may be intoxicating. Such apparently slight causes destroyed Greece and Rome, and will destroy England and America."

New musical forms do have the potential to affect culture and society—well beyond the social function of enabling people to mingle and dance, music can also make them think. While a number of its critics have contended that music literally brainwashes individuals, more temperate folks recognize songs have the ability to suggest new and different ideas to a listener. And *that* is what the control freaks cannot abide.

For example, Henry V, who became the king of England in AD 1413, promptly issued a royal decree that "no ditties shall be made or sung by minstrels or others"—likely over similar worries as articulated in a later (1543) ban there on the printing of song sheets that held the potential to "subtilly and craftily instruct the kings' people and especially the youth of the realm."

It is not uncommon for governments to develop such rationales for instituting control over forbidden forms of music, and censorship has regularly been seen in countries such as the Philippines, Vietnam, Thailand, Pakistan, Lebanon, Australia, Singapore, Trinidad, Bermuda, Puerto Rico, Cuba, Uruguay, Paraguay, Peru, Mexico, Bulgaria, Sweden, Bavaria, Zaire, Mauritania, Sierra Leone, Kenya, Ethiopia, Tibet, Bhutan, and Canada.

In the former Soviet Union, for example, music, musicians, and music fans alike were repressed for decades. The Communist Party's Central Committee once vilified several of the country's top classical music composers by describing their creations as "confused, neuropathological combinations that transform music into cacophony, into a chaotic conglomeration of sounds." Later on, Politburo member Constantin Chernenko railed that rock 'n' roll music was part of "an arsenal of subversive weapons aimed at undermining the commitment of young Russians to Communist ideology." The Beatles' music in particular was considered the "propaganda of an alien ideology." As late as 1986 Soviet leaders imposed a ban on any music that "depicts our life in a distorted way and makes propaganda for ideals and attitudes foreign to our society." Simultaneously, 41 rock bands were singled out for strict performance bans—as were their counterparts in Yugoslavia, Poland, and other nations within the Soviet political sphere. On their 1958 tour through East Germany, Bill Haley and His Comets didn't fare too well after drawing the unwanted attention of the minister of defense, who suspected that "it was Haley's mission to engender fanatical, hysterical, enthusiasm among German youth and lead them into a mass grave with rock and roll." Authorities in Spain canceled that same Haley tour after just one show. Czechoslovakia received some well-deserved international media coverage when they began persecuting a prominent rock band, the Plastic People of the Universe, in 1976. That year, and again in 1982, its members were imprisoned, and/or forcibly exiled, for their "anti-state" comments. In 1985 the authorities in Hungary imprisoned members of Coitus Punk Group (CPG) after objecting to an anti–nuclear weapons song.

Since its founding in 1948, Israel has had an informal ban on the performance or airing of music by Richard Wagner because the composer's early anti-Semitic writings had helped shape Adolph Hitler's views and the Nazi leader had adopted Wagner's music as the official soundtrack of his Third Reich. In more recent years Israeli authorities have cracked down on the ethnic culture of their Palestinian Arab population by various means, including canceling concerts, banning songs from radio, rounding up music sellers, and requiring that certain musicians not perform without formal security clearances.

Japan's initial reaction to rock 'n' roll's invasion was to cancel concert tours (by the Beach Boys, the Ventures, and the Astronauts), ban TV broadcasts of the music, threaten to ban electric guitars outright, raid dances under the power of the new Act to Control Business which May Affect Public Morals, ban objectionable groups (e.g., long-haired ones) from the state radio network, NHK, and expel students caught enjoying bands who were listed as being dangerous. China—a country that viewed the music as ideologically suspect and didn't allow an indigenous rock scene to develop until the late '80s—still tightly reins in its music industry. The work of musicians is monitored and guided (even songs simply dealing with "romantic love" or "personal feelings" are forbidden), police selectively harass nightclubs, and during a Chinese Communist Party initiative of the late 1980s called the Anti-Bourgeois Liberalization Campaign, artists who rebelled were identified, targeted, and isolated through performance restrictions. Though popular underground artists created an entire body of work in support of the pro-democracy movement in the spring of 1989, the music was no match for the People's Liberation Army's bloody crackdown at Tiananmen Square on June 4. During and after the Korean War, North Korea purged numerous song forms and even certain musical instruments—including a traditional long-stringed zither called the *kŏmun'go*—that the leadership felt were tainted by past associations with "elites." Years later, South Korea's Art and Culture Ethics Board, which was formed in 1966, produced a list of 261 "mind-numbing" rock songs that were banned outright—they even went so far as to decree that "entertainers who wear outfits which may harm the sound emotional development of youth will be banned."

The regime founded in South Africa in 1948 that instituted apartheid censored music indiscriminately for nearly half a century—particularly songs whose lyrics included words like "peace" or "power." In the '80s Nigeria outlawed independent radio and imprisoned their nation's most popular musician, Fela Anikulapo Kuti. Simon and Garfunkel's 1970 hit "Cecilia" was banned in Malawi in the '80s because the public was singing bawdy new variations on the song's lyrics that poked fun at President Banda and his mistress, Cecilia. Egypt outlawed rock 'n' roll outright in 1957, and four decades later launched a campaign against youthful heavy metal fans that resulted in nightclub raids and roundups. In the '60s President Sukarno of Indonesia outlawed Beatlemania because it was "a form of mental disease," and in 2003 Islamic authorities there urged the banning of dance performances by a young new star, declaring that her dancing "is an affront to morality and could lead to an increase in sex crimes." Malaysia's forthrightly named Censorship Board routinely bans songs and music videos for such infractions as the showing of "singers sporting long hair and mop tops, wearing earrings and bangles and playing black metal music." In India the Bombay Police Act, which forbade the "public utterances of cries, singing of songs, playing of music," was harshly enforced in 1997 in an effort to quell political protests.

The military junta that took over Argentina in 1976 not only "disappeared" thousands of young people, it also repressed youth music by tear gassing theaters during concerts and rounding up hundreds of attendees at a time, and it reportedly leaned on halls to desist from booking further shows. Under the CIA-supported dictatorship of General Augusto Pinochet (1973–90), Chile instituted strict censorship and banned entire forms of music and instruments, "disappeared" thousands of liberals, and murdered the nation's preeminent folk-protest singer, Victor Jara—who had once said: "The authentic revolutionary should be behind the guitar, so that the guitar becomes an instrument of struggle, so that it can also shoot like a gun." For two decades under a military dictatorship that began ruling in 1969, Brazil banned imported and indigenous popular music. In 1983 the military junta in Guatemala forced that nation's radio stations to abandon their formats and to begin airing nothing but martial music. Corrupt police in Jamaica have long conducted surveillance on popular dance halls, harassing patrons and exacting bribes, and at least three politically active reggae artists have been killed there by the police (or mysterious forces) since 1983.

Italy has a constitutional ban on Mafia-related songs, which are known as *canto di malavita* ("songs of a life of crime"). The military junta that in 1967 took power in Greece not only jailed and tortured its nation's most-beloved composer, Mikis Theodorakis, it also denounced all rock musicians, stating that "the state cannot allow them to set as its aim the corruption of society…. It will stop them and stamp them out to protect both society and art." In France in 1997 a court sentenced two rappers, Kool Shen and Joey Starr, to six-month prison terms for having described police as "fascists" at a concert. In 2003 new "crime-fighting" measures proposed by France's so-called security czar, and passed by the national assembly, included a law that would impose an $8,000 fine and eight months in prison for "mocking" the national anthem. In 2001 the prime minister of Cambodia ordered thousands of nightclubs, discotheques, and karaoke parlors closed in a nationwide crackdown on vice—even going to the extreme of threatening them with destruction by military tanks. Repression of the Kurdish people by the authoritarian regime in Turkey includes a ban on their traditional music.

In addition, various traditionalist Muslim countries, including Saudi Arabia, Jordan, the Sudan, and Algeria, have been brutal to pop music *fans*. Following the 1979 fundamentalist revolution in Iran, the new regime's Center for the Campaign Against Sin attacked rock music as an "immoral hobby" and banned the sale of westernized (secular) music, and the Organization for the Promotion of Virtue and Prevention of Vice was established with the authority to enter private homes to confiscate outlawed materials.

Without a doubt though, the starkest example of a thoroughly brutal anti-music policy was the one imposed on Afghanistan by an unimaginably conservative coalition of religious zealots—the now-infamous Taliban regime. After overtaking the capital city of Kabul in 1996, these ultraconservative nutcases imposed harsh cultural restrictions on the people—beginning with the barring of women singing in public—using religious decrees (or *fatwas*) enforced by the new Ministry of Justice's Department for the Promotion of Virtue and Elimination of Vice. All forms of modernity—including the use of radio, TV, the Internet, video players, film projectors, or secular music—were strictly outlawed, and the Taliban immediately began to display their disdain for westernized culture by draping trees with lengths of magnetic tape that had been ripped from confiscated music cassettes. Some musicians were reportedly so intimidated that they burned their beloved instruments, and music fans buried their cassettes and CDs in their backyards. One cleric explained that "according to Islam, one of the worst sins is to encroach on a person's consciousness. When someone listens to music, his state of mind changes." Music was considered to be so distracting from holy thoughts that the ancient and widely popular Afghan practice of keeping caged songbirds in the home was banned because of the pretty melodies they provide. The ringing of bells or chimes was outlawed. Even *humming* a tune to oneself was a risky gamble. Transgressors faced potential punishments that included severe beatings, imprisonment, and public executions.

This international roster of shame certainly gives one pause. While citizens of the United States can be proud that we've never sunk as low as most of those nations, we ought also be humble enough to acknowledge that the US *does* in fact have a blemished track record on censorship issues. While American society has thus far escaped the worst sorts of governmental intrusions, our own "secret police"—the Federal Bureau of Investigation—does have a long and well-documented history of illegally targeting musicians for surveillance.

While cultural activities are closely monitored and officially regulated by their respective governments in many countries, it remains unlikely that the US government will ever be allowed to grossly overstep its authority by, for example, generating a list of officially censored songs. The main reason—in addition to the strong free speech protections provided by the Bill of Rights—is a fairly effective (albeit informal) system of censorship that is *already* established here.

Existing not as a list of rigidly restrictive rules imposed by politicians and enforced by bureaucrats, the American system is instead based on a process comprising the everyday decisions made by artists, the record and radio industry, and retailers. It is not, however, a toothless system, and punishment for artists who cross the line is meted out in our own capitalistic terms. The price exacted for these infractions often amounts to some form of financial sacrifice. Rarely are cops brought in to bust heads; instead, the system itself turns the screws: a hostile reception from citizens groups, boycott threats, forfeiture of radio support, canceled concert tours, curtailed distribution, withdrawal of corporate promotional or advertising support. The key result: lost revenues.

Whether initially savvy about such business practices or not, most artists come to recognize the ground rules in due course. In practice, the first links in the "censorship" chain are the innumerable decisions that any artist makes in his/her creative efforts. In the process of composing, every musician makes countless choices regarding variables that include the song's potential chord structure, key, and melody contour. When crafting lyrics, the artist creates quite freely, yet some level of editing—potentially including considerations about current marketplace viability—occurs along the way, shaping the tenor, tone, and content of the lyrics. (This process, by way of example, is likely what transformed the early Beatles song "I Want To Hold Your Thing" [the original lyrics are in the archives of London's British Museum] into the rather-more-marketable worldwide hit, "I Want To Hold Your Hand.") Most such decisions are made out of personal taste and an artistic drive to express an idea in a particular way. It is when an artist makes "wrong" choices that things get interesting....

How things *really* work in America can best be illustrated by a few quick examples of artists taking controversial stands—and the "system" responding in kind. In 1989 a hard-line conservative group, the American Family Association, took exception to a new ad campaign by Pepsi-Cola that featured the pop/dance-music icon Madonna. They threatened a boycott based not on the ads themselves, but on overall objections to Madonna's penchant for mingling sacred and profane imagery in her songs and videos, such as "Like a Prayer," which depicted interracial mingling. The AFA's muscle-flexing was very effective and Madonna's contract was quickly severed.

Then in 1990 pop singer k.d. lang became the target of a boycott organized by the beef industry and a Nebraska radio station, who felt compelled to punish the "controversial" vegetarian (and lesbian) artist after she took a public stance against eating meat. However, the impact on her career was ultimately far less negative than intended—after all, how many beef-eating Nebraska rednecks were in her CD-buying demographic in the first place? Finally, a few years later, the powerful Ford Motor Company reportedly punished *The New Yorker* magazine for an article that quoted some naughty lyrics by the '90s industrial/goth/shock-rock band Nine Inch Nails. That misbehavior earned the esteemed publication six months of lost income from advertising withdrawn by the auto giant. In mid-2002 the rap star Ludacris came under attack by critics for his lyrics, and when conservative cable-TV host Bill O'Reilly called "for all responsible Americans to fight back and punish Pepsi" for featuring the hip-hopper in their summer ad campaign, the skittish soda pop company immediately yanked the piece—which had merely shown Ludacris performing

The most famous instance of a major LP being recalled and altered was the Beatles' '66 album Yesterday and Today—*which due to its gory original version has become known as the "Butcher Cover."*

and drinking pop—and officially apologized for offending anyone. O'Reilly, for one, was undoubtedly pleased with these dramatic results, but PepsiCo was about to learn that political pandering is a double-edged sword. Suddenly faced with the threat of a boycott campaign by the hip-hop community, the firm managed to wiggle off the hook—but only by donating millions of dollars to various charitable organizations.

And thus, corporate America—the major record companies included—has been made keenly aware of the power wielded by people acting in solidarity, and has learned to respond out of a sense of self-preservation—often, unfortunately, at the expense of an artist's freedom. In recent years especially, the labels have exerted an increasing degree of control over their artists' work, and as a result there have been more and more instances of albums being recalled and altered—often over concerns about the cover art rather than the music contained within. Perhaps *the* classic example is the instance in 1966 when Capitol Records rush-released the Beatles' *Yesterday and Today* album without giving much thought to the unusual cover image. The story goes that, being angered that the label had been "butchering" their

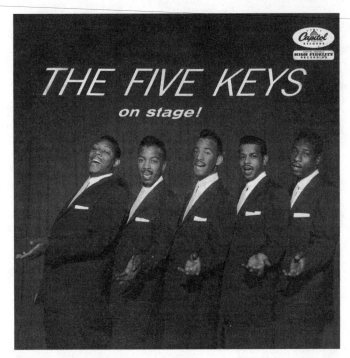

The 1957 *On Stage!* LP by doo-wop stars the Five Keys was recalled by Capitol Records after someone with a dirty mind imagined that the forefinger (seen at far left bottom) of lead balladeer Rudy West was a penis. Once the finger was airbrushed out, the LP was reissued.

work (by repackaging their original British albums for the American market in a way that juggled the songs into different, shorter, and *more* albums), the band provided a disturbing photo of themselves attired in bloody butchers smocks draped in raw animal organs. On second thought, Capitol recalled the LPs from retailers and distributors, literally slapped a new photo on the jackets, and reshipped them.

While the "butcher album" fiasco does nicely expose the gray area that exists between outright censorship and smart marketing—and it can be argued that most similar cases are really the latter—it was far from being the only time a label interceded and overruled an artist. Additional examples of the original choice for album-cover art being nixed include: 1957's *The Five Keys on Stage*, '67's *Moby Grape*, '68's *Electric Ladyland* (Jimi Hendrix) and *Beggars Banquet* (Rolling Stones), '69's *Blind Faith*, '70's *The Man Who Sold the World* and '74's *Diamond Dogs* (David Bowie), '79's *Lovedrive* (Scorpions), '89's *Appetite for Destruction* (Guns N' Roses), '90's *Ritual de lo Habitual* (Jane's Addiction), '93's *In Utero* (Nirvana), et cetera—which all were withdrawn and/or remarketed with altered graphics. For all practical purposes, the greatest incentive for the record industry to "censor" anything is probably the fear that some controversy might hurt their bottom line.

In response to corporate pressure to replace the original artwork of their 1990 hit album Ritual de lo Habitual, *Jane's Addiction replaced this cover with a minimal presentation of the First Amendment's free speech guarantee.*

Another example of the type of incident that occasionally has elsewhere been called censorship—a description that I would dispute—involves records like the Kinks' humorous 1970 hit "Lola." As originally recorded, the song included a lyrical snippet about how the "champagne" at some particular dive tastes just like "Coca Cola." Apparently pressure from the brand owner quickly forced the band to alter that phrase to the more generic "cherry cola" in subsequent pressings of the single. Although this was a fairly straightforward case of a corporation vigilantly acting to protect their legally protected trademark, some folks cried censorship—while others figured that the conservative company probably just had an aversion to being linked, lyrically, to a song about Lola: a transsexual ("I know I'm a man / *and so is* Lola"). (Whereas they apparently didn't object back in 1918 when an anti-Prohibition song—"Every Day Will Be Sunday When the Town Goes Dry"—included lyrics stating that "At the table d'hote with Lola they will serve us Coca Cola," or in 1948 when the Andrews Sisters celebrated, by drinking "Rum and Coca Cola," successive generations of native women selling their virtues to on-leave GIs ("...Both mother and daughter / workin' for the Yankee dollar..."), or in 1960 when their product was mentioned in Pat Boone's clean-cut take of "Call It Stormy Monday.")

One can only imagine the hellstorm that would have whipped down had the soda pop company been made aware of the Fugs' 1965 classic "Coca Cola Douche," or when the Rubber Dubber label issued a bootleg LP of a 1970 Jimi Hendrix concert with a blatantly trademark-infringing cover design. But in 1991 the Seattle grunge band TAD *did* run afoul of a carbonated sugar-water empire and was forced, at considerable expense, to change the cover art for their pro–drunk driving single "Jack Pepsi." Interestingly, in 1997 when the agit-prop audio-collage band Negativland—who'd already seen an earlier CD banned because of copyright lawsuits— issued their confrontational *DISPEPSI* CD (which directly dissed both the PepsiCo and Coca Cola companies by manipulating unlicensed samples from various old ad campaigns) nothing happened. It seems likely that the soda bigwigs figured that attacking *DISPEPSI* would only draw wider attention to its negative critique of their questionable corporate policies.

Copyright challenges did afflict some other bands that crossed big biz and then paid the price. In 1977 the Ramones' "Carbona Not Glue" was disappeared from their *Leave Home* album after trademark infringement claims by the named stain-removal product company; in 1992 the Melvins had to re-release the *Lysol* CD with that household cleanser's name removed from their cover art; and in 1995 the Converse company forced the Queers to desist from using a knock-off of their famous athletic shoe logo for promotional purposes—of course, it didn't help that the band had substituted the words "Fuck You" in place of the original "Chuck Taylor All Star" in the graphic. Attitude is important, though: back in 1973 Eastman Kodak's initial concerns about Paul Simon's usage of their word "Kodachrome" quickly gave way to an understanding of no-harm/no-foul, and he was left alone while the song became a nice (No. 2) hit. In recent years, trademark, copyright, and just about every other intellectual-property claim imaginable have increasingly been weaponized by corporations to silence the commentary of boundary-testing artists.

The other key facets of our unofficial censorship system are the distribution and retail marketing businesses. Whether considering a powerful-but-faceless megastore chain like Wal-Mart, or our friendly independent neighborhood record shop, one basic fact is that any rational company only stocks merchandise that it believes will interest its customer base. A similar, long-standing form of natural selection occurs in America's radio (and music-oriented cable TV) industries whereby stations have a music director who weeds through many new songs each week and selects relatively few—those recordings that will safely appeal to their clientele: the listening audience. It simply makes good business sense for radio (and MTV, VH-1, and CMT) programmers to identify songs (and/or videos) that fit their particular genre and format. Acknowledging this reality allows one to accept more peacefully that country/western (C&W) stations will opt for the Oak Ridge Boys every time over the Dead Boys, the Geto Boys, or the Beastie Boys; that classical stations logically program Ludwig van Beethoven rather than Camper van Beethoven, and that urban hip-hop and R&B stations will *never* embrace despicable old discs like the KKK label's "Why I Am a Klansman" (100% Americans) or "Nigger Hatin' Me" (Johnny Rebel).

These are the realities of the music industry, and while some free speech absolutists may resent the gatekeeper role that the retailers and corporate media have thus established, these stations have put their success as businesses first. Unfortunately, some very significant artistic and political ideas get shunted aside in the process. Controversial material is not highly regarded by your average station manager—indeed, a premium has been put on the bland and unthreatening. The ongoing consolidation of entertainment media in the hands of fewer and fewer megacorporations has resulted in a noticeable homogenization of radio content—and at the direct expense of the needs, tastes, and interests of various local/regional (or minority) communities.

A related and equally legitimate concern is that much of today's domestic cultural "censorship" is imposed not by outside political or religious forces, but rather from within the big record companies themselves. Now, whether or not those firms have any political agenda is debatable, but is there any other way to view the effect wrought by their ignoring and marginalizing of many so-called fringe or politically challenging artists than as a soft form of de facto censorship? If a mere half-dozen major labels control the majority of CD sales (as they do), don't their choices of which particular artists to sign and promote have an inordinate, and potentially dangerous, impact on the music (and ideas) that will reach the mainstream masses? And finally, with those few labels so tightly wedded to their vast parent companies, doesn't the possible risk of facing a conglomerate-wide boycott over issuing some controversial recording (see, for example, the Ice-T/Time Warner incident in Chapter 6) make them awfully vulnerable to organized pressure—and thus not a reliable conveyor of cutting-edge culture? Listen, any one of us may occasionally find ourselves irked by an idea (or song) we encounter. We all face the risk of being offended by *something* every time we leave the house. It's a simple truth that the arts encompass a broad range of expression. I as a music fan, for one, believe that most censorship campaigns throughout history got started because a certain person encountered something that wasn't even *intended* for them.

Diverse as they are, music and the other arts offer something for everybody —however, none of us will ever fully approve of everything our fellow citizens say, sing, read, or do. And so, citizens of a truly strong and just nation must agree to disagree once in a while. As long as people express themselves, other folks *will* take offense. The system of informal control is not foolproof, and that's because it relies on the judgment of individuals rather than official lists of *verboten* terms, grand jury indictments, or political inquisitions. So, while it cannot fully guarantee that any one individual's sensibilities will never be offended, all in all it serves its purpose reasonably well.

A significant hazard we face is when, in the guise of "protecting society," legitimate political expression is suppressed. *Billboard*, the record biz trade magazine, in response to the censorious goals of the conservative forces who began pushing for warning stickers on "questionable" recordings, once expressed serious concern about the threat to political discourse and free speech rights that labeling represents: "Even in cases where meaning is ambiguous, defending our children from bad thoughts can easily become a smokescreen for weeding out socially or politically oriented lyrics that are perceived to threaten the established order."

Yet that very thing has increasingly occurred in recent times. And rather than challenging those ideas head-on, censors have resorted to obscuring issues and skirting laws in their attempts to silence artists. Think about the case of that highly political '60s protest singer Phil Ochs, who saw his brilliant social satire, "Outside of a Small Circle of Friends," quashed for a mere mention of pot. Or the punk group the Sex Pistols, prosecuted for using the mildly crude term "bollocks" (Brit slang for "nonsense" or "bullshit") in their 1977 (No. 1 UK) debut album's title, *Never Mind the Bollocks Here's the Sex Pistols*. Or the politically articulate American punk band the Dead Kennedys, who were prosecuted on "pornography" charges based on a paper poster included in each *Frankenchrist* LP. In 1990 Professor Griff, a popular rapper (formerly with Public Enemy) who is admired by fans for consistently addressing *political* topics, had his solo recordings slandered as "totally obscene" and banned by retailers even though the tunes referred to *nothing* sexual or indecent.

Then there is the serious matter of politicians attempting to guide what songs we can be allowed to hear. It was apparently the accuracy of certain lyrics ("…We got CEO's makin' 200 times the workers' pay / But they'll fight like *hell* against raisin' the minimum wage…") in Iris Dement's "Wasteland of the Free," which, when aired by Florida's WMNF in 1998, reportedly inspired the state legislature to slash the public radio station's budget in recrimination.

It would seem that the greatest dangers our nation faces on the cultural front are not that some innocent may accidentally overhear a bawdy, boozy, sacrilegious, or "unpatriotic" song. Instead, we should be concerned that—in this era of ever-consolidating corporate media—less diversity of opinion and aesthetic taste are being given exposure, and that people seem so willing to undermine our civil society by habitually dragging the government and courts into every little squabble. Not only have such attempts to legislate other people's morality not worked historically, those efforts begin to edge toward downright undemocratic territory.

CHAPTER 2

Beat Crazy

Rock 'n' roll . . . is sexy music. It has something of the African tom tom and voodoo dance [about it.] It is deplorable. It is tribal. And it is from America. It follows rag-time, dixie, jazz, hot cha cha and boogie woogie, which surely originated in the jungle. We sometimes wonder whether it is the negro's revenge.

—*Daily Mail*, London, 1956

There is something in the BEAT of this music that fires up those who listen to it and releases primitive lusts within them. . . . Rock's incredible volume, coupled with screeching dissonance and the rhythmic beat of voodoo, form a battering ram that smashes the listener's mind and spirit.

—Jeff Godwin, 1988

BOOM Chuck, BOOM Chuck, BOOM Chuck, BOOM! Granted: the high decibel level of a driving drumbeat is a huge part of the "problem." But the matter clearly goes way beyond headache-inducing pulses of pounding percussion. In order to understand the violently negative reaction that music seems to periodically inspire, it might be worthwhile to consider the possible existence within humankind of a pathological, primal fear of unfamiliar rhythms.

History shows us that when a new rhythm is introduced into the music of a particular society, some folks will assuredly find it to be jarring to their sensibilities. But crabby seniors and other tradition-bound sticks-in-the-mud have not been alone in seeing the menace posed by young people's music. In fact other, wiser folks have detected serious societal threats lurking behind even minor innovations or changes in their culture's traditional "beats."

Just recall the sobering thought that the ancient Greek sage Plato tendered some 2,500 years ago: "Forms and rhythms in music are never altered without producing changes in the entire fabric of society." Or, how a thousand years later (1322 AD)

Pope John XXII issued a decree that banned the usage of descant (improvised high melodic lines) in church services. Another example of an innovative musical practice receiving a negative reception—and this time not by some authority figure, but rather by the people themselves—was in 1913 when fisticuffs broke out in a Paris theater at the debut of Igor Stravinsky's *Le Sacre du Printemps* (Rite of Spring). The altercation, which escalated into a riot that spilled out into the streets (and featured the rare sight of baton-wielding gendarmes thumping the heads of uptown arts patrons), was reportedly sparked by an audience shocked by the musical piece's then unheard of, and therefore extremely unsettling, rhythms.

America's own history provides examples of the power associated with new (or at least newly arrived) rhythms—and the concomitant threat those beats therefore posed to the Powers That Be. Surely a major thread within this long-standing sociocultural conflict is the race factor. From the time the transatlantic slave industry got rolling in the 1500s, American slave owners forbade the use of "talking drums" (and other African musical expressions and traditions), fearing that they would be used as communication tools to transmit subversive messages and fuel insurrection.

Music's ability to reinforce and sustain age-old cultural traditions was also not lost on governmental authorities in the 19th century, when the United States military undertook the forcible herding of much of the native population into regional reservations. Though the cultural practices of these peoples varied widely, the government's policy was basically one-size-fits-all, and the nations—once effectively contained—were informed that their former culture was discouraged if not outlawed, and in particular they were forbidden to express themselves through the singing of, or dancing to, their native songs (not to mention the additional bans on traditional dress, language, and religion). Thus, through official cultural genocide, untold numbers of hunting songs, love songs, healing songs, war songs, mourning songs, and others were likely forever lost.

At the end of the Civil War in 1864 a small number of bitter Confederates began forming various "underground" social organizations in order to keep the lost battles alive. "America for Americans" was the title of an anthem favored by the most feared of these violent cults, the American Knights of the Ku Klux Klan (KKK), and its title serves well to indicate what kind of motivations drove these hood-wearing night-riders to terrorize newly freed slave families (as well as Jews and Catholics). Dedicated to the separation and purity of the "white race," the Klansmen fancied themselves as good God-fearin' defenders of, in their own terms: virtue, white womanhood, and Christian values. As such, in their minds, the horrendous acts of barbarity they regularly committed were fully justified.

That same heartless mindset seems to have guided some of the poisonous responses to the emergence, in the late 19th century, of a new form of music: jazz.

Indeed, it hardly needs stating that a cruel, mean streak of raw racism runs deeply throughout most early negative critiques of the music, and the threat level that jazz apparently posed is indicated by the torrent of scorn heaped upon it by reactionary detractors back in the day. In 1899 one newspaper let loose with this censorious editorial: "A wave of vulgar, filthy and suggestive music has inundated the land with its obscene posturing, its lewd gestures. Our children, our young men and women, are continually exposed to the monotonous attrition of this vulgarizing music. It is artistically and morally depressing and should be suppressed by press and pulpit."

Today jazz is a highly honored art form that is welcomed in the world's finest concert halls, studied at universities, and widely lauded as "America's classical music." But not so long ago, jazz was seen by proper citizens as a dirty and debased back-alley abomination fit only for the street hustlers, gamblers, reefer den habitués, and ne'er-do-wells who frequented seedy dives down in the red light districts. Though its exact beginnings remain hazy, the term "jazz" was likely coined in the fabled brothels and booze parlors of New Orleans. Of those scandalous roots the snooty *Etude* magazine would once huff: "If the truth were known about the origin of 'Jazz' it would never be mentioned in polite society." This slang expression (which originally referred to the sex act) came to be applied to a new form of music, as well as its associated dance steps. It was only later that the genre's enemies applied the same word to the notion of generalized nonsense—you know, "all that jazz."

And in January 1900 *Etude* magazine published "Musical Impurity," a diatribe fulminating against the retailers who profited by foisting this jazz junk on the youth of America: "The counters of the music stores are loaded with this virulent poison which, in the form of a malarious epidemic, is finding its way into the homes and brains of youth to such an extent as to arouse one's suspicions of their sanity." In 1914 one particularly adamant foe of the music—especially its early ragtime incarnation—spewed forth, in the *Musical Observer*, a full-on anti-jazz call to arms: "Let us take a united stand against the Ragtime Evil as we would against bad literature, and horrors of war or intemperance and other socially destructive evils. . . . Avaunt with Ragtime rot! Let us purge America and Divine Art of Music from this polluting nuisance."

Though that "polluting nuisance" would eventually come to be admired for its unprecedented harmonic and rhythmic complexities, it was initially slammed as "syncopated savagery," and the entire genre was vilified just as mercilessly. Reactions to the music's growing popularity were incredibly hysterical—in 1921 one newspaper quoted a Dr. Maud Parker's learned observation that "jazz is a return to the primitive—to the savage who used music as a physical stimulant," and, furthermore, "jazz is a cross rhythm that carried far enough could so irritate the nervous system as to derange it entirely." Another doctor concurred, adding that "jazz is one of the greatest contributing factors to the recklessness of young people today." The

Christian and Missionary Alliance Conference's president claimed that due to jazz, "American girls of tender years are approaching jungle standards" Meanwhile, a teacher predicted that "if we permit our boys and girls to be exposed indefinitely to this pernicious influence, the harm that will result may tear to pieces our whole social fabric." A leader of the Calvary Baptist Church in New York City piled on, claiming that jazz was nothing less than "music of the savage, intellectual and spiritual debauchery, utter degradation." Around that time numerous towns (including Zion City, Illinois) banned public performances of the music altogether, while Chicago merely outlawed the playing of saxophones and trumpets after dark.

But it wasn't just the *playing* of jazz that aggravated the censorious—so too did the broadcasting of it. Even the famous electronics inventor and self-described "Father of Radio," Lee de Forest, once groused: "Why should anyone want to buy a radio? Nine-tenths of what one can hear is the continual drivel of second-rate jazz, [and] sickening crooning by degenerate sax players." In the '20s New York City's ad hoc Keep the Air Clean Sunday organization castigated radio station WMCA for airing jazz on the Sabbath. According to one source, these busybodies characterized WMCA's programming as "'degrading and defaming,' [and] the group launched a telephone campaign demanding that Sunday blue laws be enforced against popular music. Not only did their efforts fail, they resulted in a victory for freedom of the airwaves and the right to schedule music—jazz, classical, or whatever—when it best served a station and its listeners. Other crusading groups worried about young people becoming content to plop into soft chairs before loudspeakers. Schools and churches began forming glee clubs and choirs to combat the 'alarming and growing tendency.'" Attempting to clarify things, one professor asserted that jazz is "degenerate" because it "'expresses hysteria, incites idleness, revelry, dissipation, destruction, discord and chaos.'"

Apparently no matter what those darn kids chose to do, it was a problem: if they weren't just idly lounging about, then they were, well, dancing maniacally. Thus, in Cleveland, this fear of jazz led local leaders to adopt an extensive set of Rules and Regulations Governing Dance Halls around 1925, and Section 8 of City Ordinance No. 20456-A led off with this dandy: "Vulgar, noisy Jazz music is prohibited. Such music almost forces dancers to use jerky half-steps and invites immoral variations." Public dancing was an issue well before the wild fashions and immoderate imbibing of the Roaring '20s drew the wrath of the fuddy-duddies. It was the rise of the waltz as a popular dance step that riled up an opposition who railed and flailed in such publications as 1892's *From the Ballroom to Hell* (which included chapters like "From the Ball-Room to the Grave" and "Abandoned Women the Best Dancers"), 1904's *The Immorality of Modern Dances*, 1912's *From Dance Hall to White Slavery: The World's Greatest Tragedy*, and various pamphlets by the prolific Dr. R. A. Adams, including *Fighting the Ragtime Devil* and his damning *The Social Dance* of 1921.

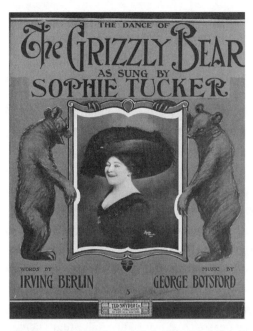

The cover of the 1910 sheet music for "The Grizzly Bear," one of the college crowd's "animal dance" songs that sparked a scandal in the early 1900s.

And much like the scandals that erupted long ago over that "reckless" new dance called the waltz, jazz dance steps too became a point of social contention. Around 1913 a number of New York City–based dance instructors—who had been quite successfully promoting old-school waltzes and schottisches—felt their livelihood was being threatened enough to come together and call for bans on new dances (as well as the halting of further publication of ragtime sheet music). And in time the censors enjoyed a few successes: A number of new dances—including the faddish "animal dances" (like the bunny hug, the turkey trot, the kangaroo hop, the camel walk, the lame duck, the chicken scratch, the raccoon, and the grizzly bear) and even the exotic tango—were formally outlawed by municipal morality codes enacted in various American cities.

In the Pacific Northwest—the area I am most familiar with and which can be seen as typical—the morality patrols were quite active. In Portland, Oregon, dancehalls were raided, dancers arrested, and trials held. In 1913 local headlines blared: "No More Tango and No More 'Wiggles'"—"Hugging Barred at Public Dances in Proposed Law"—"Dancing Position Is Deemed Menace"—"Dancehall Held Evil." [Note: It was also in Portland that the famed burlesque star and "hoochie coochie" dancer Sophie "The Last of the Red Hot Mamas" Tucker was hauled off to the local jail on indecency charges in 1916. That arrest was but one of three in her career—the first had been in 1910 for singing "The Dance of the Grizzly Bear"—and apparently was not an uncommon occupational hazard, as her peer, Mae West, also was jailed a time or two.] A press account on July 12, 1915, reported that "officers of Tunica County, Mississippi, have issued an order prohibiting young society folk from dancing a strange waltz. The dance was originated by Negro cotton pickers and is dubbed the 'boll weevil wiggle!' It is the combination of the grizzly bear, the chicken slide and a waltz."

A humorous incident in Bellingham, Washington, should have exposed the whole dance-ban trend as the ridiculous farce it was. Around 1913 local dance instructor H.O. Morrison was arrested at the Armory for doing a "four-step" dance move, when a city ordinance limited people to a "three-step." While being booked, he met the mayor and complained, asking, "What kind of laws do you have here that go against the laws of music?" The mayor showed him the rules, and then surprised Morrison by asking if he could serve as an expert witness in the prosecution of some others who'd been arrested for doing the bunny hug and the grizzly bear at a Socialist Hall dance. Morrison agreed, but actually had other ideas in mind. When the trial opened, Morrison requested of the presiding judge that a demonstration of the particular moves of the bunny hug be made. Granted the opportunity, he asked that two policemen do the demonstration. And then, just when the two clasped hands and went cheek-to-cheek, a newsman snapped a photo, and Morrison announced that the dance move they were doing was in fact the coatie park—a dance step *not* specifically outlawed—and the next day, that ridiculous image graced the front page of the local paper. But Morrison didn't stop there; he then sent a copy of Bellingham's many blue laws to a national newspaper that took an interest in the story, published the same photo, and even called the rather embarrassed judge for a quote. Ultimately the lunacy of the whole situation was clear and charges against the dancers were quietly dropped. On-campus college dances were particularly well-monitored, it seems. According to one source, at the University of Minnesota "a couple who were dancing in an objectionable fashion were given a card, distributed by the Women's Self-Government Association and the Association of Minnesota Upperclassmen, which read, 'We do not dance cheek-to-cheek, shimmy or dance other extreme dances. You Must Not. A second note will cause your public removal from the hall.'" And, "At Ohio State, an editorial entitled 'Watch Your Step' made this clear: 'Recent rumpus over dancing should make clear to students that they are being watched, constantly, closely and critically.'"

One particularly sexy new dance step, the tango (which was, early on, even banned in its place of origin, Argentina), was also attacked in America. In 1915 the Reverend Billy Sunday saw fit to aim his ire at women in particular and really took them to task: "On the ballroom floor you allow liberties to men that you never allow them elsewhere. You grant them liberties on the ballroom floor that if a man other than your husband would attempt them in your home and your husband would find you at it, he would have no trouble securing a divorce, and if he shot the man no jury in the world would convict him for it."

There were news reports of dancers being fined because "their Turkey Trots were interpreted by the courts as disorderly conduct." In another instance, fifteen working girls were fired from their jobs with the Philadelphia song publisher Curtis Publishing when they were caught doing the turkey trot—even though the dancing took place during their lunch break. Trying, one supposes, to console themselves a bit, dance teachers attending an annual meeting in 1919 solemnly "announced that jazz dancing was waning and soon jazz music would be a memory." One song of the era, 1913's "Anti-Ragtime Girl" went so far as to exalt an honorable gal who rejected any sort of new dance ("She don't do the Bunny Hug, nor dance the Grizzly

The 1913 tune "Anti Rag-Time Girl" celebrated a proper young woman who disdained up-tempo, danceable jazz music.

Bear / She hasn't learned the Turkey Trot / ... She can't tell a Tango from a Can Can or a Jig / ... She's my little Anti-Ragtime Girl").

In 1927 the London *Daily Mail* bemoaned the growth of the whole jazz fad, insisting that "Victims of the dancing craze multiply with the frequency of adapted jazz 'melodies.'" Another account of the era noted that "new steps replaced outlawed ones in rapid succession, however, as young Americans raced dance censors to the ballrooms. Recognizing the futility of the situation, authorities changed tactics and began regulating the dance halls rather than particular dances." The music's foes also tried the tactic of equating the music with chemical addictions. In 1921 some activist society ladies in Seattle declared that jazz "is a menace as serious as the narcotic menace and even worse than liquor." Indeed, one of their leaders—the music chairman of the General Federation of Women's Clubs—stated that "as dearly as she loved music, she would rather see it wiped out of existence than to have it succumb to jazz."

The war against venues that spread this "moral rot" by purveying liquor was spearheaded by various meddlesome organizations like the Anti-Saloon League and the Women's Christian Temperance Union, who stormed taverns and shattered whiskey kegs with axes. In Seattle, the First Presbyterian Church's Rev. Mark Matthews lent support to the movement with wonderfully hyperbolic invective against the saloon as a place that takes "your sweet innocent daughter, robs her of her virtue, and transforms her into a brazen, wanton harlot"—moreover, such a venue is "the most fiendish, corrupt, and hell-soaked institution that ever crawled out of the slime of the eternal pit." And just like the illicit booze that fueled America's wild partying before (and during) the Prohibition era, modern music was also regarded by some as a serious social menace. As early as 1912 one elitist, writing in *Musical America*, even equated the two, asserting about musical imbibers that "ragtime has dulled their taste for pure music just as intoxicants dull a drunkard's taste for pure water." The good Rev. Matthews gave no quarter to jazz either, asserting in 1921 that "jazz is an evidence of intellectual and moral degradation"; and around that same time a New York doctor issued a report associating the music with promiscuity, claiming that jazz "intoxicates like whisky" and "releases strong animal passions." Such, alas, was the intellectual level of the Prohibition "debate."

Then, in 1919, after a long, bitter, and intemperate propaganda campaign, the US Congress was successfully pressured into passing the 18th Amendment outlawing alcohol sales nationwide. In reality though, there would be little shortage of booze available under Prohibition—the new restrictions enabled criminal gangs to grab a monopoly over the now-illicit liquor biz. And during that decade-and-a-half experiment, the American public became generally *less* law abiding—making their own "bathtub gin" at home, acquiring it on the black market, or drinking it at "underground" speakeasy clubs.

Reason did finally prevail though, and Prohibition was repealed in 1933. But even with alcohol sales legal once again, the crusade against jazz didn't stop. One newspaper referred to college kids as "jazz inebriates," and on December 22, 1933, Congressman William A. Allen of West Seattle submitted his "Jazz Intoxication" measure (House Bill 194) to the Washington State Legislature. The intention was to establish a five-man statewide commission "to survey the havoc being wrought on society as a result of jazz intoxication." Furthermore, "If it be found that our people are becoming dangerously demented, confused, distracted or bewildered by jazz music, the commission should recommend that the governor act to bring about immediate cessation." And his proposed final solution? "All persons convicted of being jazzily intoxicated shall go before the Superior Court and be sent to an insane asylum." Allen was not the only politician to despise jazz, and newspaper headlines of the era—"Jazz Dancing Soon to Pass, Says Coolidge" and "Hoover Sees End of Jazz in Radio"—documented that even presidents can engage in wishful thinking.

It is disheartening enough that such national leaders would bother to attack cultural expressions in America, but the war against jazz was even more extreme in Germany. In 1930 the up-and-coming National Socialist (Nazi) party was victorious in some important local elections, and they quickly instituted the Ordinance Against Negro Culture with the goal of ridding the land of "all immoral and foreign racial elements in the arts." One result was that jazz music was outlawed (a move that Mussolini made in Fascist Italy as well)—as were certain classical composers, including Stravinsky and Hindemith. Hitler's brown shirts soon began disrupting concerts and raiding dancehalls to arrest jazz fans, and so began the Third Reich juggernaut....

In America the anti-jazz phenomenon was mostly just a bunch of redneck bluster—although at least one hall, the Evergreen Ballroom in Olympia, Washington (which had been the object of gripes about the jazz shows occasionally booked there), was mysteriously torched in the '30s. And even though there were suspicions about who was behind the arson—a couple of right-wing vigilante groups (the Sentinels and the Silver Shirts) were active in the area at the time—the issue wasn't pressed and the owners just chose to rebuild and start anew. The enemies of jazz, though, weren't all just hick nobodies and militia cultists. It was no less than jazz icon Duke Ellington—whose orchestra had performed at the Evergreen—who once scornfully recalled the Catholic archbishop of Dubuque, Iowa, griping in 1938 about how "jam sessions, jitterbugs, and cannibalistic rhythm orgies are wooing our youth along the primrose path to hell."

Just as certain dance venues felt the heat, the radio industry also drew the ire of the conservatives. In 1935 *Radio Guide* magazine published a distraught letter to the editor that pleaded:

Please take from the air the noisy and offensive musical trash called jazz. The young people should be taught to like good music instead of MUSICAL GARBAGE. It is wrong to offend good musical taste by putting on the air the noisy selections in which the oboe screams out a solo part which causes chills to run up your spine; then the moaning saxophone that makes your sympathetic heart wish that the suffering animal making the noise could be chloroformed; then the muted cornet, whose tones cannot be described in words, joins in. The piano accompaniment of bum, bum, bum, separates the selection into measures. The whole conglomeration reminds me of a four-member catfight in my back yard.

Apparently at least a few powerful people in England agreed with that assessment, for by the mid-1930s, jazz—or "hot music" as they called it—was specifically banned from the air by the BBC.

A decade and a half later, one radio chain manager in Washington State reportedly issued a memo to his staff that vilified such youth-oriented music with terms like "cacophonous," "neurotic," "instrumental hysteria," and "musical epilepsy." Furthermore, he banned the playing of all "be-bop, hot jazz or whatever terms apply to wailing reeds and screaming brasses." Instead, he suggested more airings of "Bach, Brahms, and Beethoven."

Upset by the detrimental influence that all this "jungle music" was having, right-wing conservative groups like the KKK and the Christian Crusade took to battling "ungodly" songs. Another far-right organization, the America First Committee, eyed the music with serious suspicion, and contended that the new cutting-edge branch of jazz known as swing music was nothing but "blood raw emotion, without harmony, without consistent rhythm, and with no more tune than the yearnful bellowing of a lonely, yearning and romantic cow in the pastures or the raucous staccatic meditation of a bulldog barking in a barrel."

Given the long-standing pattern of attacks that jazz had been subjected to down through the decades, one might have hoped that jazz fans, of all people, would show more tolerance for other sorts of artistic expression. The fact is, however, that in the 1950s when rock 'n' roll popped up, certain jazzers (having apparently learned little from their own struggle to gain respect) attacked the new music. In 1956 one memorable critic even charged in England's *Melody Maker* magazine that rock 'n' roll was "the antithesis of all that jazz has been striving for over the years, good taste and musical integrity." Such partisan angst aside, the reality was that the Jazz Age had faded and the Rock 'n' Roll Era was being born. For the next several decades this new big-beat form of music would captivate the youth—while simultaneously serving as a rich target for self-appointed censors.

What had begun as a rich variety of slurs about the "jungle" origins of big-beat music's rhythms (and their supposed "relation" to cannibalistic voodoo rites and all) over time boiled down into a simple two-word phrase of conservative code-speak that effectively signaled the Bible-thumpers' position on a whole tangle of racial, sexual, and political issues: "the beat." Indeed, by the '50s, Cold War conservatives had come to associate "the beat" with just about everything they despised—like Communists, Negroes, drug addicts, and, yes, bongo-thumping bohemian beat-niks. And so with the emergence of rock 'n' roll—a music in which "the beat" is per-haps its most pronounced and defining aspect—the same epithets that had been applied to jazz were transferred wholesale to the new music. In fact, that very same pattern would reoccur time and again. Whenever an innovative new form of big-beat music arose in the black community—consider such historic examples as blues, jazz, R&B, reggae, and hip-hop—it really only got labeled a "menace" after some uptight white folks somewhere discovered their own kids groovin' on the stuff.

In the '50s, the increasing prominence of flamboyant young stars like Elvis Pres-ley, Little Richard, and Chuck Berry provided would-be censors with an especially rich cast of beat-mongers to target. Faced with the growing popularity of those rockin' wildmen, a number of less-than-gracious Americans lashed out. In 1954 one of Alabama's White Citizens Councils distributed a handbill asserting that "rock 'n' roll will pull the white man down to the level of the negro," and a handbill pro-duced by their counterparts in New Orleans concluded that "the screaming, idiotic words, and savage music of these records are undermining the morals of our white youth in America."

In Birmingham, in 1956, the jazz/pop star Nat "King" Cole was brutally beaten with a microphone stand mid-concert at the Metropolitan Theater by thugs from the White Citizens Council. One proud member even "articulated" their position with a remark that rock 'n' roll, "the basic, heavy-beat music of the Negroes," was in-tended to appeal to the base in man, that it "brings out the animalism and vulgarity" in people, and that it was the basis of a "plot to mongrelize America." Another at-tempted to justify the attack on Cole— whose music was *far* from rock 'n' roll—by asserting that it was "only a short step... from the sly, night club technique vulgarity of Cole, to the openly animalistic obscenity of the horde of Negro rock 'n' rollers."

Meanwhile, one radio commentator of the era—North Carolina's future senator Jesse Helms—was reportedly so ticked off by Elvis's music that he smashed a record to smithereens on the air while roaring that "rock and roll have *got* to go!" Numerous other Southern radio stations no doubt agreed wholeheartedly, but being more gentlemanly, they simply banned it by politely setting the young rockabilly singer's 45s aside with the big stack of other new and unproven singles that they'd also rejected that week.

By 1957, the leader of the North Alabama White Citizens Council was so outraged by this "vulgar music" that he agitated for the confiscation and destruction of jukeboxes. It wasn't just know-nothing rednecks who were up in arms though—plenty of well-educated preachers also contributed to the holy war against big-beat music. One British clergyman roared that the act of dancing to rock 'n' roll was turning "young people into devil worshipers, to stimulate self-expression through sex, to provoke lawlessness and impair nervous stability." And in March of 1957 the "hedonistic, tribal rhythms" of rock 'n' roll drove Cardinal Stritch of Chicago to ban the music from Catholic schools. Meanwhile, the good Rev. Robert Gray of the Trinity Baptist Church in Jacksonville, Florida, calculated that Elvis Presley had "achieved a new low in spiritual degeneracy." It was, however, one Rev. Riblett of Michigan who achieved a new low in ignorant musicological postulating: "Rock and roll is the devil's diversion. It's been traced back to the jungle drums. That's where it all comes from. The headhunters use the same beat before they go out to hunt heads."

In hindsight (and with extreme reluctance) we must in fairness admit that those otherwise wrong-headed critics were dead-on *correct* in their dire predictions that should America's (white) kids be allowed to listen to "Negro music," there would be serious societal ramifications. In fact, an entire generation of white teenagers—inspired by the rockin' R&B hits of the '50s—actually did begin accepting African-American rhythms and eventually adopted other aspects of that culture's lingo, fashions, and attitudes as well. And in doing so, the white youth of America loosened up, learned to move their bodies a bit, and ultimately realized the humanity of their fellow black citizens—and many went on to join wholeheartedly in the civil rights struggle that recommitted this nation to its declared principles of fairness, dignity, and the rule of law.

Prior to the rise of the civil rights movement, few people got worked up about the content of African-American musical expressions—as long as the tunes stayed in their proper place: on "the wrong side of the tracks" where they originated. But controversies arose when white youth began taking an interest in the sexy, beat-heavy music of their black crosstown counterparts. Only then did concerns about lewd dancing, "dirty lyrics," and such reach a fever pitch.

This unprecedented social interaction—or "race mixing" as the bigots put it—alarmed plenty of folks. Savvy leaders instantly recognized the political value in demonizing music, if for no other reason than to distract the general public from more pressing social issues. The earliest official swat taken at rock 'n' roll was the spotlight placed on it by the new US Senate's Juvenile Delinquency Subcommittee in 1954. When their investigation wound down in 1955—and all the possible publicity had been successfully milked—the committee released its findings in a final report on the link between rising youth crime rates and rock 'n' roll.

It was also in 1955 that Alan Freed—America's top radio DJ and the man often credited with first applying the name "rock 'n' roll"—had his New York–based *Rock 'n' Roll Dance Party* TV show canceled by CBS bigwigs when the camera caught black doo-wop singer Frankie Lymon dancing momentarily with an ecstatic white teenage girl who had rushed the stage. As for Freed's new "competition" over in Philadelphia—the *American Bandstand* program—well, they reduced the possibility for such controversial race-mingling by establishing a policy of simply banning black teenagers from attending and dancing on the show. Never mind that under that rule a black singer could still conceivably make contact with white kids.

Variety magazine began publishing a major three-part essay in 1955 on what it derided as R&B's "leer-ic garbage," concluding with the advocacy of censorship and a warning that others would act if the music business didn't clean up its own act. The following year *Time* magazine joined in the disparagement by describing rock 'n' roll in venomous terms: "an unrelenting, shocking syncopation that sounds like a bull whip; a choleric saxophone honking mating calls; an electric guitar turned up so loud that it shatters and splits; a vocal group that shudders and exercises violently to the beat while roughly chanting a near-nonsense phrase or a moronic lyric in hillbilly idiom." In April 1956 *Variety* returned to the topic, this time flat-out linking rock 'n' roll to "a staggering wave of juvenile violence and mayhem." That same year the *New York Daily News* identified rock 'n' roll as an "inciter of juvenile delinquency." The writer asserted that the demise of the music was inevitable due to the "riots and bloodshed, slurs on the national anthem, and slowly gathering public disgust at a barrage of primitive jungle-beat rhythms, which when set to lyrics at all, frequently sound odd with double meaning leer-ics few adults would care to hear."

The 20th century certainly provided fear-inducing opportunities for cultural worrywarts. Although some level of a "generation gap" has always existed, the 1950s definitely brought additional degrees of social tension as the sizable baby boom generation began to come of age and an unprecedented "teen culture" developed. It was a time when wave after wave of silly fads ebbed and flowed. Some of them—like speaking in pig Latin and using mirror writing—seemed to develop out of the teens' need to differentiate themselves from adults, but others were obvious cases of cultural exploitation by money grubbing corporations. This post–World War II era was a period of unprecedented prosperity, and the forces of capitalism geared up to supply America's demand for novelty and began flooding it with an endless stream of products aimed strictly toward the teenage market. The summer-long hula hoop rage of 1958 was but one example of how the younger set was particularly susceptible to the manipulations of a fast-growing pop culture industry—but, as its critics were so fond of pointing out, rock 'n' roll was also easily twisted to meet purely commercial needs.

Meanwhile at mid-decade—and inspired by rebellion-stoked movies like James Dean's *Rebel Without a Cause* and Marlon Brando's *The Wild One* (not to mention *Untamed Youth, Hot Rod Gang,* and *Blackboard Jungle*), and the hugely popular Broadway play *West Side Story*—a disconcerting teenage fad erupted: hoodlum chic. Trend-addicted teens seeking to emulate the toughs depicted in those street gang productions quickly adopted the requisite surly attitude and biker fashion, including leather jackets, T-shirts, black denim trousers, motorcycle boots, and ducktail greaser haircuts. While there may have been something to justify parental concern, anyone seriously trying to identify popular music that advocated juvenile delinquency would really have their work cut out for them.

The fact is, for all the angst expressed about the suspected connection between rock 'n' roll and youth crime, very few tunes actually milked the delinquent or gang angle. And those were far from being hits. Hopelessly obscure even in their day, tunes like "Rumble Rock" (Kip Tyler and the Flips), "Street Fight" (Barry Weaver), "Stealing Hubcaps" (Billy Ledbetter), "The Greaser" and "Wolf Call" (Lord Dent & Invaders), "Gangwar" (Gene Maltais), "Ballad of a Juvenile Delinquent" (Phil Johns and the Lonely Ones), and "Juvenile Delinquent" (Ronnie Allen) are forgotten period pieces that exist today only as ultra-rare discs valued by hard-core record collectors.

No matter. The newspapers continued to stir up panic by pushing the image of legions of wayward youth and the bike chains and switchblade knives they used in alley fights called rumbles. And in the wake of all that coverage, it was soon no longer just rock 'n' roll's devilish "jungle beat" or "questionable" lyrics that drew fire from the music's opponents—now, even a song with *no* lyrics could be censored. By early 1959 Link Wray's guitar-based instrumental, "Rumble," had been banned on Boston, Detroit, and New York radio because its title was seen as a reference to *West Side Story*–type street gang fights. Which it was! Although one of the true classics of the instrumental era, it's been said that TV host Dick Clark was reluctant to book the band on his *American Bandstand* show. Clark was so risk-aversive, however, that after doing so, he managed to neglect announcing the song's *title* when he introduced Wray's performance.

The authorities' concern over gang-related matters was reasonable given that violent "gangs" had long plagued various neighborhoods. But it was troubling to see that more focus was seemingly being placed on musicians than on real street thugs. In 1956 *Melody Maker* magazine contended that "viewed as a social phenomenon, the current craze for Rock-and-Roll material is one of the most terrifying things to have happened to popular music." Rock was so threatening to some folks that a good number of learned physicians dropped any pretense of professionalism in order to take aim at a cultural phenomenon they couldn't fathom. Thus newspapers reported so-called experts like Dr. Braceland, the psychiatrist-in-chief of Hartford, Connecticut's Institute of Living, whose careful diagnosis left him with the inescapable scientific conclusion that rock 'n' roll, as a "cannibalistic and tribalistic" form of music, was a dangerous "communicable disease with music appealing to adolescent insecurity and driving teenagers to do outlandish things."

Various other censorious types also joined in the rock 'n' roll bashing. One Texas legislator of unknown medical expertise sputtered that "it's not music, it's a disease." Disgusted, the Russian classical composer Dimitri Tiomkin chimed in: "Now, in our popular music, at least, we seem to be reverting to savagery." An additional diagnosis of America's problem was provided by the esteemed Spanish classical cellist Pablo Casals, who was quoted in *Music Journal*, railing:

> "You want to know what I think of that abomination, rock 'n' roll? I think it is a disgrace. Poison put to sound! When I hear it I feel very sad not only for music but for the people who are addicted to it. I am also very sorry for America—that such a great country should have nothing better to put into the expectant ear of mankind than this raucous distillation of the ugliness of our times, performed by juveniles for juveniles. It is a terrible and sardonic trick of fate that the children of the present century should have to grow up with their bodies under continual bombardment from atomic fall-out and their souls exposed to rock 'n' roll."

Then for good measure he also predicted the lifespan of the music: "Rock 'n' roll is a disease that shall pass away as quickly as it was created. It is a sad thing for your country. It is nothing. *Nothing*." The King of the Crooners, Bing Crosby, concurred: "Rock 'n' roll seems to have run its course." Responding to such wishful doomsayers, a few groups responded with musical defenses including Danny and the Juniors' 1958 hit, "Rock and Roll Is Here to Stay," and the Showmen's 1961 hit, "It Will Stand" ("…Rock and roll forever will stand").

In such an intolerant atmosphere, radio stations became the lightning rods for those who were seeking a scapegoat for all of society's problems. They after all were seen as supplying the rock 'n' roll that innocent American children were being poisoned with via the family radio. In 1957 the author and rock 'n' roll foe Vance Packard said: "Our airways have been flooded in recent years with whining guitarists, musical riots put to switchblade beat, obscure lyrics about hugging, squeezing, and rocking all night long." He also noted that rock 'n' roll "stirred the animal instinct in modern teenagers" with its "raw, savage, tone." The following year—in testimony before the Senate Subcommittee on Interstate Commerce —he made his opinion about the music perfectly clear: "Rock 'n' roll might best be summed up as monotony tinged with hysteria." Hysteria, ironically, might also be the perfect description of anti-rock reactionaries like Packard himself and even Frank Sinatra—who at the time was dazzling mainstream adults with the antics of his own "Rat Pack" gang—but still felt it necessary to give the music a fierce pimp-slap: "Rock 'n' roll smells phony and false. It is sung, played and written, for the most part, by cretinous goons. And, by means of its almost imbecilic reiteration, and sly, lewd and in plain fact, dirty lyrics… it manages to be the martial music of every side-burned delinquent on the face of the earth."

Not everyone in a position of prominence was so dedicated in their hopes that rock 'n' roll was just some passing fad. Some folks still figured it needed a little help expiring—and, not surprisingly, it would be the city of Boston where the battle lines would be drawn. Boston, dominated by its conservative Catholic base, is famous for many things, including a licensing division that was responsible in part for public health and safety at entertainment venues. And so, with that mandate, its chief—the poetically named Richard Sinnott—reviewed all films, ballets, concerts, and strip acts (tough work, but someone's gotta do it) and single-handedly passed judgment on what was or was not fit for local consumption. Thus, between 1955 and 1982, Sinnott was so aggressive in outlawing various things that the phrase "Banned in Boston" became known nationally—and was sometimes used as a marketing technique to help boost ticket sales elsewhere. Over the years Sinnott played a role in the "dirty lyrics" scare over the Kingsmen's "Louie Louie," banned concerts by the Jackson 5 because of the supposed violence of their fans, and forbade Marvin Gaye to play Boston during the '70s school-busing crisis on this pretext: "We didn't want black and white together, so they wouldn't kill each other." But, back in May 1958, the city's immediate concern was an upcoming show sponsored by Alan Freed.

Boston's mayor had just lifted a rock concert ban imposed there after Freed's show in 1957, and the DJ wasted no time in announcing that he'd be bringing his popular traveling concert extravaganza, *The Big Beat Show* (with Buddy Holly, Chuck Berry, Jerry Lee Lewis, and others), to the Boston Arena on May 5. Miffed over this policy change, a few local cops let it be known that they weren't too pleased. Freed later recalled that "a police sergeant approached me before the show and said, 'We don't like your type of music. There are nothing but hoods in here.'" Then mid-show, when some boisterous teens began dancing, the authorities flipped on the house lights, sparking a riot—an incident that allowed Boston officials to announce a new ban on any further such events.

Said Freed: "These kids in Boston were the greatest. They were wonderful kids. But the police were *brutal*. They grabbed kids and shoved them back. I saw one of them grab a little 14-year-old girl and call her a foul name. I was shocked—after all, I have teenagers myself." Though exactly what happened may never be known, the damage to rock 'n' roll had been done, and following Boston's ban, authorities in New Haven, Connecticut, and Asbury Park and Jersey City, New Jersey, also formally banned rock shows. The whole idea snowballed, and city officials in Bridgeport, Connecticut; Atlanta, Georgia; Portsmouth, New Hampshire; and Burbank, California, all enacted laws outlawing rock 'n' roll concerts.

The authorities—figuring that they finally had Freed on the ropes—began dog-piling the DJ. At one point Boston's Rev. John P. Carroll incited his flock with inflammatory rhetoric like "Rock and roll influences and excites youth like jungle tom-toms readying warriors for battle. Inject a wrong word or misunderstanding and the whole place blows up. The suggestive lyrics on R&B records, of course, are a matter of law enforcement." J. Edgar Hoover agreed, warning the citizenry of rock 'n' roll's "corrupting influence on America's youth" and assigning FBI agents to track Freed.

Within 48 hours of the Boston event, Massachusetts Senator William Fleming charged that narcotics had been sold at the concert and demanded that further shows at any state-owned facility be prohibited. One day after that, a county district attorney exhumed a long-forgotten rule from the 1800s—the Massachusetts Anti-Anarchy Law—and used it to charge Freed with "inciting the unlawful destruction of property," a crime that would bring a fine of up to $1,000 and imprisonment of up to three years. Indeed they reportedly claimed that the concert promoter had attempted to "overthrow the United States government." While these charges were ultimately tossed out, that didn't stop the intrepid FBI from watching Freed for years.

Meanwhile, Congress thought it politically advantageous in 1957 to explore, once again, the possibilities of taming rock 'n' roll. The idea floated was to enact legislation that would have formed a review committee charged with screening all songs and clearing them for broadcast or retail sale. Jumping on the bandwagon, the Senate Committee on Interstate and Foreign Commerce launched a new inquiry into possible causal links between music and teenage crime.

Things were so edgy that some records were now being shunned simply because of rumors. In 1957 numerous radio stations voluntarily banned Donald Woods's sorrowful 1955 R&B ballad "Death of an Angel" due to its sad-sack lyrical tone, which rumors claimed had caused a few teenagers to commit suicide. The potential to inspire teen suicide was also the reason given by stations two years later when they refused to support the new, histrionically titled teen-angst single "I Think I'm Gonna Kill Myself" by rockabilly star Buddy Knox—not to be confused with Elton John's '70s tune "I Think I'm Going to Kill Myself" or Crack the Sky's more resolute "I'm Gonna Kill Myself." A grain or two of salt—and an understanding about melodramatic tendencies of adolescents in general—is helpful when considering such pop songs. With the clarity of hindsight we now see that not only are those '50s suicide reports wholly unsubstantiated, but none of the songs mentioned "promote" or "advocate" suicide one bit.

Invoking the potential for violence as a rationale for censorship is nothing new: in the '40s Billie Holiday's dark jazz number "Gloomy Sunday" was reportedly banned by radio for inspiring suicide. Four decades later the matter of teen suicide was at nearly epidemic levels, and a nervous MTV banned further airings of the Replacements' 1987 video hit "The Ledge." Then the following year, a faculty advisor, reportedly convinced that the music would inspire suicides, restricted all heavy metal from the playlist at a Newark, New Jersey, student-run radio station.

If America's censors were truly concerned about music's potential to "cause" suicides, they would have exhibited considerably more consistency in their approach and actively launched a campaign to outlaw any further pieces of suicide "promotion" such as William Shakespeare's teen tearjerker *Romeo and Juliet* and his classic *Hamlet*—not to mention classic operas like *Tosca* or *Tristan und Isolde,* which also feature suicide (and adulterous and murderous) themes. And while we're compiling lists of forbidden songs the censors might also wished to have targeted, there are probably the two most popular suicide-themed songs of all time: Leadbelly's folk/blues favorite "Goodnight Irene" ("I want to jump in the river and drown") and that 1895 Australian classic, "Waltzing Matilda" ("he up and jumped in the water hole / Drowning himself…").

Never letting facts get in the way of their crusade, rock 'n' roll's agile opponents just shifted methods in battling the music: they would attack the *messenger.* And the messenger that was delivering big-beat music through millions of cool new transistor radios across the land was the commercial radio industry. The debate was enlivened with such know-nothing parries as the one offered by a critic who sputtered in 1956 that "not only are most of the … songs junk, but in many cases they are obscene junk. … It is the current climate on radio and TV which makes Elvis and his animal posturings possible." Such concerns brought the radio industry squarely into conservative America's crosshairs.

The '50s were dicey days in the radio biz. Even though radio station managers had for years willingly participated in banning "questionable" records, now, as the censorship forces gained steam, the radio industry itself began to be targeted as a cause of all the trouble. Soon rumors began circulating within the industry that a crackdown on rock 'n' roll was in the offing, and broadcasters became paranoid about reprisals from the licensing agents of the Federal Communication Commission. Since the passage of the 1934 Federal Communications Act the FCC has been chartered to monitor the broadcast industries, radio and TV, to ensure that the "public interest, convenience and necessity" is served by those stations who seek to build up their private corporations by utilizing publicly owned airwaves.

In practical terms, one of the FCC's stickiest challenges was to forge a workable means of dealing with complaints that certain songs were "obscene" or "indecent." The main issue was that American courts had ruled that items deemed "obscene" could be prohibited, but that "indecent" items could only be regulated. However, those two notoriously elusive terms have long vexed some of our greatest legal minds—and so nailing down just exactly what "obscene" means became the crux of the matter. The central challenge is that it's just about impossible to define such a concept in terms that are objective rather than wholly personal.

The Supreme Court forged ahead though, developing by the late '60s a three-part test to help determine if something can be legally pegged as "obscene": 1) considered as a whole, would the average person find the primary theme of a particular work to be of a "prurient" nature?; 2) was the work "patently offensive" to "contemporary community standards"?; and 3) does the work lack serious social, artistic, literary, political, or scientific value?

If something meets *all three* of those criteria, it is considered legally obscene and thus has been exempted from the wide protections of the First Amendment. However, this arrangement has proven to be quite contentious and serious questions have arisen. For example, even the carefully chosen words used in those three test inquiries don't answer questions like: Who is this average person—and how are they to be identified? Why should an *average* person make the decision? Whose definitions of "prurient," "offensive," "artistic," and "value" will guide the determination? And for that matter, which community are we referring to—how might this be determined in a diverse cosmopolitan city comprising various ethnic subcultures? If a community's standards evolve over time, then what exactly would signify a definitive change?

For an industry based on rapid-fire blather, this new focus on what language was permissible over the public airwaves was unnerving. A general climate of fear pervaded the radio world, managers got spooked, and heads began to roll. Most prominently, Buffalo, New York's legendary jock Dick Biondi was fired on the air at WKBW for spinning Elvis 45s against management's wishes. In Portland, Oregon, a popular disc jockey was reportedly axed by station KEX when outraged listeners phoned in complaining about him airing Elvis's take on that Yuletide chestnut, "White Christmas." This was an orchestrated campaign supported by the song's author, Irving Berlin, who'd personally encouraged stations to reject the young rocker's version. In the winter of 1957 Los Angeles's KMPC took this a step further, banning Elvis's entire *Christmas Album*.

Then, in 1958, one major national chain, the Mutual Broadcasting Network, announced that they were dropping rock 'n' roll records altogether, citing the music's "distorted, monotonous, noisy" sounds and "suggestive" and/or "salacious" lyrics as a problem. Other critics faulted the music's generally "gimmicky" nature while still others denounced rock lyrics as "insipid" or "juvenile" even. In doing so these folks were effectively ignoring a simple truth that even a crotchety old detractor like Pablo Casals understood about rock 'n' roll: The music is an art form intended for teenagers.

Even mere references to sophomoric behavior were open to attack. In 1959 an industry trade publication, *DISC* magazine, reported that England's government-owned radio network, the BBC, had banned the Coasters' new 45 "Charlie Brown"—"a humorous rocker about a high school kid who is always goofing off"—from airplay because of the use of an objectionable word ("spitballs"). Whether or not that action decreased juvenile delinquency in England is unknown, but the record's sales established it as an international smash hit. [Note: As late as 1972, British politicians—fearful of the rebellious message of teen spirit behind Alice Cooper's songs like "School's Out"—attempted to halt his tour there by gumming up the visa process to deny the American band entry, an effort that rightly failed.]

Another subcategory of songs that caused concern were the rock 'n' roll knock-offs of the '50s horror movie fad, like that 1958 hit "Dinner with Drac" (John "The Cool Ghoul" Zacherly); the '59 hit "The Mummy" (Bob McFadden & Dor); '60's "Werewolf" (Frantics), a single whose scary rabid-wolf-like snarls were said to have been enough to cause skittish stations to drop it; or the '62 (No. 1) Halloween hit, "Monster Mash" (Bobby "Boris" Pickett), which was actually banned by the BBC as "offensive." This panic over gimmicky music led a number of radio stations to ban records such as Nervous Norvus's bloody 1956 tune "Transfusion." This humorous hipster hit, while having fun with the awful topic of a car wreck and its survivor's hospitalization, may have repulsed adults, but the kids loved its taboo aura and it raced up the charts (No. 8) without strong radio support. Then came what was known in the radio biz as "the Death Disk," Ray Peterson's 1960 (No. 7) hit "Tell Laura I Love Her." This criminally maudlin tune about a dying fella's last request received the same cold-shoulder treatment from radio, but teens bought the 45 in droves. Misgivings were also expressed about (and scattered bans placed on) a couple of drowning-oriented songs like the '58 (No. 5) hit "Endless Sleep" (Jody Reynolds) and '62's "Leah" (Roy Orbison), as well as other death-centric tunes, including that same year's (No. 1) hit "Johnny Angel" (Shelley Fabares); '64's (No. 2) hit "Last Kiss" (J. Frank Wilson); (No. 8) hit "Dead Man's Curve" (Jan and Dean); and the (No. 1) biker-gang-related hit, "Leader of the Pack" (Shangri-Las).

The critics, of course, were completely incapable of differentiating such wacky novelty songs and the real rock 'n' roll goods. To their ears, *all* of the stuff was equally lame and in their heart-of-hearts they just *knew* that only a radio station actively accepting payola from record companies would stoop so low as to air it. Eyeing the rising popularity of rock 'n' roll, American authorities tried a new way of bringing the youth-music biz to its knees. Rock 'n' roll's lyrical content ultimately became the next avenue of attack, and in June 1959 *DISC* sensed the change in the political winds and wrote: "A few months ago, the lyrics of a big rock 'n' roll record would have been a matter of small concern. Firstly they were usually completely without meaning and, secondly, they were often sung in such a way that it was very difficult to catch. It is a sign of the times that a lot more attention is being paid to the words. And deservedly."

It was in this new climate that a classic pop song—Kurt Weill's epic street saga "Mack the Knife" from *The Threepenny Opera*—became engulfed in controversy. When the same tune had been cut previously (by artists including Lawrence Welk, Ella Fitzgerald, Louis Armstrong, and Frank Sinatra), it had not been an issue. But now, recorded in 1959 by teen idol Bobby Darin, it was instantly banned by New York City radio stations concerned that its lyrics might incite violence by juvenile delinquents. The suffocating social atmosphere in the Big Apple even prompted Bronx doo-wop stars Frankie Lymon and the Teenagers to record their just-a-little-bit-defensive hit, "I'm Not a Juvenile Delinquent."

Another sign of the times was the remarkable number of stations across the country that began abandoning their winning Top-40 formats and switching to easy pop formats. Apparently spooked by all the anti-rock murmurings in the industry—and the halls of Congress—top stations all across the land suddenly announced that they were dropping all rock 'n' roll from their playlists. Stations including KSFR in San Francisco, WPIN in St. Petersburg, KDEN in Denver, KSEL in Lubbock, WZIP in Cincinnati, WLEV in Erie, WAMP in Pittsburgh, and KING and KJR in Seattle all chose to make this change. In Milwaukee things went a degree further when a number of old-school DJs celebrated their liberation from having to air such drivel by torching a reported 200 records in their station's parking lot.

The turning point came with the *Miami Herald*'s account of the debauched activities that took place at the annual national DJ convention. In an article that featured a screaming tabloid-like headline—"Booze, Broads, Bribes"—readers got a glimpse at the seamy behind-the-scenes reality of the radio industry. And it was a view that shocked some naïve readers—and one that intrigued many politicians. As it happened, that very same season several factors converged and created a great opportunity for rock 'n' roll's foes. The first was that ASCAP (an organization that licenses pop songs to radio and TV for broadcast) saw a chance to strike a debilitating blow to their more rock-oriented competition, BMI, and reportedly began lobbying certain leaders to examine the underbelly of the rock 'n' roll industry. Second, and simultaneously, some of those congressional representatives got stuck holding hearings to investigate a topic they'd really have preferred not to explore: the scandalous revelations that certain popular TV quiz shows, like CBS's *The $64,000 Question* and *Dotto*, were rigged. Those charges caused extreme discomfort in the industry, and no one was happy that the public's trust in the media—and faith in authority—would likely be diminished. How convenient then when the politicians found a potential solution to their dilemma: diverting the public's attention from corrupt TV practices to an inquisition into the despised business of rock 'n' roll radio.

Representative Oren Harris's Special Subcommittee on Legislative Oversight of the Committee on Interstate and Foreign Commerce announced on November 14, 1959, that it would shift gears and begin hearings to root out the evil in rock 'n' roll. These were the sessions that came to be known as the "payola hearings." In truth, the issue was not does "payola" exist, because the answer to that inquiry was patently obvious: yes. Payola—or commercial bribery—is a well-established business practice. Indeed the practice has been honed to a fine art by the politicians (and their industrial lobbyists) themselves. In reality, these hearings were just another election year gambit to appear tough on the godless music industry.

The stakes were high and fallout in the radio and record industries was immediate and widespread. Scores of DJs in many cities resigned their positions and/or were fired. Others showed their true colors by turning against the music. Seattle radioman Jim French, for example, opined in 1959 that "rock 'n' roll is sick. This music is often extreme, generally objectionable, and frequently vulgar. It is performed by 'artists' who seldom have any qualification other than a typically nasal, childish delivery, and a perfunctory acquaintance with a guitar or piano.... It's obvious that someone involved must take a stand."

It was Alan Freed who, when subpoenaed to testify, stepped forward to defend teen-oriented music. He flatly admitted that yes, being no fool, he'd been involved in the system: "If I've helped somebody, I'll accept a nice gift, but I wouldn't take a dime to plug a record. I'd be a *fool* to; I'd be giving up *control* of my program." Despite Freed's clear delineation of the difference between a token gift and a corrupting "pay for play" scam, his bosses at New York's WABC immediately pulled the plug on his massively popular program.

Six months were spent investigating more than 200 DJs in 42 cities—and then the Harris Committee chose to call it a day after merely bagging Freed and a grand total of five additional small-fry DJs (each of whom was charged with receiving varying amounts of illegal gratuities). This tally was hardly evidence of a national crisis. However, as the designated fall guy in the whole affair, Freed was targeted by the IRS in a brutal tax trial over the previously undeclared gifts he'd admitted receiving. In the end, Freed died a broken shell of a man in 1964.

With the payola hearings finally fading into the background, rock 'n' roll began to revive itself as noted in *DJ* magazine: "The so-called authorities that predicted the sudden death of rock 'n' roll after the senate hearings that delved into payola practices are being proven wrong.... In our opinion... music with the 'teen beat' will always be here. It has been, it shall remain so."

Meanwhile a new chapter in the saga was unfolding: around 1960 the twist—a silly but persistent dance craze like the Watusi, the freeze, the hucklebuck, and the frug—first popped up. This new dance step was based on a song, "The Twist," that had originally been cut in 1958 as a B-side to a 45 by R&B pioneers Hank Ballard and the Midnighters. It remained in relative obscurity until mid-1960, when the combo appeared in Baltimore on the regionally televised *Buddy Deane Show* and its teenage attendees went wild trying out some new steps on the dance floor. Ballard's hopes of cashing in on the fad were fleeting, though, as America's teen-dance king Dick Clark and his gang over in Philadelphia (who had also taken note of the twist fad) simply manufactured another new teen star, Chubby Checker, who recut the song. It was that version that was hyped on Clark's nationally popular *American Bandstand* TV show and became an overnight sensation, and, ultimately, a huge No. 1 hit. It also sparked a backlash from certain folks who were appalled at the sight of people twisting and shaking their bodies so publicly.

In 1962 Bishop Burke of New York denounced R&B music and announced a ban on Catholic school students doing the twist. Instantly a slew of Catholic schools—which were actually pioneers in having teen-dances in many American towns—announced that the twist would be forbidden at their weekend sock-hops. The Catholic Youth Organization (CYO) had plenty of prior experience implementing bans: as far back as 1954 they lobbied DJs to desist from spinning "obscene" records and had begun policing sock-hops—which they had pioneered as a youth activity in 1952—eventually blacklisting particularly provocative dance steps like the dog and the alligator. Despite the CYO dance ban, the twist had a reasonably long run of popularity in the US, though like all fads, it eventually faded away. America had dodged another bullet.

In less democratic countries, however, the twist met with extreme official disfavor. In China, one newspaper expressed outrage over "ugly displays" of young people twisting, and in Moscow *Izvestia* quoted a respected arts leader whining about the "disgusting dynamism of rock and roll and the Twist.... It expresses dirty feelings, dirty instincts, and poverty of thought and spirit." [Note: Even up to the late '90s rock 'n' roll music, and indeed, even music with "strange" *rhythms*, was expressly banned by Chinese broadcast media.] While South Vietnam's government simply banned it for violating their strict morality laws, in Czechoslovakia dance parties were raided, and in Damascus the Syrian Minister of Information ordered a halt to the importation and distribution of all twist records because of their "sexually provocative" nature (the Ministry of Culture and National Guidance in Cairo followed suit). Meanwhile in Beirut, the interior minister ordered a police raid of the Zeitoun nightclub district in order to "safeguard the morals of Lebanese youth."

Clearly, the fear of new and different rhythms and beats is widespread—and their condemnation by critics seems just as inescapable. Just as earlier anti-music "experts" had made claims like "the throb of the beat from the drums brings his mind to a state when the voodoo ... can enter him. This power then takes control of the dancer, usually resulting in sexual atrocities," much of the criticism hurled at disco music when it emerged in the 1970s was framed as complaints about its "unrelenting," "mindless," and "sex-fueled" beat.

The massive popularity of John Travolta and the Bee Gees notwithstanding, the "experts" certainly maintained a consistency with their forebears' conclusions. In 1970 it was asserted that "there is no difference between the repetitive movements of witch doctors and tribal dancers and the dances of American teenagers. The same coarse bodily motions which lead African dancers into a state of uncontrolled frenzy are present in modern dances. It is only logical, then, that there must also be a correlation in the personality of demons gaining possessive control of a person through the medium of the beat."

Then, in 1977, the perceived threat to society posed by those punk rock icons the Sex Pistols drew an attack by one British politician that evoked the 1950s when he warned that punk rock bands "work up the kids into a frenzied excitement, just like the witch doctors of Central Africa ... you keep banging the drums and that sort of thing, and they start foaming at the mouth." Ho-hum...

Even as late in the game as 1997, alarmists like Seventh-Day Adventist minister Louis Torres would *still* be spouting the same old stuff: "Young people don't understand what this music is doing to them.... They think it is a natural process and may succumb to the message produced by the notes, the rhythms and the beat."

These days, however, it is not just prickly preachers and crotchety old-timers who lash out against whatever new music they can't understand. Proof is provided as easily as doing a quick search on the Internet, where one can find entire Web sites operated by young rock 'n' roll fans who dedicate themselves to disparaging various other music genres. Current examples include sites like "I hate Hip Hop," "anti-rap," "Fuck Hip Hop," "rapsucks," and the "crAP Sucks Page," where we are reminded how blind ignorance is a timeless human characteristic as we read all about why this or that webmaster despises hip-hop rapping: "I will tell you the reasons that I hate rap.... First and foremost ... is the sound. I do not see how a person who grew up anywhere except in the jungles of Africa could like these jungle beats and rhythms."

Alas, the beat *does* go on....

CHAPTER 3

The Devil in Disguise

What is this thing called rock 'n' roll? What is it that makes teenagers throw their inhibitions as though at a revival meeting? Is this generation of teenagers going to hell?

—*New York Times Magazine*, 1958

Rock music is the Devil's masterpiece for enslaving his own children. By the grace of God, let's keep him from also using it as a tool to weaken the children of God...

—Frank Garlock, *The Big Beat: A Rock Blast*, 1971

T he cosmic quest to discover proof for the existence of a superior being—God—has stumped humanity for eons. And while that ultimate mystery persists, perhaps the long-sought evidence has always been swirling around us simply unrecognized. Could it be that God is manifested through such ethereal expressions as music and humor—but that we humans only sometimes hear the tunes or get the jokes? If so, it would seem that one particularly divine prank involved what was probably the first genuine hit record to ever be widely banned in America. Far from being a piece of XXX-rated musical smut, or some despicable drinkin' song, Johnny Standley's "It's in the Book" was instead a mirthful disc that drew negative attention by poking a bit of fun at pious preachers.

Upon its release in 1952, Standley's folksy tune was quickly banned by many Bible Belt radio stations who figured that their listeners wouldn't abide the gentle—if pointed—humor behind this parody of a country parson's sermonizing. Too late though; the record had already struck a chord with consumers and so, despite a lack of airplay, "It's in the Book" rocketed to the No. 1 spot on *Billboard's* charts based on retail sales alone. Our punch line? The radio industry's "moral guardians" had not only underestimated the tolerance quotient of the American people, they had also unwittingly brought things full circle by harking back to the very origins of censorship in this land.

Johnny Standley's It's in the Book *EP featured an illustration of the folksy comedian as a country preacher.*

For "mock sermons" were one of the specified targets of the earliest censorship law in the New World. Crafted by the Puritans of colonial Massachusetts—home of the infamous Salem witch-burning trials of 1692—a 1712 law criminalized the publishing of "any filthy, obscene, or profane song, pamphlet, libel, or mock sermon." Then—within a few years of the 1776 revolution that forged the United States—additional laws were enacted against blasphemy and profanity. Protecting the church from infidels who would speak ill of God and religion (or dare to use rough language) was clearly a major concern, and simply outlawing such manifestations of Satan's influence was deemed an ideal solution.

There have, it would seem, always been folks who claim to possess the ability to spot the devil's handiwork in just about anything, and history is littered with examples of such demonization. The concern that Satan is behind certain musical elements can be traced back to at least the Middle Ages, when one particular musical interval (the difference in pitch between two tones) was damned as the *diabolus en musica,* the "devil in music," and banned from church music. (That dissonant and still rather jarring tritone has nevertheless been successfully employed in such classics as Hector Berlioz's *Symphonie Fantastique*, Gustav Mahler's *Das Lied von der Erde,* Bill Doggett's R&B hit "Hold It," and Jimi Hendrix' acid-rock masterpiece "Purple Haze.")

Way back in the 1600s the Puritan settlers in the American colonies were so suspicious of music-making that the singing of psalms in their churches was conducted sans instruments. It was, presumably, a keen fear of the growing support for the introduction of organs to their houses of worship that led the good folks to establish a mid-17th-century law that "no woman shall … play any instrument except the drum, the trumpet or the jew's harp"—all three, of course, being instruments that had a snowball's chance in, well, you know where, of gaining acceptance at Sunday services. And thus it was only after years of rancorous debate that New England's very first organ was installed, in 1714. And in fact, throughout those times, instrument players were so lowly regarded that "even the name 'musician' was one of reproach"—to the extent that as late as 1788 a French visitor to Boston noted that many of the townsfolk still considered music as a "diabolical art" unfit for godly persons.

This prejudice carried over into the 19th century, when plenty of superstitious Southerners identified fiddle players (and their music) as an evil influence and the instruments themselves were specifically damned as "devil's boxes." In 1867 one prominent self-styled "prophet" rued the modern world's distractions, writing: "I feel alarmed as I witness everywhere the frivolity of young men and women.… Their minds are filled with nonsense.… They have a keen ear for music, and Satan knows what organs to excite, engross, and charm the mind." By the Roaring '20s the fear-of-God crowd likewise branded saxophones as the "devil's flute," and later, at the dawn of rock 'n' roll in the '50s, it was that new-fangled contraption, the electric guitar, that became a potent symbol in the minds of the music's foes. Amplified guitars were ear-shatteringly loud, sexy, flashy, decadent, and, thus, a tool of the devil.

Being committed literalists, religious conservatives are not exactly famous for their ability to discern when artists employ sophisticated literary devices such as irony, sarcasm, parody, symbolism, or metaphor. It seems that numerous classical composers were just plain lucky that the censors weren't aware of their work, otherwise Igor Stravinsky's "Triumphal March of the Devil" (from *The Soldier's Tale*), Giuseppe Tartini's "Devil's Trill" sonata, Ralph Vaughan Williams' "Satan's Dance of Triumph" (from *Job: A Masque for Dancing*), and Johann Strauss Jr.'s "Lucifer Polka" op. 266 would surely have also been attacked as satanically inspired material and damned right along with so much jazz, blues—and, in time—R&B and rock 'n' roll. But it didn't matter whether a song had a devilish title or contained lyrical references to Satan. The danceable rhythms and sexy beats of jazz and blues that pulled people into juke-joint parties also drew condemnations from churchgoers who tarred anything they feared as "devil's music."

Even later in the rock 'n' roll era—and still decades away from the emergence of anything that could accurately be identified as truly satanic rock—conservatives kept raising Cain about various "devil songs." From the beginning, R&B and rock 'n' roll were both considered irredeemably ungodly, and that sort of judgmental mindset led the good people of six different counties in South Carolina to take the radical step in 1953 of outlawing the operation of heathen jukeboxes within earshot of any church. When Elvis Presley came along, among the countless headlines generated were such classics as: "Did the Devil Send Elvis Presley?" In 1956 Gene Vincent's rockabilly raver "Race with the Devil" ("Well, I've led an *evil* life") was banned by a number of radio stations in conservative communities. Another song of the era that raised the hackles of conservatives was Screaming Jay Hawkins's 1956 classic, "I Put A Spell on You." This is a rare example of a rock song that actually fits the classic cliché and *is* built upon an overtly swampy, "jungle," "voodoo" theme—and its critics could have scored a direct hit by pointing just that out. Instead, they switched to a sexual and racial critique calling it "suggestive and cannibalistic." The result? A widespread radio ban—which was reportedly ignored by a DJ in Chilliwack, BC, Canada, who yielded to a devilish temptation to air the record against management's edict and was promptly fired—and retail sales of over one million units.

A revival of the unwinnable battle to try and purge the language of common curses indicates the futile extent to which some conservatives will go. In 1961, after receiving complaints from religious-minded listeners about the song's hook line ("he was *one hell of* a man"), a number of radio stations buckled and axed Jimmy Dean's "Big John." It was then that Columbia Records called Dean back into a studio, replaced that line with ("he was *a big, big* man"), retitled it "Big Bad John," and scored a No. 1 hit. Then in 1963 America's top folk group, the Kingston Trio, had their rendition of "Greenback Dollar" altered by the record company after someone took exception to their use of language ("I don't give a *damn* about a greenback dollar"). When the song was later issued as a single, the offending term had been replaced with an extra guitar strum. In the late '60s, the powerful Metromedia Group's chain of radio stations banned the Grateful Dead's "Uncle John's Band" due to the lyrical line ("*Goddamn*, well, I declare … ").

In rock 'n' roll's formative years there were a lonely few religious activists who bothered to picket concerts—and they were easily dismissed as grumpy throwbacks who were attempting to stop the world. However, the Beatles—as the world's preeminent pop band—made an irresistible target. From day one the Beatles had drawn generalized criticism from conservatives, but two years into their reign, in March of 1966, the band's most talkative member, John Lennon, carelessly gave their foes the ammunition needed to escalate the battle. Drawn into commenting that cult followings (like the Beatles' massive fan base) are similar to certain historical but extinct religions—i.e., transitory in nature—Lennon blurted out that "We're

On August 8, 1966, piles of records were torched by a crowd of 1,000 at a "Burn the Beatles" event in Waycross, Georgia, organized to protest John Lennon's flip "We're more popular than Jesus" remark.

more popular than Jesus *now*." Accurate or otherwise, *that* was a big mistake. Preachers near and far erupted with condemnations of the band, and Bible Belt radio stations like Birmingham, Alabama's WAQY reasoned that "something ought to be done to show them that they can't get away with this sort of thing." Launching a "Ban the Beatles" campaign by breaking Beatles LPs live on the air, WAQY then scheduled a "Beatle bonfire" and urged their young listeners to attend and stoke it with records, mop-top wigs, and other accoutrements of Beatlemania. The publicity that followed sparked a wave of record burning events, including one in Ft. Oglethorpe, Georgia, and those aired live by sponsoring stations like WAYX in Waycross, Georgia, and KLUE in Longview, Texas. Within weeks at least 30 stations announced Beatles bans. Bravely going entirely against this grain, Fort Knox, Kentucky's WSAG—which, up till then, amazingly enough, hadn't played *any* Beatle records—began doing so strictly in support of Lennon's right to self-expression.

Perhaps the most bellicose response though, came on August 13 in South Carolina, where the Beatles were burned in effigy and a Grand Dragon of the KKK nailed Beatles records to a flaming cross. The Imperial Wizard of the Klan also denounced the Beatles as "atheistic," and yet another of their spokesmen noted that their interest in the matter was due to the KKK's goal of fighting Communism and to "*restore* Christianity all over the world" [emphasis added]. Lennon was aghast at these extreme reactions to his flip comment, later admitting, "When they started burning our records … that was a real shock, the physical burning. I couldn't go away knowing I'd created another little piece of hate in the world … so I apologized." Contrition was not enough though, and on the 15th several fully robed and hooded members of the KKK picketed the band's concert in Washington, D.C. Then, four days later, in Memphis, someone interrupted their show by tossing firecrackers on stage. The angry protesters milling outside impressed Paul McCartney: "They were zealots. It was horrible to see the hatred on their faces." Two weeks later, and after problematic concerts in a few more towns, the Beatles quit touring forever.

The continuing death threats from, presumably, militant "people of faith," however, took their toll, and the stress Lennon felt surfaced a full three years later on a new Beatles single. "Ballad of John and Yoko" included both the pointed chorus hook ("*Christ*, you know it ain't easy") and the prescient line ("They're gonna *crucify* me")—a coupling that, incidentally, caused an estimated 50 percent of American radio stations to dump that disc. Australia followed suit, as did South Africa. [Note: The hot water that the Beatles found themselves in was but a mild harbinger of the trouble another musician, Sinead O'Connor, would spark a quarter century later. In October 1992 the Irish singer did Bob Marley's "War" on the *Saturday Night Live* TV show and then—in an act of protest against the Catholic Church's use of "marriage, divorce and, in particular, birth control and abortion to control us through our children and through fear"—ripped up a photo of Pope John Paul II, saying, "fight the real enemy" and stormed offstage. Well, O'Connor's in-your-face exercise of free speech brought down a furious hellstorm: Catholic leaders and the National Ethnic Coalition of Organizations announced a boycott campaign against her music and (after offering up a $10 bounty) collected a good 200 albums that were then destroyed by a steamroller to the roaring approval of spectators. The harassment and stress that O'Connor was subjected to reportedly led to an early, if temporary, retirement.]

Though the Beatles were not quite the agents of the devil that their detractors tried to paint them as, other bands were beginning to create music that did in fact dabble in lyrical themes related to satanic matters. Traditionally, most pop and rock 'n' roll songwriters used satanic (or occult) references as light-hearted metaphors for the unholy temptations presented by the object of one's affection—for example, "Witchcraft" (Frank Sinatra), "(You're the) Devil in Disguise" (Elvis Presley), "Devil

Doll" (Roy Orbison), "Devil or Angel" (Bobby Vee), "Devil in Her Heart" (Beatles), "Devil with a Blue Dress" (Mitch Ryder)—but around 1965 the paradigm shifted. That's when the Sonics (a legendary garage rock combo from Tacoma, Washington) released what was likely the first modern song to invoke the Evil One's name ("Satan knows what you did …He's waitin' for you") to exact vengeance on an unfaithful girlfriend. And although "He's Waitin'" thus remains a trailblazer, their earlier local hit, 1964's "The Witch" ("she's an evil chick"), also contains occult implications.

The real father of the whole "satanic rock" subgenre was the wildly theatrical British artist Arthur Brown, whose 1967 debut single, "Devil's Grip," has been credited with introducing hellish imagery to England's pop charts. While that single made no headway in America, his follow-up, "Fire" ("I am the god of hellfire"), scored a No. 2 US radio hit the following year. Around the same time another British Invasion group, the Rolling Stones, signaled an interest in the topic on the 1967 *Their Satanic Majesties Request* and in their 1968 hit "Sympathy for the Devil"—both of which drew condemnations from critics.

The first band to dedicate themselves wholly to a gothic/satanic image was Coven. Over the span of three LPs—1969's *Witchcraft Destroys Minds and Reaps Souls* (featuring songs such as "Black Sabbath," "Pact with Lucifer," "Satanic Mass," and "Dignitaries of Hell"), 1971's *Coven*, and 1974's *Blood on the Snow*—it became apparent that, unlike any of their predecessors, these musicians were in fact quite well informed about satanic matters as well as witchcraft traditions. The band's potential breakthrough moment ought to have been their headlining of Detroit's Black Arts Festival (which was touted as the Satanist's Woodstock), slated for Olympia Stadium on Halloween 1969. A coalition of local church leaders, however, conspired against the event, applied pressure to the promoter's firm, and suddenly the show was canceled. Had it gone ahead, it is easy to imagine that Coven would have become the finest rock 'n' roll whipping boy that religious censors had yet discovered. As it happened, their career fizzled without much notoriety.

The late '60s also produced a veritable flood of anti-rock propaganda, beginning with Bob Larson's 1967 magnum opus, *Rock & Roll: The Devil's Diversion.* That screed was closely followed by Frank Garlock's *The Big Beat: A Rock Blast,* and was joined by a number of wacky books penned by the dean of Colorado's Christian Crusade Anti-Communist Youth University, the Rev. David A. Noebel, including: *Rhythm, Riots, and Revolution; Folk Music and the Negro Revolution; Communism, Hypnotism and The Beatles; The Beatles: A Study in Drugs, Sex, and Revolution; The Legacy of John Lennon: Charming or Harming a Generation?* Impressive? Sure, but, the good reverend really outdid himself with an attempt to, essentially, blame poor old Karl Marx for rock 'n' roll's crimes in his 1974 *The Marxist Minstrels: A Handbook on Communist Subversion of Music.*

In 1975, Tallahassee, Florida's Rev. Charles Boykin garnered headlines for his claims that more than 98 percent of surveyed unwed mothers got into their predicament while under the influence of rock 'n' roll. The good reverend's record burning campaign against such "devil's music" was, it was explained, based on the reading of a biblical passage (Deuteronomy 7:25): "The graven images of their gods shall ye burn with fire."

While religious sleuths busied themselves trying to convince the public that the Beatles were sworn to the service of the devil, they somehow managed to overlook that *genuinely* satanic-themed groups had actually arisen on the fringes of the nascent British heavy metal scene. In addition to Coven (whose bassist, Ozzy Osbourne, was soon fronting the vastly more influential band Black Sabbath), other pioneers of the subgenre included Black Widow, Monument, Witchfynde, Angelwitch, and Lucifer. The latter's in-your-face single, "Fuck You," was reportedly confiscated in a police raid. [Note: An identically named American band who formed in 1971 cut a seminal LP named *Black Mass*.]

By the 1970s, the topic of "devil music" was largely a forgotten concern and the issue remained off the general public's mental radar screen for years. Well, at least until 1979, when three Christian brothers named Jim, Steve, and Dan Peters from Minnesota organized their first record burning rallies. About 350 folks reportedly jammed the tiny Zion Church and were fired up enough by the preaching to pile up hundreds of rock albums and torch them. International media attention instantly pushed the brothers into prominence, who claimed in their book *Why Knock Rock?*, after additional burnings, that "more than 10 million dollars worth of records and tapes have been destroyed, and countless lives have been redirected toward … a life founded on the only Rock mentioned in the Bible, Jesus Christ."

In 1981, the Reagan Era brought forth a parade of right-wingers whose goal appeared to be the destruction of America's secular pop culture and the remolding of it into a homogenized Christian nation. Over the next several years the general public had to endure the moralizing of such characters as televangelists like Jim and Tammy Faye Baker, Rev. Jerry Falwell (with his Moral Majority organization), and Rev. Pat Robertson (and his Christian Coalition organization), as well as amateur freelancers like the Peters Brothers (and their Truth about Rock Ministries). In addition there was the well-financed rise of conservative organizations like Ralph Reed's College Republican National Committee, the Concerned Women of America, the National Association of Christian Educators, and the Christian Leaders for Responsible Television.

So, it wasn't long before music was again viewed as something that could stir up a good amount of trouble. The action began to pick up in 1980 when Des Moines, Iowa's First Assembly Church of God organized a rock record burning event and ignited albums by artists including the Beatles, Peter Frampton, and the Indian sitar master Ravi Shankar, as well as the soundtrack to the movie *Grease*. Then Salinas, California's First Baptist Church's members—convinced that the Beatles *cause* crime and drug abuse—reportedly torched hundreds of rock LPs. The same thing happened in Keokuk, Iowa, where churchgoers reportedly burned albums by such "satanic" stars as Perry Como, John Denver, and the Carpenters. The following year a nightclub owner in Carroll, Iowa, announced that he'd finally seen the error of his ways and ignited $2,000 worth of records. The next year a crowd of 75 gathered at the Chapel of Peace in Lynnwood, Washington, to burn their $2,000 pile of rock records (including those by the Beatles, Peter Frampton, Led Zeppelin, and even Donny and Marie Osmond) and newspapers reported that three of the teenaged ringleaders "said they feel closer to god now."

It was also in 1981 that a new high-profile target for the conservatives' wrath emerged: MTV—the music channel that came to be branded "the one-eyed church of Satan." MTV—a cable outlet suddenly capable of spewing music videos into the living rooms of every wired home—was a *revolutionary* step in the music industry, and hence one that requires no imagination whatsoever to guess how the Religious Right (who oppose *anything* new) reacted. They attempted to ban their fellow citizens' access to the new channel. In 1983 an Emporia, Virginia–based Baptist minister pressed his city council to have MTV eliminated from their local cable system. The next year the National Coalition on Television Violence issued a report calling on the federal government to regulate music videos. In 1985 televangelist Rev. Robertson called for the regulation of rock music on both radio and TV. That same year a Utah-based Mormon bishop also made news headlines when he announced that tenants of an apartment building he owned would not be allowed access to the "pornographic" music videos aired on MTV. Soon two Massachusetts women who considered music videos to be "decadent, morally degrading and evil," called on local officials to remove MTV from that area's cable system. Though destined to fail, these efforts signaled the extent to which well-meaning folks would go in attempts to limit the variety of entertainment being offered to the wider community. Their time would have been better invested in simply learning how to use their own TV's channel selector device.

Instead, the foes of rock 'n' roll marched on, employing that tried and true tactic of banning concerts. In 1982 the ex–Black Sabbath singer-gone-solo, Ozzy Osbourne, made headlines when he was arrested while carousing through the streets inebriated and, worst of all, attired in a *dress*. The final straw, no doubt, was that Ozzy was caught urinating on the near-sacred Alamo. That incident resulted in his band being banned from performing any concerts in San Antonio, Texas, for a period of ten years. [Note: It was also in San Antonio that a councilman would in 1985 famously declare that "the First Amendment should *not* apply to rock and roll."] A magnet for trouble, Ozzy was also banned from returning to Baton Rouge, Louisiana; Boston, Massachusetts; Corpus Christi, Texas; Scranton and Philadelphia, Pennsylvania; and Las Vegas, Nevada, by local authorities who were scared witless by Ozzy's reputation.

Ever resourceful in their quest to rid America of devilish influences, Christian crusaders generated various way-out theories on the ways that Satan attempts to recruit the susceptible. Perhaps the wackiest idea was espoused by the leader of a Michigan-based street ministry, Redge Peifer, who believed that a vast satanic conspiracy was behind the numerical digits included in computerized retail bar codes that have been applied in recent years to commercial products—including musical recordings. He discovered a disc that bore those ominous three sixes that the Bible's apocalyptic Book of Revelation calls the mark of the beast—or of the devil. It would be fruitless to attempt to explain to these folks that any numbers included on a bar code are randomly applied for inventory identification and that it was inevitable that some item was going to get stuck with a "665," another with a "666," and another with a "667"on its tag.

In his 1991 book, *The Rock and Roll Nightmare*, Peifer also provided insight into another industrial process at play in devil-ridden record companies: "Satanic covens work hand in hand with the production of a lot of these HEAVY METAL and PUNK ROCK records and tapes. These workers of iniquity and evil put a satanic curse on these records asking Lucifer to draw people into drugs and the occult as these people listen to this wicked music."

Yet another nutty thesis of this ilk was the notion that some songs accomplished their intended deviltry through subliminal impact. In other words, according to the religious sleuths, evil messages were now being hidden in records through new electronic editing techniques—"back-masking"—that secretly imbedded disturbing recorded messages into songs. Not only that: these audible spoken messages were backwards.

Now let's just pause a moment to examine a couple of popular misconceptions. First, that something can be recorded and then played backwards is beyond question. None other than Thomas A. Edison, while conducting pioneering research on his new phonograph device in early 1878, noted that the recordings could be played backwards, and that "the song is still melodious in many cases, and some of the strains are sweet and novel, but altogether different from the song reproduced in the right way." So, it is possible to record something and then play it backwards. An instrumental musical passage—as Edison pointed out—might even be pleasant backwards. But absolutely *no* scientific evidence exists to demonstrate that the human brain is able to decipher spoken words when presented in reverse.

However, a full century after Edison's day a few anti-rock would-be censors came along and imagined that a song could contain lyrics that made sense both forward *and* backward. But around 1977 the concept of "backward masking" (or "back-masking" as it came to be known) was posited as a means by which artists insert "hidden messages" into their art. Under this theory *any* song could conceivably be a sort of musical Trojan Horse—one that appears to be one thing, but in actuality represents a dangerous tool used by Satan to infiltrate listeners' minds with insidious, destructive, and eternally damning notions.

In spite of the biomechanical and technological challenges that this theory fails to account for, the concept of "back-masking" became quite the issue du jour. Interestingly, the expert that censors cited as their authority on the subject, the minister and author of the book *Backward Masking Unmasked* Jacob Aranza, seems, if sincere, also confused about the nature of the phenomenon. He wrote that it was "a technique that rock groups are using to convey satanic and drug related messages to the subconscious. The technique is used by someone saying something forward which intentionally means something else played backward." Furthermore: "If someone said to you, 'Satan is God,' you would immediately reject it.… But if you heard, 'dog si natas' a number of times, which is 'Satan is God' backwards, it would be 'decoded' by…the brain and stored as fact!"

Obviously even the Religious Right's own "expert" on the matter was grasping a bit to try and explain his theory about how this technique could conceivably function. Neither Aranza nor anyone else has explained how the human brain could be capable of deciphering mysterious, barely audible (backwards) sounds while listening to a song. Nevertheless, in part encouraged by Aranza and his brethren, the ID'ing of such musical suspects became great sport. Before long it was reported that five radio DJs were fired after encouraging their listeners to try playing their own record collections backwards to see if they could discover hidden messages. In no time the news media was filled with newly discovered examples of songs that were alleged to contain such content.

All this is complicated by the fact that there have been a fair number of bands who *did* produce recordings that used backwards tracks. Typically this was done for esthetic reasons—to create mysterious sonic textures or establish a certain audio vibe. The first time the issue arose was during the short-lived panic around the rumor in 1969 that the Beatles' bassist, Paul McCartney, had died and his passing was being kept from the public. All sorts of ridiculous clues "proving" the theory were reported through the media. During the hysteria it was said that towards the end of "Strawberry Fields Forever" John Lennon says (in reverse) "*I buried Paul*," and that if you played a recording of "Revolution No. 9" backwards, the phrase "number nine" actually came out as "*Turn me on, dead man*." And from there the back-mask patrols claimed to uncover additional secret messages in other Beatles tunes, including "Rain," "Blackbird," "Girl," "Baby, You're a Rich Man," "I'm So

Tired," and "I Am the Walrus." Of these, it has been determined that the fade-out gibberish in "Rain" is in fact a reversed voice singing "*sunshine.*"

And that was but the beginning. Plenty more songs had unsubstantiated back-masking charges leveled at them, and among those reported were: Black Oak Arkansas's "The Day when Electricity Came to Arkansas," where unspecified portions heard backwards supposedly sound like "*Satan, Satan, Satan, he is god, he is god, he is god*"; the Cars' "Shoo Be Do," where "shoo be do" is said to equal "*satan*"; the Eagles' (No. 1) hit, "Hotel California," whose lyrical line "this could be heaven or this could be hell" transforms into "*Yes, Satan, he organized his own religion*"; Electric Light Orchestra's "Eldorado," where the lyric beginning "On a voyage of no return to see" reverses to "*He is the nasty one / Christ, you're infernal / It is said we're dead men / Everyone who has the mark will live*"; Jefferson Starship's "A Child Is Coming," where "It's getting better" is revealed as ("*son of Satan*)"; the Rolling Stones' "Tops," which allegedly contains the phrase "*I love you said the devil*"; and Styx' "Snowblind" where "*Satan, move through our voices*" was supposedly embedded.

Whether any of this was true or not, the concept was publicized widely and more bands began joining in on the fun, even going so far as to bait devil-hunting censors with way over-the-top pseudosatanic malarkey. Pink Floyd's "Goodbye Blue Sky" contains the humorous salutation "*Congratulations! You just discovered the secret message. Please send your answer to Old Pink, care of the Funny Farm*". The Electric Light Orchestra embedded a sarcastically cautionary message, "*The music is reversible, but time—Turn back! Turn back! Turn back! Turn back!*", in their tune "Fire on High," and on a tune actually titled "Secret Messages" they dropped in this welcoming line: "*Welcome to the big show. Welcome to the big show*". The J. Geils Band contributed "No Anchovies, Please," a song that included this reversed commentary: "*It doesn't take a genius to know the difference between chicken shit and chicken salad.*" Styx upped the ante by placing a "warning sticker" on their *Kilroy Was Here* LP that read: "By order of the Majority for Musical Morality, this album contains secret backward messages"—and indeed, the reversed message on "Heavy Metal Poisoning" said "*Annuit coeptis. Novus ordo seclorum,*" a phrase that the attentive will recall as the Latin phrase (meaning "God has favored our undertakings. A new order of the ages.") that is printed on the back of one-dollar bills. But it was Frank Zappa who best satirized the whole farce by recording an *entire* six-minute song, "Ya Hozna," backwards. Marvelous fun this all surely was, and scores of other acts were eager to give the religious conspiracy nuts exactly what they were imagining: *genuine* "satanic" invocations.

Perhaps the crowning achievement though, was provided by one of the censors' own favorite whipping boys, Prince, who confounded the search-for-all-things-satanic crowd but good when he included this backwards message in his song

"Darling Nikki": "*Hello. How are you? I'm fine 'cause I know that the Lord is coming soon. Coming, coming soon.*"

The inexact science of deciphering back-masked messages is perhaps best highlighted by the varying interpretations that devil-hunters have applied to one song in particular, Led Zeppelin's 1971 classic "Stairway to Heaven." The original lyrics played forward clearly state, "Yes, there are two paths you can go by / but in the long run / There's still time to change the road you're on", however, as anti-censorship author Martin Cloonan has astutely pointed out, the anti-rock books have not been able to come to any agreement over what are the supposed subliminal messages contained in even that one song. In *Why Knock Rock?* (Dan & Steve Peters) the "backwards" content was said to be, "*Here's to my sweet Satan, no other made a path. For it makes me sad. Whose power is Satan?*" while *The Occult in Rock Music* (Eric Barger) determined the same portion to say, "*Oh, here's to my sweet Satan. The One whose little path has made me sad. Whose power is Satan? Oh, my number, 666.*" The *Devil's Disciples* (Jeff Godwin) pegged the song as saying, "*I sing because I live with Satan. The Lord turns me off, there's no escaping it. Here's to my sweet Satan, He'll give you six, six, six. I live for Satan.*" So, three out of three experts disagree.

The good Rev. Billy Farrar of Bellingham, Washington, was quite successful in attracting media coverage for his investigation of rock records in an effort to expose "Satanic influences." Though he and other sleuths discovered what they claimed were hidden messages, Farrar also qualified his research into back-masking by explaining that to hear this stuff "you've got to listen real hard, ten or twelve times." The researcher's credibility wasn't helped much by that sort of assertion, or the one contributed by the Ohio preacher Jim Brown, who in 1986 led a public record burning after having discovered that if the theme song to the popular early-'60s TV show *Mr. Ed* were played backwards the grammatically challenged satanic message "*Someone sung this song for Satan*" was, according to him, clearly audible.

To many people the whole controversy had turned into one big game—especially the rock bands who played along by adding actual backwards messages to their songs. But certain politicians started playing for keeps. The whole farce reached its peak in 1982 when a California assemblyman introduced a state house resolution to create a statewide law banning the insertion of "back-masked" or other subliminal messages in recordings, declaring that the practice could "manipulate our behavior without our knowledge or consent and turn us into disciples of the Antichrist." Unbelievably, instead of laughing down his fellow "statesman," the Republican Congressman Bob Dornan raced a version of the silly measure ["Warning: This Record Contains Backward Masking That Makes A Verbal Statement Which Is Audible When This Record Is Played Backward And Which May Be Perceptible At A Subliminal

Level When This Record Is Played Forward."] all the way up to the hallowed halls of the US Congress.

The lack of even one iota of scientific evidence didn't stop Louisiana Senator Bill Keith from weighing in on the matter in 1983: "The sinister nature of rock and roll music is one of the burning issues of our time.... Recent information concludes that rock stars are using a technique known as backward masking to implant their own religious and moral values into the minds of the youth." Other leaders went beyond talking: the Arkansas state legislature boldly enacted a law in 1983 mandating that albums be affixed with a warning sticker if they contained any backwards messages.

By the time Reagan was reelected in 1984, his conservative supporters were truly chomping at the bit to escalate their much-longed-for battle against America's pop culture. And thus did America's entertainment industry begin to find itself in serious political crosshairs. Ironically, while the Religious Right's censors were distracting themselves with back-masking (and other silly controversies like Ozzy's pissing practices—or the imminent "threat" embodied by Iron Maiden's 1982 hit LP, *Number of the Beast*), all *hell* broke loose.

It seems that the more opponents attempted to bully the music community, the more extreme—and even specifically anti-Christian—the musicians' responses became. As the right's pressuring escalated, so too did the intensity of the music—and the nastiness of the lyrical rhetoric. It is likely the sense that conservative religious activists are forever meddling in the private affairs of their fellow citizens that generated the resentment reflected by the emergence of bands with names like the Filthy Christians, Christian Death, Nunslaughter, Creaming Jesus, Severed Savior, and Millions of Dead Christians—and voiced in dozens of rudely provocative songs, including "Hate the Christian Right!" (Team Dresch), "Kill the Christians" (Deicide), "Satan Is Jesus to Me" (Skull Kontrol), "We're Satan's Generation" (Impaled Nazarene), "Kill for Christ" (Kevorkian Death Cycle), and—heaven help us all—"Ripping the Wings off the Backs of Angels" and "Raped by the Virgin Mary" (Hell On Earth).

It might be beneficial here to recognize that this material is largely a commercial—rather than religious—phenomenon. Most of these musicians consider the whole thing as one big game. Their ridiculously wicked lyrics—some of the rudest of which are obviously designed to needle religious types—really need to be taken with a grain of salt. Certainly no reputable observer has contended that even a fraction of the rock bands that use satanic references in their music or graphics are genuine devil-worshippers.

Meanwhile as the Religious Right busied themselves fretting about radio hits like the Eagles' "Good Day in Hell," Blue Öyster Cult's "Don't Fear the Reaper," AC/DC's "Highway to Hell," Van Halen's "Runnin' with the Devil," and Santana's "Evil Ways," they all but overlooked the international dimension to the satanic phenomenon, which by 1982 had evolved into a new movement called "black metal."

Inspired by the ultra-wicked tunes recorded by a band called Venom on their first two LPs (1981's *Welcome To Hell* and then *Black Metal*), legions of bands (with names that ought to be enough to scare the bejesus out of any sensible Christian) emerged in nations all across the globe: Finland (Mercyful Fate, and Impaled Nazarene), Norway (Mayhem, Enslaved, and Dark Throne), Brazil (Mystifyer), Greece (Rotting Christ), Germany (Sodom), USA (Profantica), Hungary (Master's Hammer), Sweden (Abruptum), Japan (Sigh), and England (Satan, Grim Reaper, Cloven Hoof, and Demon).

The British group Demon released three LPs—*Raise the Dead*, *The Return*, and *Under the Sign of the Black Mark*—that have been credited with pushing the genre's form into its *next* phase, the so-called death metal trend of the late '80s. Seminal albums include Death's 1987 *Scream Bloody Gore*, Morbid Angel's 1989 *Altars of Madness*, and the 1990 classic *Deicide* by Deicide. In their wake came Malevolent Creation, Cannibal Corpse, and Cradle of Filth. Needless to say, this sort of music is an acquired taste, and very few of these satanic bands ever made much headway commercially. However in the American market, some, including Slayer, Exodus, Possessed, and Onslaught, actually developed considerable fan bases.

Although critics had long been damning certain rock 'n' roll songs for being satanic, they had, for the most part, simply been barking up the wrong tree. Had they been more skilled as researchers they might have discovered a whole slew of songs (dating mainly from the 1980s and '90s) that *finally* fit the bill. That is, songs that overtly give homage to the devil, such as "Satan" (Satan's Cheerleaders); "Devil" (Oghr); "Dance with the Devil" (Raise Hell; "Hand of Doom" and "Devil and Daughter" (Black Sabbath); "The Hellion" and "Devil's Child" (Judas Priest); "Welcome to Hell," "Possessed," and "Nothing Sacred" (Venom); "Satan Spawn" (Deicide); "Burn in Hell" and "Sold My Soul" (Mercyful Fate); "Deliver Me to Evil" and "Your Soul to Satan" (Hell on Earth); "Satan Never Sleeps" (Enthroned); "An Apprentice of Satan" (Dark Funeral); "In League with Satan" (Witchery); "Deliver Us to Evil" (Exodus); "Hymn to Lucifer" (Daemonarch); "Church of Satan" (Love Child); "History of Hell (Burning Witches); "Satan's Child" (Danzig); "Blessed by Satan" (Vergelmer); "Lucifer's Lament" (Obtained Enslavement); "Devil in My Eyes" (Obliveon); "The Devil Loves You" (A.F.I.); "Satan's Cronies" (Method of Destruction); "Satan's Spree" (Non Serviam); "Bleed for the Devil" (Morbid Angel); "Lucifer's Seduction" (Metanoia); "Satan, Ruler of Earth" (Viking Crown); "Hordes of Lucifer" (God Dethroned); "The Triumph of Satan" (Triumphator); "Lucifer Rising" (Unrest); "Servant of Satan" (Satanic Slaughter); "Satan's Vengeance" (Destruction); "Satan's Majestic Empire" (Abyss); "The Devil Is Calling" (Gorgoroth); "Satan's Curse" (Possessed); "Kill for

Satan" (Upsidedown Cross); "Led by Satan" (Hypocrisy); "Angel of Death" (Slayer); "Hail Satan" (Mindless Self Indulgence); "Satan Live within Me" (Psychopomps); "Fallen Angels" (Coven 13); and "Deep Within, I Plant the Devil's Seed" (Necrophagia). Yikes! Scary and wicked stuff, certainly *not* the type of fare that MTV supported.

Condemning MTV, however, remained a mainstay activity during the years of the Reagan Revolution. In 1985 the administration's "Culture War" took on a new vigor with the founding of the Parents Music Resource Center (PMRC). It was this organization that sparked a congressional inquisition of rock 'n' roll that placed enough pressure on the music industry that most major labels finally acquiesced and began stickering their recordings with "Parental Advisory/Explicit Lyrics" warning labels. Though the leadership of the PMRC sometimes seemed to have their hearts in battling "dirty" music, they eventually targeted songs with themes of violence, drugs, and the occult.

But the PMRC wasn't alone in this battle for the soul of America; right-wing forces were aligning in powerful coalitions, and conservative Christian leaders were inspired to do their part. In 1984 a Baptist minister named Jeff R. Steele went on the warpath and received considerable media attention by denouncing heavy metal with the claim that: "It is sick and repulsive and horrible and dangerous." Anti-rock crusader Jeff Godwin concurred: "Rock music has proven itself to be evil over and over again. It has broken down the barriers of decency and smeared smut all over radio, television and movie screens.... Rock music has splintered families and fired up teenage rage since its beginning. It has preached rebellion, hatred, drug abuse, suicide, fornication and the dark things of Satan for too many years." And furthermore: "Rebellion is the Devil's trademark.... Satan and his demons continually throw more rebellion, rebellion, rebellion onto the raging family fires and rock music is the gasoline that feeds the flames."

Others agreed, and in an approach similar to that employed by those who have established treatment programs in efforts to "cure" homosexuals by retraining them, various organizations (like the Back in Control Training Center based in Orange, California) were founded as "de-punking/de-metaling" brainwashing centers in the 1980s.

In 1985 the Rev. Jimmy Swaggart led a successful campaign that pressured the giant retail chain Wal-Mart into discontinuing the stocking of rock-related publications including *Rolling Stone*, *Spin*, *Hard Rock*, and *Tiger Beat*. Retailers, though, were far from the only entities to face the wrath of the Religious Right and their political representatives. In fact, from the very moment George H.W. Bush was inaugurated as President in 1989 a fresh wave of cultural repression commenced. That year saw a level of censorship unseen since the Comstock era of pious prudery. This time, the publicity that was drummed up in attempts to suppress new artworks such as Robert

Mapplethorpe's photography, Andres Serrano's *Piss Christ* piece, and Martin Scorsese's film *The Last Temptation of Christ* ensured that all of America would become familiar with these mostly obscure "blasphemies."

Meanwhile, the back-masking hysteria prompted a whole string of lawsuits. The teen violence angle—dormant since the original '50s hoodlum scare—was once again employed by would-be censors. Only this time, it was revived with a new and ominous twist: the general public was expected to support the banning of bands whose fans *might* conceivably harm themselves (or others) and blindly shift blame from the criminal to the *art*.

That is how a bunch of heavy metal bands came to have their music implicated in various cases of teen violence. Ozzy Osbourne (and his label, Columbia) were sued in 1985 by the distraught parents of a teenager who'd committed suicide with his father's pistol. The kid's reason? Adolescent depression? *Naw.* Unhappy home life? *Uh-uh.* Absurdly easy access to military-grade firearms? *Nope.* The culprit of course *had* to be the devil in the earthly form of rock 'n' roll—in this case Ozzy's "Suicide Solution." Osbourne's defense pointed out that the song, in fact, was specifically written as an anti–drug abuse and anti-suicide ode in reaction to the death of a musician friend (Bon Scott, from AC/DC) by alcohol poisoning—hardly a case of promoting violence. The judge agreed, ruling that rock lyrics are protected speech, and that there was insufficient evidence to tie Ozzy's song to the death. It was also in 1985 that those Australian kings of hard rock, AC/DC, were charged with producing the music that served as inspiration to Los Angeles's infamous Night Stalker serial killer.

In 1986 the British heavy metal band Judas Priest was attacked for allegedly providing the inspiration for two Nevada teenagers who'd committed suicide in 1985. Charges were leveled in court that certain songs on their popular 1978 LP *Stained Class* had embedded within them depressing messages. In particular the plaintiff's case claimed that the lyrics "Faithless continuum / Into the abyss" in the title track, when back-masked, actually said "*Sing my evil spirit*;" that those of "White Heat, Red Hot" ("Deliver us / from all the fuss") said, "*Fuck the Lord / Fuck all of you*"; and that "Better by You, Better than Me" encouraged impressionable kids with phrases such as "*Let's be dead—Try suicide*" and "*Do it.*" The whole case crumbled in 1990 when these claims proved impossible to verify and the judge rightly ruled that no causal connection had been demonstrated between the songs and the teens' deadly acts, and acquitted the band of all charges. Judas Priest and their label celebrated by promoting the band's next LP as "Awesome! Backwards or Forwards!"

The theory that songs can cause teen suicides refused to go away, and soon another band, Metallica, was dragged into this mess for their 1984 song "Fade to Black," which purportedly played a role in the case of a double teen suicide in

Chicago. When in 1995 a couple of Washington State teens killed three of their family members, the media played up the fact that one of their favorite albums was Silverchair's *Frogstomp*, which includes "Israel's Son"—a song that the band's manager immediately clarified was "never intended to provoke violence. In fact, the song seeks to criticize violence and war by portraying them in all their horror."

Another troubled teen, on trial for causing violent carnage in his school classroom, desperately grasped at legal straws by attempting to shift blame to Pearl Jam's grunge-era hit "Jeremy" as inspiration for his crimes. In point of fact, the song had been written about an incident in a Texas high school where a student named Jeremy shot himself in front of his classmates, and was Pearl Jam's sorrowful response to an event that had been reported widely in the media—the polar opposite of a call for America's youth to go on a killing spree.

As the '90s grunge movement waned, rock 'n' roll kept on evolving, and when the witch-hunting censors looked up, they faced a slew of popular new bands that would provide them with targets for a full decade. Now, the morals police could choose from ultra-angry "rage rock" (or "rap-metal") bands like Rage Against The Machine, Korn, Limp Bizkit, or variations on industrial, goth, or shock-rock acts as GWAR, Nine Inch Nails, White Zombie, and Marilyn Manson. Of that new crop, GWAR's run-ins with the law first made headlines. In 1990 their vocalist was arrested on "obscenity" charges in Charlotte, North Carolina. Then, in 1994, Manson was arrested on identical charges by Jacksonville, Florida, police. [Note: In 2001 Manson would be charged with "fourth-degree criminal sexual conduct" for his onstage behavior in Clarkston, Michigan.] In February 1996 White Zombie's concert scheduled in Johnson City, Tennessee's Freedom Hall was banned by the city council due to concerns about the band's satanic message. Singer Rob Zombie bravely spoke out, saying, "It always amazes me how these God-fearing freedom fighters are so ready to spit on the First Amendment every time they see the bogeyman." Johnson City's deputy mayor shot back: "I don't *care* if it's the First Amendment—White Zombie's music is a *disgrace!*"

Despite the escalation of these attacks on American bands, fans have one big thing to be grateful for: that they don't live in places like Egypt or Jordan. In March 1997, 40 teenage heavy metal fans were jailed by the Egyptian government for "contempt under religion," which is a crime under Islamic law and can be punishable by death. Then in May two heavy metal fans were hauled in by Jordan's General Intelligence Department and accused of being "Satanists."

That same year Marilyn Manson—out touring in support of his latest hit album, *Anti-Christ Superstar*—had appearances in Lubbock, Texas; Fitchburg, Massachusetts; Columbia, South Carolina; Normal, Illinois; La Crosse, Wisconsin; and Fort Wayne and Evansville, Indiana, that were picketed by religious activists. Pressure applied by such groups helped lead to the cancellation of one concert, enforced by school officials at New Mexico State University. But, government officials were agitated as well. The city council in Oklahoma City declared Manson's work "obscene" and then leaned on the managers of the state fairgrounds to keep a close eye on Manson's performance. Similarly, the council in Anchorage, Alaska, took the step of warning concert promoters of their potential legal liability in booking the band. With the censorious frenzy building, politicians in various towns including Washington, D.C., Utica, New York, and Richmond, Virginia, called for bans on Manson's performances. The legal standing of these acts was made clear by a federal judge who ruled firmly against New Jersey officials who had also attempted to ban Manson's scheduled appearance. Still, the ever-resilient censors were determined to fight on, and at a Crime Prevention Resource Center conference in Fort Worth, Texas, in 1998, a number of local police department representatives recommended an interesting solution: the forced hospitalization of Marilyn Manson's young fans. Then, an even more draconian proposal was floated: create a computerized database for law enforcement agencies that would monitor the Internet traffic, and musical proclivities, of suspicious youth.

So the Culture War was waged. In October 1998 the mayor of Syracuse, New York, claimed that he had a "moral obligation to the people of Syracuse" to block an upcoming concert by Marilyn Manson, and promised to try to have the Landmark Theater's permit for the concert denied. Meanwhile some Onondaga County legislators joined in by threatening to withhold $30,000 in an effort to pressure operators of the venue to cancel the date. And trouble continued to dog Manson. During a 2001 tour abroad, various Polish educational leaders and the Roman Catholic Church protested his upcoming concert, culminating in a plea by the mayor of Warsaw urging parents to forbid their kids from attending, claiming that the music contained lyrics that "promote bad ideas, bad values, and violence."

The fans of certain bands had been the focus of increasing harassment from authorities as well. In 1997 a Marilyn Manson T-shirted teenager was arrested in New Braunfels, Texas, on obscenity charges. That same year Milwaukee officials banned students from wearing goth-associated fashions, and 18 students who protested the ban of Manson (and subsequently, 2Pac Shakur and Wu-Tang Clan) T-shirts at Fayetteville, North Carolina's Southview High School were suspended. In the spring of 1998 a Zeeland, Michigan, high school student was suspended after wearing a T-shirt that sported the name of a favorite band, Korn. The assistant principal stated: "Korn is indecent, vulgar and obscene, and intends to be insulting. It is no different than a person wearing a middle finger on their shirt." That same year a teen in Westerly, Rhode Island, was suspended for wearing a T-shirt that featured White Zombie as well as the infamous "number of the beast," 666. Members of the black-metal band Cradle of Filth were arrested in Rome when officers of the well-armed

Vatican Police took offense at their "I Love Satan" T-shirts—meanwhile some of their fans were arrested in England on charges of "public indecency" for wearing the band's promotional "Jesus Is a Cunt" T-shirts. In 1999 a Portsmouth, New Hampshire, school superintendent banned goth attire in general and Manson T-shirts in particular. In 2000, police in Northwood, Ohio, informed a teenaged rap fan that his Insane Clown Posse T-shirt was an outlawed item and that if he didn't remove it, they would, and he would be arrested. Needless to say, civil rights lawsuits were filed in several of these cases.

Not all such incidents were so serious though, and some humor was to be found when in 1997 that veteran of '50s pop Pat Boone had the unsettling experience of feeling the intolerant heat of his fellow people-of-faith. After releasing his obviously tongue-in-cheek "comeback" album, *Pat Boone in a Metal Mood—No More Mr. Nice Guy*, the Christian-run Trinity Broadcasting Network abruptly sacked the singer's long-running weekly gospel show. A somewhat chastened Boone was later quoted saying that "they didn't get the joke."

It is apparent that the 18th-century French philosopher Voltaire nailed the situation perfectly when he posited that "God is a comedian playing to an audience too scared to laugh."

CHAPTER 4

Token Drug Song

"Who loves not wine, women and song,
He is a fool his whole life long."

— "The Credo," William Makepeace Thackeray (1811–63)

t all began with one itty-bitty puff—the modern era of America's "War on Drugs" that is—and when alarmists decried the folksy '60s pop hit "Puff, the Magic Dragon" as nothing but an insidious ode to the "evil weed," marijuana, it was a certain sign that the new crusade against "drug songs" would become a key battlefront. Fact is though, societal skirmishes over the notion that music can help seduce new recruits into a squalid life of chemical addictions dates back much, much further.

For eons, and in many distant lands, various regulations, rules, and laws have been established in attempts to restrict the recreational use of mind-altering substances—including booze. One very early example, the Code of Hammurabi (c.1780 BC) included an interesting item about public drinking and its consequences in ancient Mesopotamia: "If a ['sister of god'] open a tavern, or enter a tavern to drink, then shall this woman be burned to death." Despite such harsh regulatory efforts, alcohol managed to establish itself worldwide as a very popular intoxicant. Indeed, to this day liquor remains the most pervasive drug scourge—other than tobacco—on earth, and the two are the only powerfully addictive drugs that can accurately be deemed a nationwide health epidemic in America. Most troubling of all though, alcohol remains a dangerous drug that, in spite of all this, is still (unlike tobacco) socially sanctioned for recreational use.

This is not to say that in modern times various well-meaning folks haven't done their level best to oppose liquor's ready availability—and music played a significant role in those political struggles. Prohibitionist forces in the early 20th century not only condemned songs that referred to, celebrated, and even promoted drinking liquor, but those folks also fought back with their own anti-booze anthems. So clearly, music has been used as a weapon in these social struggles, in addition to its more common roles as pure artistic expression and as a dance motivator.

Certainly the busy intersection where the arts and mind-altering substances cross paths is not exactly uncharted territory. Most people know that many great artists have squandered their talents—or at least damaged their reputations—with drugs. One need only recall the troubles of jazz titans (Charlie "Bird" Parker, Miles Davis, Billie Holiday, Ray Charles, Chet Baker, Stan Getz), C&W stars (Hank Williams, Keith Whitley), and rock icons (Elvis Presley, Jimi Hendrix, Janis Joplin, Jim Morrison, Kurt Cobain) to begin measuring the human cost of such self-abusive behavior.

Less publicized than all the drug overdoses that we read about are the examples of artists whose dabbling with intoxicants to explore altered states may have actually been a bit of a blessing to their work. With no desire to glorify drug use, we can still acknowledge the fact that many creative types found the recreational use of various drugs to be relatively beneficial. For example, among those inspired by use of the now widely outlawed hallucinatory herbal elixir absinthe were immortal poets (Verlaine, Rimbaud, Wilde, and Poe), brilliant painters (Degas, Manet, Lautrec, van Gogh, Monticelli, Gauguin, and Picasso)—and even the esteemed composer Victor Herbert, who created his "Absinthe Frappé" tribute.

By now no informed person can still harbor the mistaken notion that it was godless rock 'n' rollers (or even decadent jazzniks, or moonshine-swillin' banjo-plunkin' hillbillies) who can be blamed for introducing recreational drug use to the world of music. Rather, it is more appropriate to give credit squarely where it's due and acknowledge the respected European classical composers—including Wolfgang Amadeus Mozart, Franz Schubert, Modest Mussorgsky, Hector Berlioz, and Robert Schumann—who were pioneers in experimenting with various intoxicants (usually wine and liquor) in attempts to further explore their consciousness and innate creativity. History records rumors that circulated in their day that Niccolo Paganini was a drug addict, and, on the other hand, that Monsieur Berlioz was merely experimenting with opium when he created his revolutionary *Symphonie Fantastique* in 1831. And let's not forget some of the other classic party-hearty anthems such as Johann Strauss's 1869 smash hit "Wine, Women, and Song," Ludwig van Beethoven's *Music, Love, and Wine, Op. 108/1,* Sir Arnold Bax's *Sonata No. 3 In G#: In a Vodka Shop,* or Geirr Tveitt's *Suite No. 1:8, Lament for an Empty Whisky Keg.* And those tunes are but a drop in the proverbial bucket....

It should be no surprise that of all so-called drug songs, those about alcohol are most plentiful. By *far.* Songs about alcohol have thoroughly permeated western culture. Without giving it a second thought, generations of American parents have allowed their children to be socialized with an alcohol-centric mindset through role modeling, media advertising—and, yes, music. Any doubts? Just recall the perennial campfire classics such as "Ninety-Nine Bottles of Beer on the Wall" or other sing-along faves like "Drink Chug-a-Lug" and "What Shall We Do With a Drunken Sailor?" Or how about dancing a round or two when a combo strikes up "Beer Barrel Polka" or "Roll Out the Barrel" at your county fair? Not yet convinced about the saturation of pro-alcohol messaging today? Well, when was the last football game you attended where the pep band didn't blat out a version of the Champs' 1958 (No. 1) rock 'n' roll hit, "Tequila," to the crowd's roaring approval?

Harmless fun? Perhaps. Comforting mainstream traditions? Maybe. But, by ap-plying the "logic" used by America's Drug Warriors—that songs referencing a mind-altering substance are, by definition, dangerous drug songs—it would seem that even old family favorites (as noted above) would cross that simple evidentiary threshold and deserve condemnation. But no—of all the drugs available, it is alcohol that seems to get a free pass.

Now, booze obviously is legal and certain other popular recreational drugs are not. Any further debate about the equity of that situation will have to occur else-where—but it doesn't seem unreasonable to wish that America's Drug Warriors would exhibit a bit more consistency in their opposition to drug-associated music. We have seen decades of attacks on just about any song related to illegal drugs while those same critics rarely dare to damn tunes that feature pro-liquor-abuse themes—a notable exception being Webb Pierce's "There Stands the Glass" ("that will ease all my pains"), which by its very prominence as a No. 1 C&W hit attracted enough negative attention that numerous Bible Belt radio stations ended up ban-ning it in 1954. Clearly, the bulk of the moralists' selectively applied ire has been re-served for rock 'n' roll (and, more recently, reggae and hip-hop) songs.

By focusing so narrowly, the censorious have managed to overlook some of the richest veins of potential targets. In fact, by their having generally given a free pass to C&W music and classical/opera—which have long featured plenty of content about debauchery and intoxication—they've missed a golden opportunity to broaden the battlefield. Instead of focusing all their angst on how the likes of a fic-tional dragon named Puff—or the evil pro-herb hip-hopper Puff Daddy—might in-fluence the young why not work up at least *some* indignation when Camille Saint-Saëns's *Melodies Persanes*, op. 26, no. 6 "Tournoiement (Songe d' opium)" is performed in classical concert halls? Or, hey, how about launching a boycott cam-paign against record companies and radio over Garth Brooks's and George Jones's huge 2001 hit "Beer Run" and any of the countless other blatantly liquor-themed C&W tunes?

Let's face facts: Americans have always been conflicted and had a love/hate relationship to recreational drug use. The roots of our *original* War On Drugs, the Prohibition movement, date back to 1789, when New England's puritanical busybodies formed a temperance society with the aim of controlling the alcohol consumption by—well, who else?—their fellow citizens. On the opposing side of the issue were a number of prominent fans of various "spirits" including President George Washington (who was well-known for brewing up his own batches of beer at Mount Vernon) and Thomas Jefferson (whose fabled wine cellar was simply second to none in the States).

There's no stopping "moral guardians" though, and the prohibitionists marched on, rallying the troops of sobriety with anti-booze tunes, including "The Temperance Crusade," "Young Man Shun That Cup," "Don't Drink Tonight Boys," "Take That Sparkling Wine Away," "Vile Wine-Cup, I Ne'er Can Forget Thee," "I'll Never Get Drunk Anymore," "The Lips That Touch Liquor Will Never Touch Mine," "Empty Is the Bottle, Father's Tight," "Come Home, Father," "Poor Drunkard's Child," "The Drunkard's Funeral," and "King Alcohol."

As catchy as some of those tunes may have been, they were no match against a truly formidable cultural force: the centuries-long tradition of common folks enjoying a bit of Dionysian revelry—and *singing* about it. For example, the British Isles produced a particularly rich vein of witty sing-along pub songs that reveal many attitudes about alcohol and its effects. Timeless classics from Ireland: "The Drinking Song," "Good Ale," "Drink It Up Men," "Whisky, You're the Devil," "The Jug of Brown Ale," "The Juice of the Barley," "Three Drunken Maidens," and "Tom's Tavern"; from Scotland: "Here's To Scottish Whisky," "The Charms of Whisky," "The Ale Is Dear," "Drunken Piper," "In Dispraise of Whisky," "Whisky in the Jar," "Fare Thee Well Whisky," and "Welcome Whisky Back Again"; and from merry olde England, the centuries-old "Five Nights Drunk" as well as "A Drop of Good Beer," "John Barleycorn," and "A Tankard of Ale."

As a nation founded by immigrants originating from many of those cultures, America's song traditions drew on those time-proven standards. Favorites within the early American folk canon include toe-tappers such as "Nothing Like Grog" and "There Is a Tavern in the Town." (Even America's foremost early bandleader John Phillip Sousa included in his sets such pieces as "The Whiskies: Scotch, Irish, Bourbon, and Rye" and "Convention of the Cordials, Wines, and Whiskies.") Certain forces, however, resented the taverns in *their* towns and after a long crusade—one that featured violent vigilante action by Ms. Carrie Nation and other members of her Women's Christian Temperance Union who invaded saloons to shatter beer barrels, whisky kegs, and bar counters with their axes—the 18th Amendment to the United States Constitution was passed by Congress and Prohibition (of the production and sale of alcohol) became national law in January 1920. It didn't take long for the criminalization of alcohol to backfire horribly. Government repression actually increased demand and Prohibition itself ended up breaking down general law and order by creating a profit motive for criminal activity. Suddenly good citizens were forced to interact with unsavory sorts simply to wet their whistle, and those criminal gangs ultimately corrupted the political structures of entire cities and states. The incredible power wielded by racketeers like Chicago's Al Capone and Detroit's Purple Gang was initially based on their ability to control the supply of illegal whisky that mainstream citizens sought.

The Prohibition era coincided with the rise of the recording industry in the 1920s and '30s, and as a result we were provided with some of the finest "drinkin' songs" ever committed to disc. Pioneering white mountain musicians contributed early country classics like "John Makes Good Liquor" (Fiddlin' John Carson), "Black Jack Moonshine" (Darby and Tarlton), and "Rye Whisky" (Roy Acuff), while African-American contemporaries were literally defining blues and jazz on such boozy numbers as "Hittin' the Bottle Stomp" (Mississippi Jook Band), "Ruckus Juice and Chittlins" (Memphis Jug Band), "Moonshine" (Memphis Minnie), "Good Liquor" (Washboard Sam), and "Gimme a Pigfoot and a Bottle of Beer" (Bessie Smith).

The last-named song also squeezed in an enthusiastic endorsement of "reefer" and, as there are vintage liquor songs, musical salutes to marijuana also have a long tradition. Early standouts include: 1927's "Willie the Weeper" (Frankie "Half Pint" Jaxon); '29's "Muggles" (Louis Armstrong); '32's "Reefer Man" (Cab Calloway Orchestra); '33's "Texas Tea Party" (Benny Goodman Orchestra); '35's "The Stuff Is Here and It's Mellow" (Cleo Brown) and "Blue Reefer Blues" (Richard M. Jones & his Jazz Wizards); '36's "The Weed Smoker's Dream" (Harlem Hamfats); '37's "The Stuff Is Here" (Georgia White); '38's "Jack, I'm Mellow" (Trixie Smith); "Light Up" (Buster Bailey's Rhythm Busters); "That Cat Is High" (Ink Spots); "Weed" (Bea Foote); "Reefer Head Woman" (Jazz Gillum and His Jazz Boys); "Reefer Hound Blues" (Curtis Jones); "I'm Feeling High and Happy" (Gene Krupa and His Orchestra); and "Ol' Man River (Smoke a Little Tea)" (Cootie Williams and His Rug Cutters); '41's "Knockin' Myself Out" (Lil Green); '43's "Reefer Song" (Fats Waller); '44's "Save the Roach for Me" (Buck Washington); '45's "Sweet Marijuana Brown" (Barney Bigard Sextette); and '47's "Lotus Blossom (Sweet Marijuana)" (Julia Lee).

At some point even the clueless Prohibition Bureau saw that public demand for booze was *so* strong that the laws were impossible to enforce, and in 1933 Congress finally stepped up and repealed the discredited liquor ban. But by then the G-Men were already recalibrating their investigational crosshairs to aim at other targets—in particular the drugs favored by pesky "outsiders" (e.g. foreigners, "colored folks," bohemians, and musicians), namely marijuana and cocaine.

And cocaine was—just as reefer and alcohol were—the subject of a considerable number of blues and jazz tunes, including "Cocaine Habit Blues" (Memphis Jug Band), "Cocaine Blues" (Luke Jordan), "Take a Whiff on Me" (Leadbelly), "Wacky Dust" (Chick Webb Orchestra with Ella Fitzgerald), and "Minnie, the Moocher" (Cab Calloway). These artists weren't the only ones to be musically inspired by cocaine, though. Even the famed psychologist Sigmund Freud penned his famous "Song of Praise" for the stuff way back in 1884!

Appreciative fans aside, the federal government deftly turned from banning liquor to launching a demonization campaign against the comparatively harmless drug marijuana. Mainly to have a legal hammer over the heads of certain population blocs. And to justify the continuing increases in annual budgets for an already bloated federal law enforcement bureaucracy.

Which brings us to the Reefer Madness era and the founding of the Federal Bureau of Narcotics, which was zealously lead by Chief Harry J. Anslinger. The chief made it absolutely clear in 1929 that one of the reasons he delighted in battling pot smokers was that "reefer makes darkies think they're as good as white men." And with that as a premise began the government's long propaganda campaign that would make hysterical claims about what now can be prescribed as a medicinal herb, and ultimately establish policies leading to the destruction of many people's careers, lives, and families. Those same policies would help pervert and corrupt the governments of numerous neighbor nations, and also help further break down the American public's sense that their government was democratic, rational, fair, and responsive to reason.

Rank propaganda films like *Marijuana: Weed with Roots in Hell*, *Devil's Harvest*, and the all-time classic *Reefer Madness* did their part in the '30s to try and convince everyone of the insanity that is triggered by even one single puff of pot. A sizeable portion of the populace, however, wasn't buying that line. Personal experience proved otherwise. Ironically, it was Prohibition's squeeze on the availability of booze that led some folks to first try marijuana as a recreational drug. And why not? The plant was then still fully legal—and best of all: reefer was also free, as it grew like a weed in many areas of the country.

In 1937, Anslinger's years of hard work finally paid off for him (and for the cotton barons who feared the rise of a competitive hemp fiber industry) when the US Congress was pushed into passing the Marijuana Tax Act. Purposely mistitled, the new law had *no* intention of taxing whatever marijuana industry existed—its goal was to ban the herb outright. And that would have been the end of the story, except for the result of so many of our military troops traveling to exotic and far-flung places around the globe after the nation got involved in World War II in 1941. A goodly number of them returned home quite a bit more worldly. Indeed, plenty of the soldiers saw, heard, and did things that changed their outlooks forever. Some stationed in Europe had their first-ever opportunity to drink British ale or French wine; others, sent to the African or Asian fronts, discovered marijuana for the first time.

And so upon the Allies' triumphant victories in 1945, many of the GIs returned home with new tastes in music and party favors. But while they had fought valiantly to defeat fascism abroad, the America that they returned to was becoming less free. The Cold War that soon developed would bring forth new hazards on the home front. While American families were being scared into building homey little bomb shelters, Republican Senator Joseph McCarthy began suggesting that citizens should fear that their neighbors could be genuine card-carrying closet Commies. Sadly, before the senator could be effectively discredited, he created a poisonous political atmosphere that had a huge impact on our culture—nearly ruining the careers of singers such as Woody Guthrie and Pete Seeger along the way. The songs that those artists created couldn't be erased simply by "blacklisting" the singers from performing. The folk traditions that they were part of were resilient enough to withstand a governmental inquisition. The content of those songs had resonated deeply with many Americans—especially, as it happened, an entire generation of young people who found folk-oriented music to be their calling. Thus, by the late '50s a genuine folk music revival began, and the Kingston Trio's phenomenal success in bringing folk standards to the pop charts was followed by the emergence of legions of folkies including Bob Dylan, Joan Baez, and Peter, Paul, and Mary.

And so, the War on Drugs reared its ugly head once more, seizing as its musical target that sing-along classic from 1963, "Puff, the Magic Dragon" (Peter, Paul, and Mary). A popular song that had sold a reported half million copies within a month and raced to the nation's No. 2 chart slot, "Puff" became the grist of rumor mills that contended that the mild childlike ditty—with its oblique and fanciful lyrics—"Puff the Magic Dragon lived by the sea / and frolicked in the autumn mist in a land called Honalee / Little Jackie Paper loved that rascal Puff..."—was actually *not* so benign. According to the drug sleuths: "Puff" is code for marijuana; "Dragon" is code for inhaling, or "draggin'"; "Jackie Paper" refers to a cigarette rolling paper; "mists" refers to clouds of exhaled smoke; et cetera. Thus what can be called the Great Drug Lyric Scare was off and running.

The case of poor ol' "Puff" raises several questions. First, how could a song that seems to be plainly about mythical dragons and mystical islands endanger a listener unaware of any theoretical drug connotations? Second, lyrics can be poetry and one attribute of poetry is that it often has the potential for multiple interpretations. Whose interpretation ought we accept—the author's (who, in this case, consistently denied that any drug references existed) or that of some self-appointed and overly aggressive morals police? Third, isn't there an intrinsic danger in having cultural bullies attempting to determine what any particular song lyric is *really* about? Beyond this: Where is the evidence that any drug addicts developed their bad habits *because* of music? And, where is the acknowledgment that countless drug addicts have gotten hooked without any musical inspiration whatsoever, and that plenty of folks can listen to "drug songs" all day long and not be tempted in the least to indulge?

The ultimate concern here has to be: couldn't just about *any* song be twisted into something else entirely if an ax-grinding analyst wanted to apply new meanings to every term in the lyrics? And the answer to that is yes. The published track record of the Drug Warriors reveals their so-called logic on this matter, as well as the way they willingly kick aside the rights of any artist to define his or her creations. It was the executive director of one American drug prevention organization who blithely informed a worldwide convention in 1995 that "the author's intended meaning, however, is irrelevant to the issue of how the lyrics might influence the public. People react and behave in response to their perceptions—not to reality. If listeners believe that the lyrics to a song have a drug-related meaning, they will be influenced by those beliefs, regardless of what the lyricist intended." As surreal as this seems, truth is, in fact, stranger than fiction. In 1999 a school board member in Belen, New Mexico—objecting to the fact that the graduating class voted "Goodbye to Romance" by Ozzy Osbourne as that year's class song—sputtered that he didn't *need* to hear the actual tune. He wanted the kids overruled because "Ozzy could be singing 'Mary Had a Little Lamb' and I would have a problem with it because of his history."

So, let's pause to see if we've got this all straight: anyone anywhere can interpret any lyrics (or even a band's name!) to mean *anything* they wish. Right? According to the Drug Warriors, what matters most is not what the lyric writer intends or even what he/she actually writes or sings. What gets their higher consideration is what the offended *thinks* may have been read or heard. And yet, in the conservatives' pipe dream of utopia, that originating artist is to be still held responsible for the content of that song? In other words, artistic intentions—and the US Constitution—be damned: we think we heard what we think we heard. As one Drug Warrior Web site reiterates: "People act on perceptions, even if they are inaccurate or completely wrong"—affording us with a perfect description of their own well-meaning, but clueless, efforts. [Note: Imagine the surprise this mindset induced in a Seattle '60s hippie group with the artful name Crome Syrcus when they read in a newspaper one day that a Rev. Richard Christiansen had avowed their moniker was "an allusion to a hypodermic needle."] At the very least it would be nice if such Drug Warriors would employ the technical skills of academics trained in text analysis, or semantics, or cryptology, or linguistics, or orthography, or something other than under-informed paranoia.

This brings us to one of the most confounding aspects of the Great Drug Lyric Scare. What on earth causes the Drug Warriors to go to such extremes in an effort to detect any possible clues—hidden, visible, audible, or otherwise—to help them

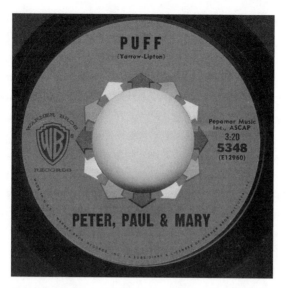

Peter, Paul & Mary's 1963 folk song, "Puff, The Magic Dragon," seemed to be a benign little radio hit to most listeners – until Drug Warriors tipped everyone off that is was a nefarious drug paean in disguise.

prove the obvious? Which is that drug songs definitely do exist. They are plentiful. They are popular. Why invest so much sweat in seeking veiled meanings, or strain the brain trying to decipher alleged druggy encryptions, or even bother trying to break these supposed word puzzles, when there is a massive body of recorded work that represents absolutely overt couldn't-possibly-be-more-in-your-face drug tunes (such as the scores of songs about liquor and/or other inebriants in country, classical, jazz, and mainstream rock 'n' roll)? The correct answer: the Drug Warriors are not on any kind of productive public-health-enhancing medical crusade but rather they are pursuing a selective sociopolitical agenda.

In the 1960s the newly emerging psychedelic rock 'n' roll scene bumped up against America's mainstream booze culture. "Psychedelic" is a medical term that describes the "abnormal stimulation of consciousness"—a state associated with the use of certain drugs, especially LSD (or more accurately LSD-25), otherwise known on the streets as acid. It was in the late '60s that the terms "psychedelic rock" and "acid rock" were adopted to describe new, wildly eclectic, and highly innovative forms of rock experimentation that became popular at the time. Telltale sonic elements of this music included feedback, droning chords, meandering lead guitar solos often spiced with sitarlike modal-scaled noodling, exotic percussion, and oblique tripped-out lyrics. Classic examples were created by artists like the Beatles, the Jimi Hendrix Experience, Jefferson Airplane, and the Electric Prunes.

The first rock 'n' roll that had the earmarks of what became codified as musical "psychedelia" was a handful of particularly innovative Beatles tracks, like "Tomorrow Never Knows," "Rain," "Yellow Submarine," and "Strawberry Fields Forever." But, by the time that 1967's Summer of Love came around, freaky-sounding tunes were popping up like hallucinogenic mushrooms. June brought us: "White Rabbit" (Jefferson Airplane) and "Light My Fire" (Doors); July: "All You Need Is Love" and "Baby You're a Rich Man (Beatles); August: "Purple Haze" (Jimi Hendrix Experience). Then as summer gave way to fall, the Drug Warriors had all the more to puzzle over: "She's a Rainbow" (Rolling Stones), "Incense and Peppermints" (Strawberry Alarm Clock)....

All in all, it was a magical season that yielded a bumper crop of psychedelic rock masterpieces, but it would be the Beatles—probably due to their prominence in '60s youth culture—who provided the richest source for imaginative drug sleuths. Indeed, the mind boggles when reviewing the list of their songs that became targets: 1965's "Day Tripper," '66's "Tomorrow Never Knows" and "Yellow Submarine" (slandered as a supposed reference to yellow Nembutal barbiturate capsules), '67's "Penny Lane" ("a pretty nurse is selling *poppies*)", "Strawberry Fields Forever," ("it must be *high* or low"), "With a Little Help from My Friends" ("I *get high*"), and "Fixing a Hole" (purportedly a reference to mainlining heroin—a particularly heinous

Jimi Hendrix's psychedelic debut 45, 1967's "Purple Haze," was inspired by a science fiction comic-book plot about a futuristic weapon—but ended up inspiring the street name of one type of LSD.

lie that was specifically denied by its author, Paul McCartney). In Britain the BBC joined in this folly, trying their luck at lyrical analysis on the *Sgt. Pepper's* LP and banning "A Day in the Life" from airplay: "*blew his mind* out" and "I had a *smoke* and fell into a dream" and "I'd love to *turn you on*". Interestingly, it seems that the one early Beatles song that could have been attacked more justifiably for promoting drugs—yet wasn't—was 1966's "Dr. Robert" ("If you're down he'll pick you up"; "*Take a drink* from his special cup." Ironically, the one 1966 Beatles song—"Got to Get You into My Life"—that McCartney *did* eventually admit was "an ode to pot" ("I took a ride") doesn't seem to have attracted the attention of the critics.

Eventually the Drug War crazies contended that the Beatles' beloved No. 1 hit from 1968, "Hey Jude," was nothing more than a pernicious paean to heroin. They went so far as to assert that the song's title was a reference to "Judas Iscariot—the friend who betrays you"—a claim that, if true, would seem to suggest a *negative* message about the drug. Their propaganda also manages to misquote the lyrics, but the authentic ones show what triggered their mental radar: "... the minute you let her under your skin / then you begin / to make it better ...". Paul McCartney's recollection, however, is contrary to their hypothesis: as the hit's author, he has consistently maintained that he penned the tune while thinking about Julian, the young son of his musical partner, John Lennon. Case closed.

But of all the Beatles' songs targeted, it was 1967's "Lucy in the Sky with Diamonds" that was attacked for the nuttiest reasons. Ignoring for a moment Lennon's perfectly plausible explanation that the title phrase erupted wholly from the innocent mind of his son Julian, who had just shown his father a childish sketch he'd made with that subject matter and title, the song's lyrics were, in fairness, sufficiently psychedelicized to invite scrutiny ("flowers that grow so incredibly *high*"). But then somehow some overly imaginative people got the harebrained notion that the initials of the song spelled out a message. "Lucy in the Sky with Diamonds" was thus made out to be a coded reference to the drug of the season, LSD.

The censors acronymic insanity was easy to ridicule, and London's outrageous new American expat rock star Jimi Hendrix led with a direct shot. The psychedelic shaman recorded a freaky new tune, "Stars that Play with Laughing Sam's Dice," that theoretically one-upped the Beatles by "encoding" within the song title the initials of the latest hybrid hipster drug, STP-LSD. However, it was a different Hendrix original that was instantly recognized as a world-shaking, genre-defining classic: "Purple Haze." Those disorienting guitars and unorthodox lyrics were very effective in driving Drug Warriors absolutely batty. And, even though the AM radio industry helped keep the tune rather low on the charts (No. 65), the song was hugely popular on record (and underground FM radio), ultimately coming to define the era as few others could. Other British acts that helped introduce musical psychedelia include the

Who, the Yardbirds, Manfred Mann, and the Pretty Things, each of whom recorded songs actually titled "LSD-25."

Stateside, the first psychedelic rock that many heard was by San Francisco's highest-profile hippie band, Jefferson Airplane, who'd managed to bag a major label recording deal that provided them with wide distribution and some promotional support. Their debut LP from 1966, *Jefferson Airplane Takes Off*, was actually recalled by their label when RCA executives belatedly took notice of two "suggestive" songs. When the album was reissued, the song "Runnin' 'Round this World" ("the nights I've spent with you have been fantastic *trips*") was deleted, and "Run Around" ("that sway as you lay under me") reappeared in altered form without any references to free love or metaphorical descriptions of drug experiments. The band's next LP, *Surrealistic Pillow*, was the real stunner. The lead single, "Somebody to Love," broke into the national Top-40 in April of 1967 and helped set the stage for the coming Summer of Love. But it was the second single released, "White Rabbit," that rocketed the whole topic of drug songs right into the headlines.

By the mid-'60s the FBI was actively building dossiers on the Airplane's activities and conservative critics had a field day. Far from being impressed with the unusual level of literacy evident in the band's work—the lyrics to "White Rabbit"—"one pill makes you larger, one pill makes you small" and "remember what the dormouse said: 'Feed your head'"—were based on Lewis Carroll's classic children's books (1865's *Alice's Adventures in Wonderland* and 1871's *Alice Through the Looking Glass*)—critics only saw the danger of Pied Piper–like musicians using such cute devices in attempts to disguise their pro-drug messages. (Even as late as 1999 "White Rabbit" was still hampered with so much Drug War baggage that the Fort Zumbald North High School band in St. Louis, Missouri, were informed that they couldn't play the song even as an *instrumental!*)

A leading conservative media figure of the Aquarian Age, the popular afternoon TV host Art Linkletter, showed little patience for the counterculture. And when it came time to squarely pin the blame for a personal tragedy, he wasted no time in trying to scapegoat the hippies. In 1969 Linkletter's despondent 20-year-old daughter dove out of a Hollywood apartment window to her death. This incident was sad on its own, but matters were only made worse when the family repeatedly insisted—contrary to the autopsy report's findings—that their deceased loved one had experienced a "bad trip" on LSD. It was simple: drugs were at fault. And it was the grieving father himself who attempted to set the news media straight about the "facts" of the case: "It isn't *suicide* because she wasn't herself. It was murder. She was murdered by the people who manufacture and sell LSD."

Another controversy of the era involved the emergence of a multimedia art form intended to simulate (or stimulate) a hallucinogenic drug trip. Though they were used as far back as the '50s by avant-jazzers and electronic composers, what became known as light shows are widely associated in the public's mind with the Haight-Ashbury hippie dance scene. Once adopted by Andy Warhol's artsy circle in New York City, the fad took off, and artists from coast to coast began expressing themselves by projecting awesome collages of lights and images on screens erected behind bandstands. One newspaper account gushed: "They can make radiant, pulsing stars and balls, dancing squares, rotating fingers and waves, and galaxies of exploding droplets—all in time to the music."

Less impressed were the authorities in various towns. Light show bans soon became just another tool that politicians would use to try and clamp down on the rising counterculture. In Seattle, for example, an ultimately unsuccessful effort was made in 1967 to shut down hippie dances by enforcing a nearly forgotten 1929 municipal code forbidding a form of risqué entertainment called shadow dancing. Another effort at halting hippie dances and concerts through the use of old blue laws was attempted the following year in Philadelphia, Pennsylvania. Citing a city ordinance dating from 1879, the mayor asserted that he could unilaterally ban any show that is "immoral in nature or unpleasant and harmful to the community."

But the battle against light shows was merely a sideshow. The favored target would remain the music. And, once on a crusade, Drug Warriors find clues everywhere they gaze. Here is a partial list of songs from that era that the drug sleuths have claimed were designed to convert the innocent to narcotics enslavement: "Candy Man" (Sammy Davis Jr.); "Good Vibrations" (Beach Boys); "Bend Me, Shape Me" (American Breed); "Mr. Tambourine Man" (Bob Dylan, and later, the Byrds); "Eight Miles High" and "5-D" (Byrds); "Trip, Stumble, and Fall" (Mamas & the Papas); "Magic Bus" and "I Can See for Miles" (Who); "Mellow Yellow" (Donovan); "Good Measure" (Lovin' Spoonful); "Magic Carpet Ride" (Steppenwolf); "Buy for Me the Rain" (Nitty Gritty Dirt Band); "Up, Up, and Away" (Fifth Dimension); and the Association's "Windy," allegedly about "Windowpane" type LSD, and "Along Comes Mary," allegedly a reference to marijuana, aka "Mary Jane." Rumors such as these spread like wildfire, and the Association were even intimidated from performing the last-named tune once when forces from California's Orange County sheriff's department monitored their show at Disneyland.

As this Great Drug Lyric Scare picked up momentum, the list of suspect songs blossomed: the hit "Whiter Shade of Pale" ("We *tripped* the light fandango") (Procol Harum); the No. 1 "Bridge over Troubled Waters," which was slandered as a promoter of heroin (Simon and Garfunkel); "Crystal Ship" ("Before you slip into unconsciousness"), "Break On Through," and another No. 1 hit, "Light My Fire," (Doors) were targeted. Booked for a September 1967 appearance on CBS-TV's *Ed Sullivan Show,* the Doors' singer Jim Morrison had been instructed to drop his "druggy" lyrical line ("Girl, we couldn't get much *higher*") from "Light My Fire," and he agreed to substitute alternative lyrics—but at the last moment he rebelled and sang the line as originally written. Ed Sullivan was so furious that he skipped his traditional post-song handshake ritual.

Now, let's recap for a moment. We've now established the existence of drug songs—that is, songs that have been named after drugs, songs that mention drugs in passing, and songs that condone, celebrate, or advocate drug use and/or abuse. However, few of the songs just listed are *those*. Some targeted tunes like Dylan's "Mr. Tambourine Man" ("Take me on a *trip*"), "Proud Mary" (Creedence Clearwater Revival), "Stairway To Heaven" ("with a word she can get *what* she came for") (Led Zeppelin), even that plainly innocent, back-to-nature hit "Rocky Mountain High" (John Denver), Blue Swede's (No. 1) hit "Hooked on a Feeling" ("*I'm high* on believing"), and Queen's "Another One Bites the Dust"—which censors alleged contained a hidden instruction for listeners to "decide to smoke marijuana" or, alternately (depending on which Drug Warrior was ranting), "it's fun to smoke marijuana"—were wrongfully snagged in a paranoid dragnet cast indiscriminately. [Note: While most folks never considered the squeaky clean John Denver to be a blatant druggie, others apparently had their suspicions, and the recent release of formerly secret FBI files has revealed that as late as 1990 the first President Bush's legal counsel, C. Boyden Gray, prepared a memo that questioned the singer's drug use and possible ties to the mob.]

It's pretty clear that by this point the "moral guardians" had gone off the deep end. And, unfortunately, three decades later, a different generation of musicians would face censors with a similar low capacity for discerning nuances in music. Indeed most censors, far from actually being trained experts of any sort, are usually just folks whose antennae are wired for taking maximum offense at the emergence of anything new, unusual, or just plain different in the culture. Perhaps this helps explain why they are sensitive enough to worry about "drug songs" but apparently not able to discern when a particular song might actually carry a not-so-secret message *against* the misuse of substances. In fact, censors have long pounced on songs that, had they taken a moment or two to listen before condemning, would actually deserve recognition as being (to varying degrees) thematically *anti*-drug.

It would be hard to find a more plainly stated personal rejection of a drug than in the lyrics to Cole Porter's pop gem, "I Get a Kick Out of You": "Some get a kick from cocaine / I'm sure that if I took even one sniff / That would bore me terrifically too, but..." Though far from promoting cocaine use, the mere mention of the substance was enough for radio station censors to shun the 1935 recording of the song by Jeanne Aubert in favor of a tamed version recorded by Broadway star Ethel Merman that substituted the irrelevant phrase "Don't want no perfume from Spain."

Despite conventional wisdom to the contrary, there have been many songs during the rock 'n' roll and hip-hop eras that contain negative messages about drug use. That list would even include "Mother's Little Helper" by the Rolling Stones. This was another song widely attacked—and even banned by the BBC—for promoting drug use when in fact it did quite the opposite ("...there's a little yellow pill...And if you take more of those / you will get an overdose..."). Other such cautionary cuts from recent decades are: "Artificial Energy" (Byrds), "Sunny Goodge Street" ("violent hash-smoker") (Donovan), "Pammie's on a Bummer" (Sonny Bono), "Round, Round" ("Today you are just high / Tomorrow you are dead") (Jonathan King), "The Pusher" (Hoyt Axton), "The Addicted Man" (Game), "Signed D.C." (Love), "Amphetamine Annie" ("you ought to know...*Speed Kills!*") (Canned Heat), "Poppies" ("and death takes another youth") (Nina Simone), "My Girl Hates My Heroin" (Iggy Pop), "Apothecary" (Ambrosia), "Pusherman" and the hit "Freddie's Dead (Theme from *Superfly)*" (Curtis Mayfield), "Shakin' with Linda" (Soul Survivors), "Cold Turkey" (John Lennon), "No No Song" ("I don't smoke it no more") (Ringo Starr), "Medicine Jar" (Paul McCartney), "The Long Road" (Genesis), "Needle and the Damage Done" (Neil Young), "(Stay Away From) The Cocaine Train" (Johnny Paycheck), "Monkey on Your Back" (Aldo Nova), "White Lines (Don't Do It)" (Grand Master Flash), "Dope Smokin' Moron" (Replacements), "Heroin Girl" (Everclear), "Not If You Were the Last Junkie on Earth (Heroin Is So Passé)" (Dandy Warhols), "Crack Addict" (World MCs), "Get Off That Crack" (Jigsy King), and "Stop Crack" (Nightmares on Wax).

Back in 1966, the censors raced each other to condemn Paul Revere and the Raiders' tune "Kicks." Based on the title alone, Drug Warriors assumed the tune extolled the "virtues" of seeking thrills—or kicks—through drug use. In fact, the lyrics clearly warn that "...you *don't* need kicks girl / to get you through this world each day...that world goes *nowhere*...". Though the song became a big hit with the Top-40 teeny-bopper crowd, music by that pop combo held zero interest to the actual drug-using counterculture the censors were opposing.

Even though Steppenwolf's 1968 epic "The Pusher" featured an unmistakably anti-drug lyrical message ("*goddamn* the pusherman"), it was still widely condemned as a drug tune. We may never know whether it was the band's prominent usage of profanity that boggled conservatives' minds—but authorities in North Carolina took it upon themselves to personally warn singer John Kay not to sing his lyrics in a local concert. In light of that threat, the band played an instrumental version that night with vocals provided enthusiastically by their supportive audience. One can only imagine the uproar that would have occurred had Drug Warriors ever discovered "Snowblind Friend," another of Steppenwolf's songs, which bore a specifically *anti*-cocaine message.

Then there is the Velvet Underground's tune from 1968, "Heroin." This underground hit presents a fine illustration of the multiple, and potentially mutually exclusive, interpretations that a song can inspire. Of course, its title alone limited any commercial potential, but fans who'd figured the plodding song portrayed an unattractive glimpse at the hidden world of desperate substance abusers were puzzled to learn that critics were charging the New York–based group with promoting the use of the drug. The eye (and ear) of the beholder was obviously a significant factor in all this.

As has been widely noted elsewhere, 1968 was a turning point in world politics, with many nations experiencing turmoil and revolution. In America, Richard Nixon clawed his way into office on a tough-talking law-and-order platform and a cynical campaign promise to make peace in Vietnam. By that year the war had become a central political issue, though drugs remained a fixation for the political right wing. Not unsurprisingly, the two issues melded into one on more than one occasion.

Take the case of poor Phil Ochs. Here was a notable protest singer, a veteran of myriad civil rights and peace rallies, an effective rabble-rouser, and a genuine thorn in the side of the Establishment—a fact greatly appreciated by his fans, though less so by the FBI. After having been a recording artist with a major label contract for a half-decade (and with several albums to his credit), by 1968 he had yet to score with any kind of "hit" record. That's when he finally came up with his best-ever shot at scoring on the charts—a brilliantly cynical masterpiece featuring sing-along lyrics about the hypocrisy of modern society, all wedded to a fun, rollicking, ragtimey tune called "Outside of a Small Circle of Friends." Upon its release, the darn thing was embraced by a promising number of radio markets and began climbing a few regional sales charts. Hopes were high among fans that he'd finally gotten the shot at the "big time" that he'd always deserved.

But then the tides suddenly shifted. Overnight, it seemed, various stations began axing the song from their playlists. Initial word was that the disc was being shunned on the grounds that it "promoted drugs"—a criticism which, for once, was technically accurate since the lyrics *did* feature a comparative evaluation ("Smoking marijuana is *more* fun than drinking beer"). This explanation seemed a bit disingenuous though, especially when stories began to filter out that Nixon was leaning on the (theoretically independent) FCC, who were strong-arming radio managers and advising them to shun Ochs in general. While it can be debated which of Ochs's ideas troubled them the most, it is certain that the drug lyric issue could be the most easily employed as a rationale for governmental intervention. This would not be the first time, nor the last, that a political gadfly has been trumped by the playing of the drug card.

The historic moment in 1970 when the President met the King—and Elvis Presley offered Richard Nixon his services as a secret narcotics agent.

As the mid-term congressional elections approached in 1970, Nixon revved up an aggressive attack on rock 'n' roll and the emerging counterculture. Nixon also enlisted his VP, Spiro T. Agnew, who kicked off this battle against the purveyors of rock with some suspiciously reasonable terms: "We should listen more carefully to popular music, because at its best it is worthy of more serious appreciation." Then, truer to form, he added the zinger "and at its worst it is blatant drug-culture propaganda." Left unsaid was that it would be the likes of Agnew—who for all his posturing would, under threat of multiple criminal charges, soon be resigning from office in disgrace—and his ilk who would be determining which was which. This judging process would have been led by a man who believed that song lyrics—including, specifically, those to "Eight Miles High" (Byrds), "White Rabbit" (Jefferson Airplane), "That Acapulco Gold" (Rainy Daze), and "With a Little Help from My Friends" (Beatles)—were "threatening to destroy our national strength."

Nixon was the first president to ratchet this rhetoric up to a fever pitch—indeed he gets the credit for being the first to declare an official War on Drugs. And one great admirer of his efforts was the "King of Rock 'n' Roll." It was in late 1970 that Nixon cautiously granted a reception in the Oval Office as requested by Elvis Presley. By then Elvis had been largely irrelevant to the music scene for nearly a decade. And for his part, Nixon needed *any* opportunities he could find to associate with anything remotely youth-oriented because the 1972 election was coming up and for the first time ever 18-year-olds would be eligible to vote. Elvis wanted the president to appoint him as an honorary "federal agent at large" in the War on Drugs. According to White House files, Elvis asserted: "I have done an in-depth study of drug abuse and Communist brainwashing techniques, and am right in the middle of the whole thing where I can and will do the most good." Despite Presley's personal poly-pharmacological activity, er, "study of drug abuse," Nixon was impressed enough that day to award the hypocrite an honorary Bureau of Narcotics and Dangerous Drugs badge.

In a visit to FBI headquarters soon after, Elvis informed his hosts that he enjoyed meeting with college kids and community groups, where he made himself "accessible for talks and discussions regarding the evils of narcotics and other problems of concern." The same internal FBI report notes that "Presley indicated that he is of the opinion that the Beatles laid the groundwork for many problems that we are having with young people by their filthy unkempt appearances and suggestive music." White House memos similarly note that Elvis informed Nixon that the Beatles were guilty of spreading anti-American sentiments among the youth. The president agreed, adding that: "Violence, drug usage, dissent, protest all seem to merge in generally the same group of young people." [Note: Nixon's mindset on such matters was revealed decades later when yet another batch of his secret White House tapes was released showing that at a March 14, 1972, staff meeting in the Oval Office, the President stated: "*Look*: People get drunk. People chase girls. And the point is, it's a *hell* of a lot better for them to get drunk than to take drugs. It's better to chase girls than boys. Now, that's my position and let's *stop* this crap! *Understand?*" Another tape has him riffing about how reasonable people simply "drink to have fun" while lowly drug users just want "to get high."]

In 1971 Nixon established the Drug Enforcement Administration (DEA), and he also had the FBI keeping tabs on various rock musicians, including Elvis Presley, John Lennon, the Grateful Dead, Jefferson Airplane, and the Doors' singer, Jim Morrison. At one point he reportedly made a personal appeal to the radio industry to review and ban songs that dealt with drugs—and more ominously, the untidy topics of violence and war! Nixon also took the time to publicly condemn—and, in doing so, inadvertently highlight (Hey! If Nixon hates it, it's gotta be good!)—Brewer and Shipley's "One Toke over the Line." Many stations took the hint and quickly dropped it from their playlists, an act that was counterbalanced by the prominent coverage the administration's antics got on prime time network news, ultimately resulting in a solid Top-Ten placement on the charts.

It was in May 1971 that the FCC reportedly telegrammed *every* radio station in America with an infamously pointed memo which, in essence, warned the industry that "broadcasting songs 'promoting' or 'glorifying' the use of drugs could endanger station licenses." Not only would the stations be expected to reject overt drug language, but—in this new age of psychedelic wordplay—they were also being asked (as with "foreign language broadcasts") to "ascertain the meaning of words or phrases used in the lyrics." Well, here's a big "goo goo g'joob" to you guys!

Now granted, broadcasters have always technically been accountable for the content of anything they allow to be aired, but this blunt reminder definitely made station owners sit up and take notice. To assist in this purge, the missive even helpfully provided a list (that had been prepared by that great arbiter of cultural taste, the US Army) of 22 songs purported to have drug connotations. It was this list (and a similar one issued the same year by the Illinois Crime Commission) that revived the flickering embers of "drug-song" paranoia about such fading oldies as "Puff, the Magic Dragon," "Yellow Submarine," "Lucy in the Sky with Diamonds," and "Eight Miles High."

This threat to their operating licenses by the FCC had an immediate chilling effect on radio stations as well as record companies—one big label, MGM Records, even called a press conference to announce that they'd taken direct action by dropping from their talent roster 18 different bands who'd been identified as singing songs that promoted drugs. It was noted that the company had less-than-sterling reasons for the move. It seems none of those artists had been very profitable—unlike the hit-making Eric Burdon (formerly of the Animals) who sold tons of records (including one, "Sandoz," specifically named in honor of the company where LSD was invented) and who remained untouched on the MGM talent roster.

That's about the time that another classic case of misidentification occurred and once again a song with a negative message about drugs was lumped in with *pro*-drug songs and banished. It was Bloodrock's 1971 record "D.O.A." that was dropped from the playlist at station WDAS in Philadelphia after just one airing. The paranoia driving the Great Drug Lyric Scare apparently prevented that station manager from seeing that the Top-40 hit actually had a clear—and graphic (replete with an ambulance siren's wail, etc.)—*anti*-drug theme. Bloodrock would not be the last act to ever have an anti-drug song misinterpreted by trigger-happy censors. Later examples include 1977's "Carmelita" ("I'm all *strung out* on heroin") (Linda Ronstadt) and "That Smell" ("There's *too* much smoke and *too* much coke ... the smell of *death* surrounds you)" (Lynyrd Skynyrd).

Another hot issue of the times regarded that new countercultural innovation the rock festival and the increasing opposition it faced from various authorities. From the very first outdoor, overnight concert event that promoted itself as a rock festival—the Sky River Lighter than Air Fair of August 1968 in Sultan, Washington—right on up through August 1969's legendary Woodstock Music and Art Fair in Bethel, New York, they had never been popular with the authorities. By 1972 scores of major festivals had been produced, leaving hundreds of thousands of young people with fond memories of peace, freedom, brotherhood, and great music.

Conversely, outsiders were having visions of all the anarchy, indiscriminate sex, and free drugs that their imaginations could conjure, and active opposition began directly in the wake of Woodstock. Seattle's Roman Catholic diocese sponsored a giant ad in a major metropolitan newspaper in 1969 demanding that rock musicians be prosecuted and the "drug-sex-rock-squalor" of rock festivals be banned. The *Seattle Post-Intelligencer*'s editorial board vented their collective spleen claiming that "the orgiastic aspects of the rock festivals... violate accepted public morality and they rip and tear at those standards of human conduct evolved through the centuries which separate mankind from the rest of the animal kingdom."

Various organizations held rallies in Atlanta, Chicago, Houston, and Tucson to protest the legality of giant rock festivals. In 1972, the Indiana legislature—stampeded by an attorney general who pegged rock festivals as "drug supermarkets" operated by the mob—quickly enacted legislation that banned such large gatherings. Too swiftly it turned out: in their haste, the learned representatives had also managed to outlaw just about any large public event, including their state's main claim-to-fame—the Indianapolis 500 auto race! Prohibitions against music festivals in particular would need to be more exacting to be effective, and the legislatures of Illinois, Washington, and several other states rose to that challenge and enacted laws that by about 1972 made such festivals all but extinct.

Nixon's re-election in 1972 promised conservatives "Four More Years" of additional time to hound their preferred targets—and New York Senator James L. Buckley chose to begin 1973 by investigating a new "drugola" scandal. This updated version of the old payola charade amounted to nothing much more than allegations that radio DJs were being bribed with cocaine to favor certain songs. Though his final report failed to document any proof that rock 'n' roll and drugs were linked, that didn't stop him from threatening the record industry by stating that federal action might be necessary unless more firms fell into line and policed their artists.

This was no small thing to demand given that songs that artfully hinted at—or even flatly stated—their references to drugs were being created by the label's top revenue-generating acts. The fact is, as bands produced more and more "drug songs," the censors just couldn't keep pace, *and* the record-buying public loved it. A comprehensive, if imaginary, *Drug Liberation Greatest Hits* album of the late '60s and 1970s would have contained such memorable numbers as: 1965's "Mary Jane" (Janis Joplin); '66's "Rainy Day Woman No. 12 and 35" ("everybody must get *stoned*") (Bob Dylan) and "Bass Strings" ("won't you pass that reefer round") (Country Joe & the Fish); the '67 hit "That Acapulco Gold" (Rainy Daze), "Night of the Long Grass"

(Troggs), and "Amphetamine Gazelle" (Mad River); the '68 hit "Goin' Up in the Country" ("where *mari-ju-an-a* grows") (Canned Heat), and "I Like Marijuana" (David Peel); "Talkin' Vietnam Pot Luck Blues" (Tom Paxton), and "Don't Step on the Grass, Sam" (Steppenwolf); the '69 hits "Cloud Nine" (Temptations), "Coming into Los Angeles" (Arlo Guthrie), "Don't Bogart Me" ("Don't bogart that *joint*, my friend") (Fraternity of Man), "Stoned Woman" (Ten Years After), "Get Back" ("California *grass*") (Beatles), and "I Want To Take You Higher" (Sly and the Family Stone); 1971's "Sweet Leaf" (Black Sabbath), "High Time We Went" (Joe Cocker), and "Illegal Smile" (John Prine); the '72 hit "Hi, Hi, Hi" (Paul McCartney and Wings)—a single which the BBC *did* slap a radio ban on—and "30 Days in the Hole" (Humble Pie); the '73 (No. 1) hit "The Joker" ("I'm a midnight *toker*") (Steve Miller Band), and that year's "(Down to) Seeds and Stems (Again)" (Commander Cody and His Lost Planet Airmen) and "Panama Red" (New Riders of the Purple Sage); '74's "Willin'" ("give me weed, whites, and wine") (Linda Ronstadt) and "Too Rolling Stoned" (Robin Trower); '75's "Roll Another Number (For the Road)" (Neil Young), "Pass It Around" (Smokie), and "Light Up" (Styx); the 1976 (No. 9) hit "Magic Man" ("Let's get high a while") (Heart); 1977's "Reefer Madness" (Hawkwind), "Twigs and Seeds" (Jesse Winchester), and "Homegrown" (Neil Young); '78's "Bustin' Out" (Rick James); and, from 1979, "Billy Bardo" (Johnny Paycheck) and "African Reggae" (Nina Hagen).

After the watershed 1980 election, the "Reagan Revolution" swept across America and the new administration proceeded to launch a "culture war" against liberals and all of pop culture. By 1982 the president had formalized his administration's approach to drug control—initially focusing on their concerns about marijuana. In fact, Carlton Turner, Reagan's first Drug Czar, once—while clearly channeling the spirit of Harry J. Anslinger, who'd asserted back in 1948 that "marijuana leads to pacifism and communist brainwashing"—insisted that pot use was inextricably linked to "the present young-adult generation's involvement in anti-military, anti–nuclear power, anti–big business, anti-authority demonstrations."

And with that simple declaration, we see revealed the right wing's true agenda. They couldn't care less about the health, safety, and welfare of individual pot smokers—the goal was to break up (by mass jailings if necessary) alliances of people who were involved in leftist (albeit *legal*) political activities. It seems that marijuana arrests were seen as a convenient way to eliminate huge numbers of the Republicans' opposition. The Reagan anti-drug policy that was launched in 1982 consisted of accelerated arrests, prosecutions, and incarcerations of casual users, along with an active "educational" facet that largely amounted to the much-lampooned head-in-the-sand Just Say No campaign—a simplistic mantra so feeble that it was easily countered by one scruffy punk band, Bitter End, and their defiantly contrary song "Just Say Yes."

Another facet of the War on Drugs was the FBI's new Drugs Demand Reduction Program that sought the assistance of pop culture figures to appear in televised ads. One band who stepped up to volunteer, the Beach Boys (who had already performed at Reagan's 1984 inaugural gala), were actually rejected. Internal FBI documents reveal that an investigation ensued, and the final report sent to Director William Sessions noted that various members of the popular band had had "drinking problems," and that leader Brian Wilson "was disdaining all moderation in food and alcohol and was careless about the amount of drugs he consumed." The G-Men's final recommendation? "Because of this adverse information...an FBI/Beach Boys video relating to drug abuse prevention would be an unfavorable endeavor." The band's manager was quoted years later as saying: "You could make the counter-argument that actually there is some *benefit* to having prior experience before making an anti-drug message.... What good is it to have a priest up there who's never experimented in any way, shape, or form?"

Good point. But one that was overlooked while Reagan's charismatic speeches continued to dazzle the citizenry. A number of other conservatives—both Democrat and Republican—joined forces to launch the Parents Music Resource Center's (PMRC) anti-rock campaign in 1985. They announced their concerns over several aspects of modern music, including content that they considered to be advocating sex, violence, drug use, and even matters of the occult. As congressional hearings—and other efforts that the PMRC sparked—played out over the next few years, it became apparent to observers that the moms who were behind it all mainly had their hearts in battling artists who'd gone too far with sexual matters. Objections to the other issues, including drugs, seemed to be afterthoughts to their initial horror at discovering "dirty" lyrics in modern songs. Then again, maybe the PMRC realized that they could get unlimited media attention for their cause by playing up the sex aspect—or, that the drug issue was a bigger battle on which others would have to provide leadership. (One song of that era that was condemned was the Bangles' 1985 No. 1 hit "Walk Like an Egyptian." The offending lyrics? "Foreign types with *hookah pipes* say / Ay oh whey oh.")

Then in 1986, Reagan launched yet another War on Drugs. First Democrats and liberals had to be cowed (through a process of having Republicans tar them as "soft on drugs") into supporting what became the 1986 Anti–Drug Abuse Act. This established mandatory minimum sentences—a disastrous transfer of power from federal judges to prosecutors—and greatly increased the penalties for drug offenses, which would clog our courts and prisons with relatively harmless stoners for decades to come. Fortified with these harsh new policies and laws, the Reaganites got busy and Drug Czar Turner personally raised the stakes by telling Americans that "marijuana leads to homosexuality...and therefore to AIDS." Although that was one of the exceedingly few times that the A-word would ever be mentioned publicly by any high-ranking member of the Reagan administration during their eight long years in power—reportedly, the president himself never let the offensive term pass his lips—the statement itself was a perfect example of the right wing's habitual reliance on opinion rather than scientific data.

Next on the right's agenda was to bolster the FCC's ability to restrict "indecent" language on radio and TV. In 1978, during Jimmy Carter's administration, the FCC's authority to regulate "indecent" speech on the airways was upheld by the Supreme Court, and the agency promptly began enforcing a curfew on rude language. Radio stations could only air the stuff after the kiddies had gone to bed: 10:00 p.m.–6:00 a.m. But in 1987 the FCC began a clampdown: new warning letters were sent to a few specific stations, and hints went out to all broadcasters that the airing of "indecent" material—even at ten o'clock—*might* trigger a governmental response. Then after much legal wrangling, a federal court of appeals judge ruled that the FCC needed to establish exactly which hours would comprise a "safe harbor" for mature program-ming. That's when Sen. Jesse Helms rammed through a bill placing a complete 24-hour ban on such broadcasts—a radically unconstitutional abridgment of the First Amendment that was quickly tossed aside by another court.

Meanwhile, many musicians were busy creating works that became ever more blatant with their messages of drug liberation. It was Jamaica's Rastafarian reggae bands in particular who first found a way to rhetorically counter the prohibitionists. The famously easygoing reggae culture has long extolled the use of their sacrament, marijuana, and simply by creating songs that note the pleasurable virtues of smok-ing weed—in the process ignoring its illegal status—they managed to, in effect, de-criminalize its usage by denying the need for approval by whatever authorities. Trend-setting songs in that rich tradition include "Legalize It" (Peter Tosh) and "Kaya" (Bob Marley).

In the 1990s the "alternative rock" and hip-hop scenes produced a whole new wave of reefer songs, including "Smoke 'Em" (Fun Lovin' Criminals), "Who's Got the Herb?" (311), "I Wanna Get High" (Cypress Hill), "Blunt Time" (Doctor Dre), "Pack the Pipe" (Pharcyde), "Marijuana in Your Brain" (Lords of Acid), and "Because I Got High," (Afroman). This revived tradition of having a "drug song" or two on an album is probably why one group, Pop Will Eat Itself, once recorded a tune humorously ti-tled "The Token Drug Song."

As the decade unfolded, a new form of social gathering known as a rave and an attendant rave culture were created by a generation who'd come to prefer "dance music" to plain old rock 'n' roll. Various schools of ultramodern, synthesized, elec-tronic-based disco—now called house, trance, trip-hop, etc.—were forged through live performances on record turntables by DJs at events ("raves") that were typically held in unorthodox venues like old abandoned industrial warehouses. This was a new generation—replete with their own forms of music and new drugs like MDMA or, as it's known on the street, ecstasy (or "E"). Their unregulated events soon attracted the unwanted attentions of the morals watchdogs.

And so for several years authorities across the country struggled to find ways of repressing this new youth scene. Raves were shut down for all of the government's traditional excuses: noise and/or fire code ordinance violations, permit "problems," the presence of drugs, etc. However, the Drug Warriors were desperate to come up with a magic bullet. They sought a foolproof means of squashing raves once and for all. In early 2001 they devised a radical new tactic: attempting to apply federal "crack house" laws to raves and hold the event promoters liable for any public drug usage. At about the same time a joint investigation by the New Orleans police department and the DEA was launched—Operation: Rave Review.

The unlucky first targets were a music promoter and the manager of that city's State Palace Theater who had staged a number of events at the hall. Charged by the DEA, the duo faced up to 20 years in prison and $500,000 in fines. A subsequent press release from the defense noted that "passed by Congress in 1986 to combat crack cocaine, the federal 'crack house' law was designed to punish the owners or operators of houses used for the manufacture, storage, distribution or use of illegal drugs. Yet Congress specifically rejected using the crack house tactic last year when it passed the Ecstasy Anti-Proliferation Act." Furthermore, by the time that act was passed in October 2000, lawmakers had wisely "eliminated a controversial provision that would have limited speech about ecstasy and other drugs. Raves are a legitimate cultural event just like rock concerts, art exhibitions and film screenings, and can be an important outlet for young people."

The American Civil Liberties Union (ACLU) stepped in, saying that it opposes such prosecutions on constitutional grounds: "Holding club owners and promoters of raves criminally liable for what some people may do at these events is no different from arresting the stadium owners and promoters of a Rolling Stones concert or a rap show because some concertgoers may be smoking or selling marijuana." Of additional concern was the fact that "prosecutors around the country are watching the case and have already publicly announced an interest in applying the same strategy in their districts." And, "if the government is successful in shutting down raves, what's to stop them from applying this tactic to other music genres, such as hip-hop, heavy metal and jazz, where drug use is known to exist?"

What indeed? In July 2002 another legislative assault was mounted in the form of US Senate Bill 2633—the Reducing America's Vulnerability to Ecstasy Act (RAVE Act) was passed by a committee and was being steered towards a full vote. According to the Drug Policy Alliance Action Center this bill would expand the "crack house statute" and "give federal prosecutors new powers to shut down raves or other musical events they don't like and punish business owners for hosting or promoting them." Violators could face prison sentences and a $250,000 fine. "The RAVE Act punishes businessmen and women for the crimes of their customers and is unprecedented in US history.... If the bill becomes law, property owners may be too afraid to rent or lease their property to groups...putting on all-night dance parties, effectively stifling free-speech and banning raves and other musical events." Well, welcome to George W. Bush's "new Domestic Order" where—after congressional passage of the act in April 2003—dance promoters, rather than those using or selling drugs, are now at heightened risk of prosecution.

Having apparently learned not one darn lesson from this nation's failed experiment with alcohol prohibition, or the blatant hypocrisy of the *Reefer Madness* propaganda farce, the senseless and corrupt "War on Drugs" has been stubbornly supported by every recent federal administration despite the lack of any genuine progress. Hope lingers, however, that one day the citizenry will come to understand that the Drug Warriors' main obstacle to success is their flawed premise: that the criminal justice system is an effective way to solve what is a patently educational and medical matter that ought to be dealt with as such.

CHAPTER 5

Let's Talk About Sex

There's a definite relationship between illicit sex and any music with a
syncopated beat.

—Reverend Charles Boykin, 1976

SEX. Yes, without a doubt, songs about sex (love, romance . . . *whatever*)—more
than any other type of taboo music—have provided the best opportunity for
people to take offense down through the ages. The simple fact that such private
matters are ever addressed in public song is enough to rile some people—while for others,
hearing a good "dirty" song on occasion can be a hoot.

Indeed, at one end of the societal spectrum we have the good and decent folks who
would likely object to the idea of any song addressing any topic that had anything whatsoever to do with sex. To their view, it is all equally inappropriate as subject matter for
songwriters—from the rudest old fornicatin' blues tune imaginable to a tenderly romantic
love ballad. Other people have felt differently. Some, for example, might prefer a mature
and sophisticated overture (". . . Oh, my love / I hunger for your kiss . . .") like the Righteous
Brothers' 1965 hit "Unchained Melody" or a smooth piece like Marvin Gaye's invitational
'73 (No. 1) hit "Let's Get It On," while for others, Ice-T's rather-less-than-suave '88 hip-
hop pitch, "Girls, Let's Get Buck Naked and Fuck," does the job perfectly well.

Somewhere in between those extremes, we find a number of other approaches, including sex-related songs that are lighthearted, humorous, or downright goofy, such
as Jewel Akens's 1965 hit "The Birds and the Bees," Tommy James and the Shondells'
'66 (No. 1) hit "Hanky Panky," the Fugs' '65 classic "Boobs a Lot" and their "Wet Dream"
of '67, and Chuck Berry's '72 (No. 1) hit "My Ding-A-Ling." Then there are those danceable
funky favorites like Hot Chocolate's '75 hit "You Sexy Thing," George Michael's '87 (No.
2) hit "I Want Your Sex" (which was banned by radio stations in Cincinnati, Denver, New

Orleans, Minneapolis, Pittsburgh, and New York City), Madonna's '90 hits "Hanky Panky" and "Justify My Love" (which MTV banned, sparking the sale of 400,000 videos), Bell Biv Devoe's '90 (No. 3) hit "Do Me!," Salt-N-Pepa's admirably forthright '91 hit "Let's Talk About Sex," Sir Mix-A-Lot's '92 (No. 1) hit "Baby Got Back," the All Saints' '98 hit "Booty Call," and Destiny's Child's '01 (No. 1) hit "Bootylicious." Not to mention the rude rockers like: Jimi Hendrix's '67 hit "Foxy Lady," Lou Reed's '73 hit "Walk On the Wild Side," Ian Dury & the Blockheads' '77 hit "Sex and Drugs and Rock and Roll," Joan Jett's '82 hit "Do You Wanna Touch Me (Oh Yeah)," Mötley Crüe's '89 gems "Sticky Sweet" and "Slice of Your Pie," the Divinyls' '91 hit "I Touch Myself" ("…when I think about you…"), Nine Inch Nails' '94 (No. 4) hit "Closer" ("…I want to fuck you *like an animal*…"), Christina Aguilera's "Dirrty" (which was a worldwide radio hit in 2002—*except* in the USA), or Custom's controversial '02 radio hit "Hey, Mister" ("…I really like your daughter / I want to eat her like ice cream…"), a video that was instantly banned by MTV.

It wasn't the banning of "dirty" songs (or their associated videos), but the outlawing of books dealing with sexual matters that comprise the most significant censorship cases in American legal history. In either case, the underlying motivations have remained consistent, and lurking beneath just about every censor's outrage about the "throbbing beat" and "lurid lyrics" in youth-oriented music has been a fixation on the carnal desires of *other* people—people that the would-be censors have no jurisdiction over. It's clear that "moral guardians" not only disapprove of songs that refer to even monogamous heterosexual relationships, they also abhor those that deal with any aspect of human sexuality.

A few quick examples will help set the stage. The great American composer Cole Porter wrote witty lyrics that occasionally touched on aspects of love and sex. And so, during his lifetime (and since), a number of his songs have had certain verses altered or suppressed for public performances—to the extent that today it is quite a challenge to even locate the complete lyrics to some of his best-known tunes with their naughty portions intact, such as "You're the Top" ("…You're the rhythmic beat of a bridal suite in use…") or "Too Darn Hot" ("…every average girl you know / prefers her favorite doggy to court / when the temperature is low…"). But it was "Love for Sale"—a Porter song that showed sympathy ("…Love for sale / appetizing young love for sale…") for a hooker's lot in life—that not only raised a few eyebrows back in 1931 when initially recorded by Libby Holman, but could still cause an uproar as late as 1956 when Billie Holiday's rendition was subjected to a radio ban. Initiated by the powerful ABC Network, other stations then followed suit, and it has been reported that recording studios also shunned the song. The hypocrisy of the situation is unavoidable when one considers that popular songs about *male* prostitution such as Porter's "I'm a Gigolo" or Irving Caesar's hit "Just a Gigolo" ("…If you admire me, please hire me…") faced no such reported resistance. Some radio stations reportedly shunned Eric Burdon and the

Animals' (No. 1) 1964 remake of that old American folk-blues classic, "House of the Rising Sun," due to its story line about a New Orleans brothel—this in spite of the fact that no foul words are sung and the moralistic lyrical message is one of disapproval.

Then there was Loretta Lynn's trailblazing C&W song "The Pill," which dealt with the then-touchy, though perfectly legal, topic of birth control but was nevertheless targeted by—presumably—population explosion proponents, and still went on in '75 (even after being banned by conservative radio stations) to attain the No. 5 position on the charts based on strong retail sales. Consider the furious controversies that raged a decade later regarding Madonna's No. 1 hit about a pregnant teenager's desire to *keep* her baby, "Papa Don't Preach." (Remember: This was a time when America's vice president, Dan Quayle, condemned a fictional TV character, Murphy Brown, for portraying an unwed mother.) Or the time that the UK's near-monopolistic pop network, Radio One, placed a ban on "Relax," a tune by an overtly gay British band, Frankie Goes to Hollywood, after belatedly realizing—it was already a (No. 2) hit thanks to Radio One's heavy rotation broadcasts—that the tune was about delaying an orgasm ("…Relax, don't do it / When you wanna *come*…"). Or the incident in 1997 when Nashville's WQQK-FM banned further airings of the hip-hop single "My Baby Daddy" (B-Rock and The Bizz) after about ten listeners complained that the song (then charting in the Top Five) *promotes* "having kids out of wedlock," a claim that seems about as on-target as the one made exactly three decades earlier: that Cher's hit, "You Better Sit Down, Kids" *celebrated* broken homes.

But all that is merely the tip of the proverbial iceberg: songs about sex—whether subtle and romantic or boisterous and crammed with gutter language—are bounteous, popular, and even *traditional!* The proof is that many societies around the world have, over the centuries, developed a taste for erotic and/or ribald folk tunes. Especially it seems, prudish societies like Victorian England, where despite the oppressive decorum of the period—like the quaint practice of covering the *legs* of pianos with drapery so as not to put any refined folks in a tizzy—an estimable musical canon of vintage raunch emerged including popular favorites like: "Old Fumbler," "My Thing Is My Own," "Sir Walter Enjoying His Damsel," "I Gave Her Cakes and I Gave Her Ale," and "My Man John Has a Thing That Is Long." The practice was so popular that as early as 1847 the Towns Police Clauses Act was enacted to inflict "a fine of 40S. or imprisonment for fourteen days on any person who 'publicly… sings any profane or obscene song or ballad.'"

America's split personality regarding adult entertainment dates back to the Colonial era when—just as today—some folks were "fer" it, some were "agin" it. But it was—again, just as today—society's religious zealots who were intent on locking their personal tastes into a legal code affecting everybody. Examples include the establishment of blue law restrictions that affected many aspects of daily life, including prohibitions on bachelors sharing a residence (or entertaining guests), or young people flirting in public. In 1646 a concern about seamen and Boston's townsfolk enjoying themselves with "much waste of Wine and Beer" resulted in the killjoys formally outlawing dancing at taverns and inns—with the prescribed punishment being that of a sizeable five shillings fine.

Though the colonies developed social mores that primarily concerned religious blasphemy or profanity, it took more than a century for concerns about obscene images or speech to manifest in law. It was in 1815 that legal issues of "obscenity," "public decency," and the "dignity and peace of the community" were first explored in an American court of law. That was the year that a Philadelphia, Pennsylvania, man was tried and convicted for running a small-time enterprise where the curious paid to visit his parlor in order to view some erotic illustrations, or, "dirty" pictures. And thus began our country's long slide down the slippery slope of governmental censorship. In 1821 the state of Vermont passed the nation's first statute against "indecent" literature, and in 1842 the United States Congress amended our customs laws to ban the importation of indecent graphic materials. Then in 1865 Congress passed a law prohibiting the mailing of obscene materials.

But the war on smut didn't fully commence in America until around 1872. That was when a former freelancing anti-alcohol crusader, Anthony Comstock, instigated (in cahoots with New York's YMCA) the formation of the Committee for the Suppression of Vice. Within a year—and armed with catchy slogans like "Morals, Not Art and Literature!"—Comstock successfully pushed the US Congress into passing the "Act of the Suppression of Trade in, and Circulation of, Obscene Literature and Articles of Immoral Use" (aka the Comstock Act) governing the mailing of "obscene or crime-inducing matter." Before long individual states fell into line and passed their own versions of what collectively have come to be known as the Comstock Laws. These new blue laws employing such subjective definitional terms as "lewd," "lascivious," "indecent," and "obscene" have provided fodder for over 100 years of legal debate.

For all his valiant efforts, Comstock was rewarded with a new job as a special agent for the US Postal Service in 1873. And thus for the next 42 years Comstock had free rein to make raids and confiscate materials that were indecent—a damn lucrative deal since he was granted a handsome kickback out of any fines that were collected resulting from convictions that they'd assisted with. This was enough to guarantee that Comstock and company would go about their task with zeal—to the extent that the epithet "Comstockery" came to signify such moral censorship. For his part, Comstock went on to greater things, eventually serving as an advocate in court trials for the banning and burning of art books that included erotic illustrations. No matter to him or the prosecutors that the titles in question had by then long been accepted as literary masterpieces by much of the civilized world.

Of no apparent concern to Comstock—or for that matter, his modern-day counterparts—was the issue of whether or not any particular essay, poem, or song even contains what might be fairly judged as "obscene" or "indecent" language. If their sensibilities were offended, by God, *that* was evidence enough.

Just as scores of classic books have had censorship campaigns launched against them, even though they contained no overtly foul words, many tunes shared that same fate. From the very dawn of the recording industry, tunes that contain nary a vulgar, lurid, lascivious, lewd, crude, or rude term have been attacked by moralists. This is not to say that the overall topics of these tunes were innocent. In truth, some of the saltiest songs around made their risqué points through the use of clever euphemisms, double entendres, sly lyrical innuendoes, and downright juicy metaphors. In this one aspect the censors have been correct: it doesn't require the use of "filthy" terms to create something salacious. However some listeners (or readers) may need to study the thing considerably in order to decipher it.

Being initiated in some African-American slang can help, and plenty can be determined by "reading between the lines." Let's try this by starting out with a few easy ones. First, one needs to grasp that in the early jazz and blues cultures a term such as "jelly roll" had come to be a sweet little nickname for a woman's lower privates. Registering that fact, you then begin to understand why one jazz pioneer not only wrote the classic "Jelly Roll Blues," but even went so far as to adopt the moniker as a stage name, Ferdinand "Jelly Roll" Morton. The metaphor was so popular that scores of additional tunes emerged with similar "coded" references including "I Got the Best Jelly Rollin' in Town," "Nobody in Town Can Bake a Jelly Roll Like Mine," and "I Ain't Gonna Give Nobody None of My Jelly Roll."

Another effective songwriting trick is demonstrated by a couple of classics that shared the metaphor of a Victrola record player to disguise their sexual subtext. Cliff Carlisle's "That Nasty Swing" ("…Place the needle in that hole / and do that nasty swing…"), and Robert Johnson's "Phonograph Blues" ("…we played it on the sofa / Now we played it 'side the wall / My needles have got rusty baby / They will not play at all…").

Now, while it is possible that some casual listeners never recognized the off-color lyrical subtext of such songs, many other song lyrics (also without "indecent" terms) still had an aggregate meaning that required no secret decoder ring to decipher. What else under the sun could the laughably lewd ol' blues tunes like the following have been about other than making whoopee: "Banana Man Blues" (Memphis Minnie); "Banana in Your Fruit Basket," "Please Warm My Weiner," "Don't Mash My Digger So Deep," and "Pin in Your Cushion" (Bo Carter); "Sweet Honey Hole" (Blind Boy Fuller); "Doodle Hole Blues" (Charlie Lincoln); "Wipe It Off" (Lonnie Johnson); "Hard Lead Pencil" (Honeydripper); "Show Me What You've Got" (Kansas City Kitty); "Let Me Play with Your Poodle" and "It's Tight Like That" (Tampa Red); "One More Greasing" (Georgia Pine Boy); "You Put It In, I'll Take It Out" (Papa Charlie Jackson); "I Ain't Givin' Nobody None" (Mae Glover); "She Showed It All" (Napoleon Fletcher); "You Stole My Cherry" and "Press

My Button (Ring My Bell)" (Lil Johnson); "Let Me Squeeze Your Lemon" (Charlie Pickett); "Somebody's Diggin' My Potatoes" (Leadbelly); "I Wonder Who's Boogiein' My Woogie Now" (Oscar's Chicago Swingers); "Shake That Thing" (Ethel Waters); "Ride, Daddy, Ride" (Fats Noel); "Drill, Daddy, Drill" (Dorothy Ellis); "Ride, Jockey, Ride" (Lamplighters); "It Ain't the Meat" ("... it's the *motion* ...") (Swallows); "Keep on Churnin' (Till the Butter Comes)" and "I Want My Fanny Brown" (Wynonie Harris); and "I'll Keep Sittin' on It (If I Can't Sell It)" and "Get 'Em from the Peanut Man (Hot Nuts)" (Georgia White)?

One example that should more than suffice in indicating the extent to which some of these artists would go is Lucille Bogan's old blues number "Shave 'Em Dry," which featured extremely graphic lyrics ("... I got nipples on my titties big as the end of my thumb / I got somethin' 'tween my legs'll make a dead man cum ..."). *A-hem....*

One whole subcategory of discs that came to be known as "party records" featured comparatively harmless blues-derived ditties about titties, musical romps about rumps, silly songs about long dongs, et cetera—tunes that were specifically produced to fuel fun at house parties. Party records were mainly, but not exclusively, sold from shops that catered to a black clientele. And the shops that stocked them—reportedly at the risk of arrest in some towns—took steps to ensure that their customers who had more delicate sensibilities were not confronted by the discs. Stored under the counter and brought out only by request, these records were also brown-bagged at the point of sale. Though their limited appeal and a low-key distribution system ensured that such tunes would never chart on the *Hit Parade*, some of these raw records enjoyed a re-markable level of commercial success.

A good number of mid-20th-century artists managed to carve out careers by specializing in such triple-X tunes. A few of the more notable of these were: Ruth Wallis, LuWanda Page, Bella Barth, Rusty "Knockers Up" Warren, Big George, Rudy Ray Moore, Redd Foxx, and the era's most popular drag queen, Ray Bourbon. Even the vastly better-known jazz diva Dinah Washington joined in the fun by offering a couple naughty numbers, "Long John" and "Short John."

Crowd-pleasers from this realm included Bourbon's "Her First Piece," Cliff Edwards's "Give It to Mary with Love," Pure and Simple's "All the Horsemen Knew Her (Riding My Sister)," "Hole in One," "I'm the Guy that Put the Dix in Dixie," "Nudist Colony (Bare Facts)," and "Bridal Suite (First Night)," and Ben Light and His Surf Club Boys' "The Girl from Atlantic City," which featured naughty lyrics ("... Every morning she'd come / This trim little *lass* / And give us the pleasure of / Seeing her *an* ... tics in the water ...").

Meanwhile Ruth Wallis emerged as America's queen of the genre, releasing numerous records in the '50s that included classics like "Long Playing Daddy" (which spoofed the term for those still-rather-new 12-inch record albums—or "LPs"), and "She's Got Freckles on Her, But She Is Nice"—which, like most of Wallis's records, was banned in the notoriously prim Boston-area radio market, thus inspiring her career's magic marketing hook: *BANNED IN BOSTON!* But perhaps her most widely known "hit" was the mildly titillating "blue" tune from 1949, "The Sweater Girl" ("…Loretta's a sweater girl / Loretta's a better girl now / How does she steal away each fellow's heart? / She's got *two* outstanding reasons … she's *cute* and *smart*…").

Though many folks found these kinds of records humorous, the entertainment mainstream did not. As early as 1928 Sophie Tucker's recording of "He Hadn't Up Till Yesterday" was widely banned, and in 1931 *Variety* magazine—a publication that preceded *Billboard* and *Cash Box* in regularly posting charts of the best-selling records—determined that trends were already getting too wild and began excluding certain songs that crossed the line, including rude and racy blues favorites like "I'm Gonna Shave You Close" and "Hoochie Coochie Man." Other folks also reckoned this kind of stuff had simply gone too far, and police raids on nightclubs where such artists were employed were not uncommon. In fact, Ray Bourbon felt enough negative pressure in Los Angeles that he took his "Boys Will Be Girls" show north to Tait's Cafe in San Francisco in 1932 and, it's been said, managed to make radio history of sorts when the revue was halted by a police raid that happened to be broadcast live by a radio station that had set its gear up in the venue. Apparently the station hadn't given much thought to their own liability issues in airing such racy stuff.

But you didn't need to be a drag queen to be condemned. *Variety* even found fault with certain tunes by mainstream country stalwart Gene Autry and the esteemed "father of country music," Jimmie Rodgers, who saw his 1931 song "What's It?" banned by radio for its story line about how well his 200-pound, "corn-fed," "dog-faced" gal could pet and "… neck where it is dark …." Later, in 1940, the giant NBC Network compiled a list of 147 banned recordings—including pop, blues, and jazz classics by the likes of Cole Porter, Duke Ellington, Bessie Smith, Billie Holiday, and, in particular, the Andrews Sisters' novelty number "Keep Your Skirt Down, Mary Ann."

Later, in 1950, a frisky West Coast country band, the Maddox Brothers and Rose, recorded a popular stage favorite, "Sally Let Your Bangs Hang Down"—whose mildly suggestive lyrics ("… I saw Sally changin' clothes / She was in a perfect pose …")—triggered bans at many radio stations, including one in Bakersfield, California, where a DJ was reportedly fired for airing it. Then, in 1951, Dean Martin's cocky "Wham! Bam! Thank You Mam!" ("… I hope you're satisfied …") was banned by a number of Los Angeles stations, and another Capitol Records artist, Dottie O'Brien, saw her version of an old tune, "Four or Five Times," meet the same fate. The banning of the latter disc, disregarding whether or not the song was actually about serial sexual encounters ("… what I like most / is to have someone who is true / who will love me, too / four or five times …"), revealed a gender-based double standard at play. Apparently when males, white or black (for instance, Brymn's Black Devil Four, the McKinney's Cotton Pickers, Jimmie Lunceford, Sidney Bechet, Lionel Hampton, Woody Herman, Bob Wills, and others), chose to record

"Wham! Bam! Thank You Mam!" was merely Dean Martin's first troubled record—in 1960 his "Ain't That a Kick in the Head" was banned by radio for its "adult" theme.

the tune it was considered acceptable—and, in fact, back in the '20s the Chocolate Dandies even cut a stakes-raising knockoff, "Six or Seven Times"—but, now, when Dottie O'Brien gave it a spin, well, *that* was a whole 'nother matter.

Given such an uptight social climate, it is easy to see why a top-tier '50s folk group like the Weavers had to clean up Leadbelly's classic "Goodnight Irene" by dropping altogether the reference to morphine and turning the line ("… I'll *get* you in my dreams…") into ("…I'll *see* you in my dreams …") when they recorded their hit version. Then in 1954 pop singer Rosemary Clooney's mildly lusty number "Mambo Italiano" ("…Shake-a baby, shake-a / 'cause I love-a, when you *take-a* me…")—though already a hit on various other networks—was rejected by ABC, which stated that the song did not meet its "standards for good taste." That same year Johnnie Ray's "Such a Night" ("…Just the thought of her lips / sets me a fire …") was also banned—a restriction that failed, though, to keep the disc's retail sales from pulling it all the way up to the No. 19 slot on *Billboard*'s popularity charts.

The stakes were raised by a September 1954 issue of *Billboard* magazine. In an editorial titled "Control the Dimwits," the use of double-entendre sex references was energetically condemned. Incredibly, the immediate result was the enactment of bans on public jukeboxes in various towns across the country—and the actual confiscation of them (and fines levied on their owners) by the police departments in Long Beach, California, and Memphis, Tennessee. (In addition to being one of America's hotbeds of musical tradition and innovation, Memphis was also a bastion of rednecks. Way back on February 8, 1948, the city's police department launched an anti-pornography campaign—one that received press coverage for raids on a number of record shops where discs deemed to be "obscene" were seized and smashed to smithereens. This was an act that civil libertarians would today likely point out as a violation of the 4th Amendment's protection from "unreasonable searches and seizures." Unreasonable in this case if for no other reason than it apparently involved honky cops cursorily judging the content [or simply the titles] of records aimed at the black community, whose cultural standards they couldn't understand and surely didn't respect. In any case, it would hardly seem that grabbing and busting records willy-nilly out in the alley amounted to anything like "due process of law.")

Memphis's radio giant WDIA produced a list in 1954 of about 40 records banned due to so-called offensive lyrics. Interestingly, though the station felt strongly enough about those songs to ban them, they nevertheless found it advantageous to identify the banned songs—by title—in self-congratulatory promotions! In some communities, banning R&B and/or early rock 'n' roll was good business, and over the next months a good number of radio stations clamped down: Mobile, Alabama's WABB publicized their list of banned

A Memphis, Tennessee, policeman holds pieces of "obscene" R&B 78s seized and destroyed in a record shop raid on February 8, 1948.

R&B hits, and Shenandoah, Iowa's KMA launched The Crusade for Better Disks, which resulted in such harmless songs as "Dim, Dim the Lights (I Want Some Atmosphere)" Bill Haley and His Comets) being axed. [Note: Haley also had his records banned in St. Paul, Minnesota, and his live shows outlawed in Jersey City, New Jersey.]

The broadcasting of "dirty" records was one issue—but soon the act of *mailing* them became another. In February 1954 a bill was introduced to the House of Representatives by Michigan's Republican Rep. Ruth Thompson whose intent was to specifically outlaw the shipping through the US Mail of phonograph records that were "obscene, lewd, lascivious, or filthy." It remains unknown exactly how big of a problem this was at that time, but the congresswoman proposed that a fair and reasonable punishment would be fines up to $5,000 and five years' imprisonment. The anti-rock crackdown continued the following year when the five-Grammy-Award-nominee *Blackboard Jungle*—which featured Bill Haley performing "(We're Gonna) Rock Around the Clock"—was withdrawn from the 1955 Venice Film Festival at the request of US Ambassador Clare Boothe Luce, who reportedly felt the film was "an unflattering look at American school life."

In 1956 the San Antonio Parks Department condemned rock 'n' roll records as "jumpy, hot stuff" unsuitable for teens' ears and then proceeded to purge the suspect discs from the jukeboxes then located at various public swimming pools because "the music attracted a lot of undesirable people who loitered around the pool with no intention of going swimming." Beyond that, the Juvenile Delinquency and Crime Commission of Houston, Texas, produced a list of 26 songs they identified as being obscene and threatened to bring down the FCC enforcers on any local station that disagreed.

The cultural climate had reached the point that even rock 'n' roll's original wildman, Little Richard, and his producers knew that in order to have half a chance at getting some radio support for his new single—1956's "Tutti-Frutti"—they'd have to tone down the saucy lyrics before recording it. Given that the lyrics ("…I got a girl named Sue / She knows just *what* to do…") of that Top-20 hit were naughty enough to draw fire from critics, the objections would likely have been even more heated had the *original* lyrics ("…Tutti-Frutti, good booty…If it don't fit, don't force it / You can grease it, make it easy…") been retained.

Before long, yet another list of popular teenage hits came under attack, this time by Catholic Church leaders. This list even included such mild pieces as Jimmie Rodgers's 1957 (No. 3) hit "Secretly" and Elvis's '58 (No. 2) hit "Wear My Ring around Your Neck" with the charge that tunes such as these worked to lower the moral standards of teenagers by sanctioning, of all things, *going steady*.

As the morals police compiled their beloved blacklists, the music world provided them with a plethora of popular hits that, far from being innocent, were in fact blatant examples of macho braggadocio regarding sexual prowess and stamina. Among those specifically vilified by critics were: "Sixty Minute Man" ("…then you'll holler *"Please don't stop! ...*") (Dominoes), "Get It" ("...I wanna *see you* with it...") (Royals), "Work with Me, Annie" ("...Please don't cheat, give me all my *meat*...") and "Sexy Ways" ("...Shake baby... till the *meat* falls off yo bones ...") (Midnighters [with Hank Ballard]), "Honey Love" ("...I need *it* in the middle of the night...") (Drifters), "Big Ten Inch Record" ("...She loves my big ten inch—*record* of the blues...") (Bull Moose Jackson), "Sweet Little Sixteen" ("...all the cats wanna *dance* with ...") (Chuck Berry), "Rock Me Baby" ("...all night long...") (B.B. King), "I Got a Woman" ("...both day and night...") (Ray Charles), "Rock Around the Clock" ("...we're gonna ...") (Bill Haley and His Comets), and Elvis Presley's rendition ("...meet me in a hurry behind the barn...") of Wynonie Harris's R&B hit, "Good Rockin' Tonight."

Though Elvis's sheer prominence made him a most tempting target, it wasn't just the music that was drawing the scorn of conservatives. There was also the issue of his pelvic thrusts and crazy-leg "dancing." From the moment Elvis Presley's career began in the mid-'50s, his peculiar moves—ones that would earn him the unflattering nickname "Elvis the Pelvis"—were a big part of his attraction, and another big reason for con-servatives to revile him. The fact that during one of Elvis's first national TV appearances in 1957 the cameramen were directed to only show him "from the waist up" in order to not broadcast that famous pelvis into every American home is part of every Rock History 101 course.

But what is often overlooked is that Elvis's sexy style had *always* brought him grief. While on tour in Florida, Elvis was "advised" by local vice squad officers that his show would be monitored and, furthermore, he'd be arrested if he didn't refrain from doing his usual "vulgar performance." Later, on his first West Coast tour, a local vice squad reportedly told his management to "clean up the show—*or else.*" [Note: A full decade later Jimi Hendrix heard the same exact threat from British tour promoters who told him "to clean up his act, because it was 'too suggestive.'"] This controversy followed Elvis all the way up to his Pacific Northwest dates, including one in Seattle that nearly wasn't allowed to happen at all. Determined not to have local youth exposed to Elvis's evil influence, the city council announced that they would attempt to prohibit Elvis Presley from performing in their town—a position that was promptly reversed when they were presented with a protest petition signed by 30,000 citizens. The August 1957 show ultimately went off successfully, but while in Seattle he was baited by a local reporter who asked how his mother felt about his onstage behavior. Offended by the implication of wrongdoing, Elvis shot back, "Suh, I'd *never* do *anything* to shame my Mutha." That same year a Nashville DJ got so riled up over Elvis that he held a record burning event in a city park and publicly torched 600 of the singer's records.

Elvis was merely one of the first white boys who faced the bureaucratic impediments and social humiliations that "Negroes" experienced regularly. Black musicians had long been hassled in podunk towns as well as major metropolises all across America, and now young white rockers would also experience harassment from local authorities. Gene Vincent—whose 1956 rockabilly number "Woman Love" includes the lascivious lyrical line ("…lovin' and a *fuggin'* and a kissin'…")—was banned by some US radio stations as well as the BBC. Vincent was actually dragged off stage (while singing another of his sex-drenched hits, "Lotta Lovin'") and jailed by an Arizona sheriff, and in 1956 he was tried and found guilty of breaking public lewdness and obscenity laws after a performance in Virginia.

In a similar incident around 1957, R&B veteran Hank Ballard was actually hauled off of the Eagles Auditorium stage by Seattle police officers mid-concert when he and members of his band were engaged in a playful little skit in support of their old 1954 hit, "Annie Had a Baby." It seems Ballard—in an act that the band had been doing without incident for years—was goofing onstage as Annie and at just the right moment he pulled a baby-doll out from under his skirt. Well, that was enough for the SPD. The show was halted, the enthusiastic audience sent home.

Almost ten years later, in 1966, a peer of Ballard, the revered R&B pioneer James Brown (creator of such funky hits as "Sex Machine" and "Sexy, Sexy, Sexy") was informed by some cops that his dancing was "obscene." *That* was an opinion simply not shared by the paying audience. They loved Brown's every wiggly move. So, when well into his show, the singer (as usual) invited up a few gals from the audience join in the onstage fun, the cops charged the stage and announced that the concert was canceled. Perhaps the ensuing riot—replete with stone-throwing, knife assaults, and a reported 20 arrests made—gave them pause later to consider the audience's opinion before overreacting in such a way again.

Back in 1957, Jerry Lee Lewis's (No. 3) hit "Whole Lotta Shakin' Goin' On" was met with bans at many stations—as was its '58 follow-up, "High School Confidential." Both were shunned for their salacious lyrics and tone, but their popularity established them as classic rockabilly hits regardless. In due course both Lewis and Chuck Berry were blacklisted by various AM stations and concert promoters for nonmusical reasons. Lewis had married his 13-year-old cousin, and Berry was convicted of taking a minor over state lines for "immoral purposes." In 1957 the Everly Brothers' "Wake Up, Little Susie" (dating teens wake up to discover that they'd fallen asleep while at the drive-in movie) was banned by a number of stations in Boston—though the rest of the nation rewarded the song with No. 1 chart status. Around that same time Jerry Byrne's single "Lights Out" (teenagers attempt a front-porch smooch) was banned by various radio stations in Florida as he was touring along with the Big Bopper and the Champs, effectively hampering his chances at stardom.

For a spell in 1957 things got so crazy that radio stations drew complaints from prudes offended over the airing of Bill Justice's popular No. 2 hit, "Raunchy." Funny thing though, the issue couldn't have been a matter of "dirty lyrics"—the song is an *instrumental.* Some actual teen dating or petting songs that caused concern in their day were Fats Domino's 1956 No. 2 hit "Blueberry Hill," the Fleetwoods' '59 No. 1 hit "Come Softly to Me," and Mel Carter's '65 Top-Ten hit "Hold Me, Thrill Me, Touch Me."

The easiest way to avoid controversy, of course, was to self-censure a song *before* releasing it. And it could even be argued that Bill Haley and His Comets' taming of Big Joe Turner's earthy "Shake, Rattle, and Roll" in 1954 is what allowed it to become the seminal hit it was. Another performer who achieved success by taming a previously raunchy song was Pat Boone. In his 1956 hit cover version of Little Richard's "Tutti-Frutti," the line ("…you don't know what she *do* to me…") was cleaned up and recorded as ("…Pretty little Suzie is the girl for me…") and, similarly, the line about drinking wine in T-Bone Walker's blues classic "Call It Stormy Monday" was sanitized into a product placement opportunity for ("…Coca Cola…").

Then there was the case of Ray Charles's 1959 classic "What'd I Say," which was also trimmed to meet commercial standards. Originally cut as a seven-plus-minute epic of call-and-response style grunts and groans ("… Unnnh … *Unnnh* … Ohhhh … *Ohhhh* …") exchanged between Ray and his girl singers, the piece was rightly deemed too long by Atlantic Records and was edited down to a 5:04-minute, two-part (two-sided) record. Once distributed, though, the label quickly heard back from distributors who wanted to return their record shipments because radio was rejecting the tune—based both on its length and subject matter—and sales had stalled out. Facing this resistance the label went back and edited out a few of the repetitive lyrical ("… shake that *thing*…") segments, and completely deleted the red-dressed gals doing ("… the Birdland all night long …"). This new, even-more-shortened (4:16) version was shipped, and "What'd I Say" raced up to the No. 1 slot on the R&B charts and became a true classic of the era.

So, we see how various entities—radio professionals, record industry figures, and the artists themselves—have all played roles in policing music over the years. Governmental intervention has happily remained a rare event in American music. One record, however, whose lyrics did attract the unwanted attentions of politicians and the federal law enforcement agencies was that 1963 garage-rock classic "Louie Louie," by Portland, Oregon's Kingsmen. This single, with its severely mumbled vocals, became a topic of rumors in schoolyards soon after breaking out as a radio hit in Boston.

The original copyrighted lyrics of that until-then obscure '50s R&B tune tell a nice tale of a lonesome sailor pining for his gal (and whining to his bartender)—but that's not what students across the nation thought they heard. Unable to make out what the band was singing, their dirty minds began hearing all sorts of things. And when school kids started whispering and passing scrawled notes with various lyrical interpretations to each other on the playgrounds of America, parents, preachers, principals, and police were soon frothing.

The Kingsmen's '63 hit single, "Louie Louie," sparked a two-year FBI investigation based on flimsy rumors that it contained "dirty words."

Letters and phone calls expressing outrage inundated the offices of US Attorney General Robert F. Kennedy, the FCC, and governors of various states. One example offers a general sense of the hyperventilating outrage: "Dear Mr. Kennedy... My daughter brought home a record of 'LOUIE LOUIE' and I... proceeded to try and decipher the jumble of words. The lyrics are so filthy that I can-not enclose them in this letter.... We all know there is obscene materials [sic] available for those who seek it, but when they start sneaking in this material in the guise of the latest teen age rock & roll hit record these morons have gone too far.... This land of ours is headed for an extreme state of moral degradation.... How can we stamp out this menace????"

This frenzy led the governor of Indiana to announce a statewide radio and live performance ban in February 1964, claiming that the record was so obscene that it made his "ears tingle." His press secretary concurred, saying that the lyrics were "in-distinct—but *plain* if you listen carefully." It was at this point that things went totally nuts: President Lyndon Johnson allowed FBI Director J. Edgar Hoover to unleash a number of G-Men on the case, launching a two-year investigation. The FCC and US Postal Service jumped in with short-lived investigations, as did Boston's infamous censor, Chief of the Licensing Division Richard Sinnott. The "negative" publicity this frenzy generated worked so well to boost sales that the band's label pitched in to help keep the controversy alive. Pouring gas on the fire, Scepter/Wand Records offered

FEDERAL BUREAU OF INVESTIGATION
WASHINGTON, D. C.

To: FBI, Indianapolis (145-335)

Re: UNSUB; PHONOGRAPH RECORD
RECORDED BY THE KINGSMEN
ENTITLED "LOUIE LOUIE"
ITOM

Date: **April 17, 1964**
FBI File No. 145-2961
Lab. No. **D-446412 AV**

Q2 destroyed
"Also Submitted" retained
in Bufile 5/22/64

Specimens received **3/30/64**

Q2 Wand record entitled "Louie Louie (Richard Berry) the
Kingsmen" on one side and "Haunted Castle (Lynn Easton)
the Kingsmen" on the other side

ALSO SUBMITTED: Typewritten lyrics to record "Louie Louie"

Result of examination:

Two additional copies of the phonograph record
described above as specimen Q2 have been submitted to the
Laboratory. One of the previous records was submitted by
the Tampa Office with a letter dated 2/17/64, and captioned
"Unknown Subject; Phonograph Record 'LOUIE LOUIE' Distributed
By Limax Music, NYC; ITOM." The other record was submitted
by the San Diego Office with a letter dated 3/17/64 and
captioned "WAND, 650 Broadway, New York, New York; ITOM."

Because the lyrics of the song on the record, Q2,
could not be definitely determined in the Laboratory
examination, it could not be determined whether Q2 is an
obscene record.

Sample page from the 118-page file compiled during the FBI's one-and-a-half year (1964-1965) investigation into "pornographic lyrics" charges made against "Louie Louie."

to "help" by posting a $1,000 reward for anyone who could provide a copy of the purportedly "pornographic" lyrics.

The FBI, alone now in their zealous quest to nail *somebody*, combed the nation interviewing the song's original author, R&B singer Richard Berry, the Kingsmen, and various record execs. They also confiscated copies of the purported "Louie Louie" lyrics as transcribed by school kids, and the FBI's internal files—obtained through the Freedom of Information Act (FOIA)—reveal that numerous variations of these "dirty" lyrics included gems like these:

("... Louie Louie, oh no. Grab her way down low ..." and "... on my chair I'll lay her there / I feel my bone ... ah ... in her hair ...")

("... Tonight at ten I'll lay her again / Fuck you girl, oh, all the way / Oh my bed and I lay her there ...")

("... Every night and day I play with my thing / I fuck your girl all kinds of ways ...")

("... May you bitch / Hey lovemaker now hold my thing / it won't take long ...")

("... Hey señorita I'm hot as hell / I told her I'd never lay her again ...")

The investigation wound down in mid-1965. A bureau document, dated May 25, states that they "were unable to interpret any of the wording in the record and, therefore could not make a decision concerning the matter." Adding "the FBI Laboratory advised that because the lyrics of the recording, 'Louie Louie' could not be definitely determined in the Laboratory examination, it is not possible to determine whether this record is obscene." The FCC meanwhile busied themselves trying to extract the "pornographic" lyrics from the recording by testing the 45 rpm disc at both faster (78 rpm) and slower (33 1/3 rpm) speeds, ultimately exonerating the song in a report that concluded that the vocals were so muddled as to be "unintelligible at any speed." Chief Sinnott concurred, stating that try as he might he just "couldn't understand it." The punchline? In the end, the record hit No. 1 in *Cash Box* magazine's charts, has sold an estimated 12 million copies over the years, and became established as the quintessential garage-rock classic. Without a doubt, there are music fans who will always look down on *any* form of rock 'n' roll—and, interestingly, as late as 1970 one "expert" was still befuddled enough to write that the Kingsmen's song was "one of the most obscene songs ever recorded for the teenage market. Frankly as an American I hung my head in shame"—but for some of the rest of us, "Louie Louie," in its simple grandeur, is nothing short of a cosmically inspired expression of teen spirit.

The "Louie Louie" inquisition coincided with the commencement of the British Invasion. The Beatles spearheaded a creative movement that would re-energize rock 'n' roll in particular—and pop culture in general. Another significant result of the rock 'n' roll renaissance was a definite sharpening of what became known as the generation gap. If the social conservatives had been gnashing their teeth over the likes of Elvis and the other early rockers, now the outrages seemed to be compounding themselves. To these critics it seemed there were suddenly hysterical "Beatlemaniacs" everywhere, and a shaggy parade of new mop-topped bands—the Rolling Stones, the Animals, the Kinks, and others—were storming our shores and capturing the hearts of teenage America.

Another British band, the Pretty Things, had the misfortune of seeing their 1964 hit single, "Don't Bring Me Down," stall out completely in the American market after various influential radio stations objected to lyric fragments ("… and then I laid her on the ground …"). This contributed to their status as perhaps the finest band of their era to *never* tour the States. Highlighting the hit-or-miss nature of censorship in action, British radio had no problem with that 45, however it did take exception to Manfred Mann's 1965 rendition of Bob Dylan's "If You Gotta Go, Go Now," because of the lyrics ("… or else you gotta *stay all night* …"). That same year Daytona Beach, Florida's Night-crawlers saw their "I Don't Remember" banned by regional radio, reportedly because a few DJs mistakenly thought the line ("… it was you …") was ("… fuck you …"). Also that year the Rolling Stones' single "(I Can't Get No) Satisfaction" was banned by numerous stations—it achieved No. 1 hit status even so. Another classic British Invasion single, the Who's "Pictures of Lily," was also shunned due to its theme of adolescent masturbation.

By mid-decade the record companies were increasingly meddling—electronically or production-wise—in their artists' work. In 1965 a radio station revived an old trick for sanitizing "questionable" lyrics from a song. As the major labels did to the small-time independents back in the '50s, they would just get a new group and produce a more refined "cover" version and attempt to steal the hit. The song in question, "Gloria"—that garage-rock masterpiece by the Irish band Them—was racing up the charts at every station that gave it a shot in 1965. *But,* those lyrics stating that ("… she *comes* in my room …") were deemed unacceptable by Chicago's AM giant WLS. Not wanting to miss out on the action altogether though, the station simply recruited a local combo, the Shadows of Knight—who cut a cleaned-up rendition—and the new 45 was promoted like crazy. And, ultimately, it overtook the original, going Top Ten nationally and leaving Them's version in the dust. In 1966 the Troggs' "I Can't Control Myself" was banned by BBC due to its theme of a lack of personal discipline and their singer's orgasmic gasps as the song climaxes.

In 1967 a "sexy" song called "Try It" by the California garage-rock combo the Standells was rejected by a local radio station. One DJ, however, really liked the tune and was given permission to air a censored version he'd made by adding "beep" tones over the objectionable lyrics. It was that version—*and apparently the novelty of those beeps*—that attracted young listeners, and the tune became a No. 1 hit there as well as in Texas and Florida.

That same year, "Brown Eyed Girl," the Top-Ten solo hit by Them's former lead singer, Van Morrison, had its lyrics—which had been criticized for "promoting premarital sex"—altered by Bang Records. The line ("… *makin' love in the green grass…*") was excised and replaced with a snippet from a different verse ("… *skippin' and a jumpin'* …"). Then, the Rationals' "Hold On Baby" single was rejected by a number of local Michigan stations who objected to a lyrical line ("… gonna get up and *do the thing* with you, baby…") and they were given no opportunity to fix it. At least when Lou Christie's 1966 ode to heavy pettin' at Lover's Lane, "Rhapsody in the Rain," stirred up trouble—*Time* magazine charged that it was "corrupting the youth"—he was given a second chance by MGM to recut it with tamer lyrics. That alteration changed the lines ("… we were *makin' out* in the rain…") to ("… we *fell in love* in the rain …") and ("… *our* love *went much too far*…") to ("… love *came like a falling star*…"). Same with the Swingin' Medallions, whose 1966 hit "Double Shot (Of My Baby's Love)"—which clearly was utilizing booze as a metaphor for the disorienting nature of young love—nevertheless initially met with radio resistance and the band was forced by Smash Records to sober up the offending line ("… The worst *hangover* I ever had…"), changing it to ("... The worst *morning after* I ever had ..."), and ("... She *loved* me so long and *loved* me so hard ..."), which was altered to ("... She *kissed* me so long and *kissed* me so hard..."). Good thing the censors never took note of that same year's nasty cover version of the song by that popular Black Southern frat party band, Doug Clark and the Hot Nuts, "Double Stroke (Of My Twelve-Inch Pet)."

During one of his nationally televised specials the Rev. Billy Graham specifically condemned the Rolling Stones' new hit "Let's Spend the Night Together." Such pressure forced Mick Jagger to succumb and sing it as ("... let's spend *some time* together ...") during the Stones' January 1967 appearance on the *Ed Sullivan Show*. For his part, Jagger did try to maintain some artistic credibility by rolling his eyes as he mumbled his way through the doctored line. [Note: As late as 2003 the Chinese government—which had refused for four decades to allow the Rolling Stones to appear there—ordered the band to ax four specific songs from their shows' set lists due to sexual references in lyrics. In addition to "Let's Spend the Night Together," that no-no list included "Honky Tonk Women," "Brown Sugar," and "Beast of Burden."]

At one point, an entire chain of radio stations banned a number of songs because of supposed sexual content. These tunes included the Beatles' "Penny Lane" ("... all the people that come and go ...") and "Day Tripper" ("... She's a big teaser / she took me half the way there ..."), and Mitch Ryder's "Sock It to Me Baby!" In 1967 British radio outlawed the Beatles' "I Am the Walrus" because Lennon's wordplay ("... Boy you've been a naughty girl / You've let your knickers down ...") crossed the line. Additional Beatles songs—including "I'm Only Sleeping," "Drive My Car," and "Why Don't We Do It in the Road?"—were also suspected of having sexual overtones.

The funny thing is, had those American adults who'd been so traumatized by the emergence of the long-haired British Invasion bands known what radical musical and cultural trends would emerge in the following years, they would have never believed it. Who could have foreseen the rise of a full-fledged peace-and-love/flower power/ free love/psychedelic counterculture led by freaky artists like Janis Joplin (and Big Brother & the Holding Co.), Country Joe & the Fish, Jefferson Airplane, the Grateful Dead, and the Doors. These bands took music and live performance to whole new heights. Each had their share of run-ins with the law—all but Joplin even earned FBI files based on their level of perceived threat to the Establishment—but it was Country Joe McDonald, Joplin, and Doors singer Jim Morrison who were literally prosecuted.

McDonald first attracted attention in 1967 for his sarcastic anti-war record, "Feel-Like-I'm-Fixin'-to-Die Rag." This was the tune which was prefaced by the infamous "Fish" Cheer—a sly take on a standard cheerleader chant ("... Gimme an *F*; gimme a *U*; gimme a *C*; gimme a *K* ... / What's that spell? ..."). This audience-participation intro was intended to break down language taboos as much as to express general outrage over LBJ's Vietnam policies. The authorities took note, weren't pleased, and after one live performance McDonald suddenly found himself fined $500 and charged with being a "lewd, lascivious, and wanton person in speech and behavior." Of his free-spirited generation, McDonald certainly wasn't alone in *that* regard.

Morrison was famously arrested onstage by officers in New Haven, Connecticut, and in 1968 charged with the crime of making "lewd gestures" and "obscene" comments. The following year he was nailed again during a concert in Miami. This time Morrison was charged with "lewd and lascivious behavior in public by exposing his private parts and by simulating masturbation and oral copulation." Although eyewitness testimony conflicted on these points, Morrison was convicted ($500 fine and six months imprisonment) and was still appealing the case when he died while visiting Paris in 1970. That same year, Janis Joplin—another countercultural icon who brought dismay to the elders with her bawdy lifestyle—was collared by Tampa, Florida, officials and slapped with a $200 fine for uttering "obscenities" publicly. The incident occurred after she'd witnessed some cops abusing her concert audience and objected by saying, "Don't fuck with those people! Hey, Mister! What are you so uptight about?" Indeed.

The Sexual Revolution of the '60s and '70s—both cherished and condemned for its free love ethos—had loosened up many of American society's mores, but when it came to the commercial realm, to the marketing of corporate product, plenty of roadblocks were still in place. Even a song with a mature theme but no foul words—like Tanya Tucker's 1974 No. 1 C&W hit, "Would You Lay with Me (In a Field of Stone)," was widely banned by Bible Belt radio stations. And thus songs that *did* contain rough or rude language were still necessarily matters of considerable concern to the record industry. Then too, there was the old "pardon my French" problem: while Jane Birkin and Serge Gainsbourg's 1969 tune, "Je T'aime (Moi Non Plus)," received some airplay in the USA—by radio stations who apparently hadn't bothered to conduct a translation of its lyrics—in the UK the song was flatly banned by the BBC, who presumably took exception to her sensual sighing and his *ooh-la-la* lines about, one surmises, anal sex ("… I come between your kidneys…"). Regardless, the single went on to No. 1 hit status across Europe.

It was in 1971 that the British progressive-rock band Jethro Tull discovered that Chrysalis Records had edited the lyrics to their song "Locomotive Breath." Scared that the song wouldn't receive radio support with rude lyrics, the label excised an offending word "… got him by the *balls* …" and through electronic engineering grafted in its place the word "*hands*," which they'd copied from an entirely different song. Yikes! Ironically, the line in its original form seems to be a perfect description of the contractual relationship the band was locked into with Chrysalis. [Note: Chrysalis went on in 1978 to bleep out the common term "bastard" from Tull's song "Hunting Girl."] In 1973 the Rolling Stones, in a devilish effort to test the will of Atlantic Records, submitted a tape of their intended next single. Imagine that label's poor sales execs mulling over the marketing challenges they'd face releasing a song titled "Starfucker." True to form, the firm reacted by changing the song's provocative title to "Star Star" and deleting the word "pussy" from the lyrics ("…I'll bet you keep your *pussy* clean…") as well. In 1976 the B-side of Patti Smith's second single, "My Generation," was censored for the UK market by Arista Records with the elimination of the punky rant ("…We don't need their fuckin' shit, hope they die because of it!…").

In addition to such examples of corporate muscle-flexing, another modern tactical trend in censorship battles has followed from the censors' recognition that they usually lose court cases that get defended with First Amendment arguments. Frustrated that their opponents—the defendants—almost always prevail, the plaintiffs have increasingly shifted to basing their challenges on the grounds of being "obscene" or "indecent" lyrics because this is a rare area of personal expression that American courts *have* determined is susceptible to regulation. And so it was that in 1973 the issue of so-called indecency on the radio exploded into the national consciousness. That was the year that comedian George Carlin's infamous "Filthy Words" monologue—which he claimed was based on the FCC's list of the "seven dirty words" (shit, piss, fuck, cunt, cocksucker, motherfucker, and tits) that had been banned from US radio and TV airwaves—landed the Pacifica Radio network in legal hot water.

The case wasn't resolved until 1978, when the Supreme Court ruled that those words are not, by definition, legally "obscene," however they *can* be considered "indecent" and ought not be broadcast when children could likely hear them. The FCC's position is that obscene material cannot be broadcast at any time and that "indecent broadcasts" ("language or material that, in context, depicts or describes sexual or excretory organs or activities in a patently offensive manner as measured by contemporary community standards for the broadcast medium") can be restricted "during times of the day when there is a reasonable risk that children may be in the audience." So, "indecent material" is theoretically restricted to the nighttime block of 10:00 p.m. to 6:00 a.m.

But, it's that tricky phrase, "community standards," that once again becomes the issue. And that's because an inexorable fact in life is that the social boundaries defining what is "acceptable" in polite society—e.g., community standards (and cultural norms)—are rather like hairstyles, fashions, ideas, and philosophies. They are not static. They do evolve and change over time. Sometimes dramatically.

Needless to say, times *have* changed. Conservatives—ever wistful for the "good old days"—choose to believe that modern society has only gotten coarser, ruder, and more violent in recent decades. Progressives, on the other hand, would counter that, for example, with the halt of lynching as sport, the forced end of legal racial segregation, the banning of cruelty to animals, and the ongoing efforts to establish that women, children, seniors, and gays all have legally enforceable civil rights, our society is arguably gentler now than, say, back in the '20s and '30s. To the chagrin of those conservatives, there has indeed been a liberalization of mores and social customs in America, and as a result we have created a significantly kinder, more compassionate, and tolerant place because of it. And music—because it is capable of giving voice to otherwise marginalized folks—has played a not insignificant role in that progress.

One cultural norm that has evolved considerably over the years is society's take on homosexuality. And an important factor in the growing tolerance for sexual diversity was the phenomenal popularity of a new form of dance music that was first forged in the 1970s: disco. An amalgam of urban black, gay, and European musical aesthetics, disco was a natural target for conservatives of all types: politicians, media pundits, radio disc jockeys—and even conservative rock 'n' roll fans.

One early controversy engulfed pioneering disco diva Donna Summer, who in 1975 saw her tune "Love to Love You Baby" banned by the BBC. Their intensive research reportedly determined that the tune contained a total of 23—though *Time* magazine's sleuths counted only 22—simulated orgasms by the singer. Uncertain mathematics aside, one numerical figure is established: the disc rose to America's No. 2 chart position, while the extended 17-minute marathon remix version was a huge international club hit.

That same year the industry once again faced the dilemma of dealing with a hit whose lyrics weren't even in English, but rather a foreign language that the vast majority of American kids couldn't comprehend. LaBelle's "Lady Marmalade"—a disco song that included the "controversial" chorus hook ("...Voulez vous coucher avec moi ce soir?...")—was promptly banned by radio stations when some smarty figured out that LaBelle's lyrical inquiry translated from French to: ("...Would you like to sleep with me this evening?..."). Judging from retail sales—which pushed the tune to No. 1—the answer from disco fans was a resounding "Yes!"

For every urban hipster who embraced disco there were probably hundreds of dyed-in-the-wool rock 'n' rollers across America's heartland who despised the stuff. Beyond the fact that the disco scene had differentiated itself from the mainstream rock world with flashier fashion styles, new lingo—and yes, that incessant foursquare *beat*—the anti-disco backlash that rose up had more than a tinge of anti-black and anti-gay sentiment to it.

By 1977 it reached the point that even the veteran civil rights leader Rev. Jesse Jackson began railing against disco (or "sex-rock" as he mislabeled it) with the claim that it promoted both drug use and promiscuity. In particular he cited such tunes as the (No. 1) hit "Shake Your Booty" (KC and the Sunshine Band), the (No. 1) hit "Let's Make a Baby" (Billy Paul), and the Top-20 hit "I Want'a Do Something Freaky to You" (Leon Haywood). Then in 1978 Dick Clark's *American Bandstand* declined to air the Trammps' classic hit "Disco Inferno," thinking that the lyrical hook ("...burn the mother down...") was too inflammatory. Following a trend begun when the Bee Gees revived their flagging careers by jumping on the disco bandwagon, several more rockers (the Rolling Stones and Rod Stewart) took risky gambles and released new disco-fied songs—material that both won them new fans and drove away some of their former ones.

The Stones, never a band renowned for their enlightened views on women (consider their '60s put-down songs "Under My Thumb" and "Stupid Girl"), returned to form with the title-track hit "Some Girls," which contained a number of crudities and even overt slurs ("… Black girls just wanna get fucked all night …"). If that LP wasn't the band's finest moment, it still served to introduce a portion of the rock audience to a few of disco's musical elements in a fairly nonthreatening way. The same situation surrounded Stewart's (No. 1) disco hit from that same year, "Da Ya Think I'm Sexy?"

A significant portion of the rock audience at that time wanted nothing to do with disco culture, and a few punk songs recorded in reaction to this disco-fication of the marketplace summed things up nicely: "Disco Sucks!" (D.O.A.), "Do You Think I'm Disco?" (Steve Dahl & Teenage Radiation), "Kill the Bee Gees" (Accident), and "Disco's Out, Murder's In" (Suicidal Tendencies). Beyond that sort of reactionary response, the anti-disco fervor was also stoked in the mainstream audience by a number of opportunistic rock radio DJs who began promoting Death to Disco events at huge sports stadiums. One infamous "Disco Demolition Night" promised to blow up records at the midpoint of a doubleheader at Chicago's White Sox Park on July 12, 1979. Of the 50,000 in attendance, about 7,000 rampaging rockers wearing *Death Before Disco* buttons rushed the field chanting "Disco Sucks!" and setting fire to mounds of discs—a display of bigotry by participants who, one writer noted, were seemingly oblivious to the "parallels to Nazi Germany"—ultimately necessitating the cancellation of the second ball game. Though this knuckleheaded behavior was appalling, things *could* have been still worse: in Africa a total radio ban on airing disco music was imposed in 1979 by the government of Rhodesia (now Zimbabwe).

In 1980, America's political tides shifted and President Carter was bounced out of office in favor of Ronald Reagan. Reagan's conservative followers quickly showed that they just couldn't wait to go gunnin' for rock 'n' roll—and *all* of untamed pop culture. It was Reagan himself who led the charge against music, bellowing that "I don't believe that our Founding Fathers ever intended to create a nation where the rights of pornographers would take precedence over the rights of parents, and the violent and malevolent would be given free rein to prey upon our children."

Though virtually no one of good will would likely argue with his premise, plenty of us took umbrage with his blithe equating of musical artists to criminals. Furthermore, it can be argued that Reagan and others who so regularly invoke the safety of "America's children" in the service of their own narrow sociopolitical goals are, in actuality, the ones guilty of exploiting those voiceless innocents. For their part though, conservative zealots only heard in Reagan's words the battle cry that they had long been waiting for. The new president had kicked open the door and the posse elbowing their way into the media spotlight along with him were scads of right-wing organizations including: the Citizens for Decency through Law, the Citizens Advocating Decency and a Revival of Ethics, the National Federation for Decency, Save Our Children (led by Anita Bryant), the American Family Association (led by Rev. James Wildmon), Focus on the Family (led by James Dobson), the Eagle Forum (led by Phyllis Schlafly), the Moral Majority (led by Rev. Jerry Falwell), and the Christian Coalition (led by Rev. Pat Robertson).

Preaching to this anti-rock choir, author Jeff Godwin once asserted that "all the smutty and degenerate emphasis on sexual lust in rock music is designed to fire up teenage imaginations and hormones, leading to active fornication." But it was the histrionic Rev. Robertson who really set the low tone of the civic debate, stating that "rock groups are singing about drugs and every kind of sex. [They] don't *care* about free speech. They're just trying to see what they can get away with. They need to be told that they can't go any further than a *certain* point." The censors' patron saint, Mr. Comstock, would have been *so* pleased that such an anti-democratic attitude had survived.

In 1981 Reagan created his Presidential Task Force on the Arts and the Humanities and empowered them to "review" the National Endowment for the Arts and the National Endowment for the Humanities. "Review" in conservative code meant to gut and destroy the mission and operations of those popular agencies. It didn't take long at all for the entertainment industry to catch the repressive drift of the Reagan Revolution, and radio stations in Salt Lake City and Provo, Utah, banned the airing of Olivia Newton John's disco hit "Physical," making it the only state whose residents did not help push that tune to its status as a nearly worldwide Top-Ten hit. Sensing this aggressively prudish zeitgeist in Reagan country, the US government's global propaganda radio network, the Voice of America, even rejected Marvin Gaye's huge 1983 (No. 3) comeback hit, "Sexual Healing." By 1985 MCA Records had second thoughts about one of their recent releases. Even though radio was already supporting Al Hudson's sexy "Let's Talk," MCA took the step of mailing stations with the urgent request that they desist airing the hit due to internal legal concerns over its lyrical content. An unusual move to be sure, but understandable given the tenor of the times.

In 1983 some members of the Parent Teacher Association (PTA) raised the issue of objectionable music at their national convention. The following year, a nice Cincinnati, Ohio, couple instigated formal action by means of that organization. As the media reported, Mr. and Mrs. Rick Allen had become disenchanted with their purchase of Prince's 1982 hit album, *1999*. Mind you now, this was the same Prince who had been recording songs along the lines of "Orgasm," "Do It All Night," "Do Me, Baby," "Jack U Off," and "Head" on albums with titles like *Come, Controversy,* and *Dirty Mind* since the late '70s. The Allens, however, were offended when explicit lyrics in "Let's Pretend We're Married" were *nearly* overheard by their children. It was their complaint to a local PTA group that began rallying other local PTAs to stampede the 1984 national convention into passing a resolution demanding that the record industry institute a system for rating and labeling music that contains "profanity, sex, violence, or vulgarity."

Conservative momentum was building, and that same year the National Coalition on Television Violence released a report condemning MTV-style rock videos—citing in particular such questionably "violent" pieces as "Penny Love" (Lionel Richie), "Come Dancing" (Kinks), "Anxiety" (Pat Benatar), and "Eat It" (Weird Al Yankovic).

Then only a few months after President Reagan's second inauguration promised four more years of conservative rule, a number of people from both political parties saw a great opportunity for capitalizing on the rising trend of social repression. And thus some old-line conservatives joined together with some up-and-coming politicos in an easy, and certainly headline-grabbing, attack on—what else?—rock 'n' roll. In order to justify the launching of a successful pop culture inquisition though, it would require an easily digestible narrative angle to command the public's attention.

The thing is, their chosen story line that was spun out for the public was just so darn tidy that it immediately begged credulity. In essence, we were expected to simply accept that the immediate problem all began one bright sunny morning when Democratic Sen. Albert Gore's wife, Tipper, took her young daughter shopping and then hurried home—in a sweet Norman Rockwell moment if ever there was one—to play their new LP together. As fate would have it, the particular album that they just had to have was the new one, *Purple Rain,* by the very same artist that had earlier ticked off the Allens in Cincinnati—Prince! What a co-hinky-dink! Well, before you knew it, Tipper had joined up Reagan Treasury Secretary James Baker's spouse, Susan; Dixiecrat Senator Strom Thurmond's spouse, Nancy; and 20 other "Washington wives" in launching their grandly named front group, the Parents Music Resource Center, or PMRC. Knowing they had the clout of their powerful husbands behind them, the wives immediately began throwing their weight around, ultimately instigating America's biggest rock 'n' roll witch hunt yet.

At first the PMRC came off as just another bunch of perhaps ditzy, if well-connected, busybodies who tried to present a reasonable "we're not censors—just *concerned parents*" vibe and seemed to want some sort of "review" of the issues regarding dirty lyrics and nasty album-cover art. But we would soon learn otherwise. Their targeting of specific musicians began with the issuance of the list of the infamous "filthy fifteen": AC/DC, Black Sabbath, Def Leppard, Sheena Easton, Judas Priest, Cyndi Lauper, Madonna, the Mary Jane Girls, Mercyful Fate, Mötley Crüe, Prince, Twisted Sister, Vanity, Venom, and W.A.S.P. And, to be sure, it was not just lyrics and album covers that offended; also at issue was the *style* employed by the musicians—as the oh-so-scandalized Baker herself said of Easton: "You should hear the way she sings those lyrics, using this very sexy, *erotic* voice—Well, you don't have to be much older than ten to know what she means."

Likewise, savvy music industry leaders knew exactly what it meant to see these pow-

Prince's '83 hit 1999 became a favorite target for worrisome parents—including Tipper Gore and her PMRC cohorts—in the Reagan Era frenzy over "dirty" lyrics.

erful women aligned against them, and in May 1985 (the very month that the PMRC had incorporated) the Record Industry Association of America (RIAA) responded favorably to the group's first overture to meet and discuss various issues—including the adoption of a rating system—maybe one, say, based on the film industry's (G, PG, PG-13, R, and X or NC-17). That the RIAA caved so quickly on this led thoughtful observers to wonder whether the looming congressional vote on their pet "blank tape tax" proposal was a factor—indeed, the specific concern was that, seemingly, "the association's swift acquiescence was prompted, in part, by the industry's fear that a nationwide debate over bawdy rock lyrics could affect the industry's campaign for government legislation protecting it against record piracy, copyright violations and granting record companies royalties from the sale of blank tapes."

A good and fair question. But with the PMRC unwilling to accept the RIAA's "yes" for an answer, all of the pieces fell magically into place on September 19, 1985, for the commencement of a formal inquiry into dirty song lyrics and record labeling options before the Senate Committee on Commerce, Science, and Transportation. In such a public and high-profile setting, unforeseen consequences should have been expected, and attendees and TV viewers certainly weren't disappointed. The imperious inquisitors—who foolishly assumed that the nation would hear nothing but devilish idiocy coming from the mouths of their intended prey—were forced to deal with the intelligent and articulate testimony, passionate parries, and aggressive counterattacks offered on behalf of music, artistry, and freedom of expression by the odd trio of musicians John Denver, Dee Snider, and Frank Zappa.

Snider, as the frontman for one of the PMRC's "filthy fifteen," Twisted Sister—and as a fellow who'd been arrested in Amarillo, Texas, on charges of "public profanity" in 1984—seemed a relevant choice. As for Denver, well, his direct experience with censors centered around the false drug rumors that had been directed at his 1972 ode to the beauty of his Colorado home, "Rocky Mountain High." But, of the three, Zappa—the iconoclastic leader of the Mothers of Invention—had the most personal experience as an artist who'd seen his work censored over the years. Back in 1965 his label, MGM, objected to a direct slam on the record biz in the lyrics to "Money" ("... I'm not going to do any publicity *balling* for you ...") and requested they be altered. But when Zappa wouldn't budge, company execs sidestepped him and had the reference deleted. Then in 1967 the label excised eight entire bars of music from one of Zappa's songs, "Let's Make the Water Turn Black." The execs had *somehow* concluded that the straightforward lyrical line about a waitress writing down meal orders ("... And I still remember Mama with her apron and her pad, feeding all the boys at Ed's Café ...") was instead a coded reference to a sanitary napkin. And, again without the artist's approval, an edit was made.

While the hearings made for riveting TV viewing, the inquisition's peak drama had to be when the PMRC leadership brought forward one of their expert consultants, a Virginia minister named Jeff Ling, to make a slide-show presentation. And thus, with the apparent goal of highlighting the general depravity of rock 'n' roll, Ling did the un-thinkable: With the eyes and ears of the whole world's press corps—not to mention those of God and the ghost of Anthony Comstock—intently focused on him, this "moral guardian" proceeded to recite the lyrics to a little ditty called "Golden Showers" by an unpopular band, the Mentors ("... Listen, you little slut, do as you are told / come with daddy for me to pour the Gold. Golden showers. All through my excrement you shall roam. Bend up and smell my anal vapor. Your face is my toilet paper. On your face I leave a shit tower. Golden showers ..."). *A-hem....*

And so, some of what must be the vilest rock lyrics ever penned were instantly mainlined straight into the minds of millions of innocents. As Tipper Gore noted in her magnum opus, *Raising PG Kids In An X-Rated Society*, "Our strategy was simple. We felt it was crucial to publicize the excesses in song lyrics." Well, mission accomplished. Indeed: due to these misguided tactics by the PMRC, vast exposure was given to the filth contained in what had been, up until that moment, some of the most obscure lyrics in existence. In one high-profile presentation, that pathetic and scatologically misogynistic band received more media attention than they'd ever enjoyed in their nearly decade-long career.

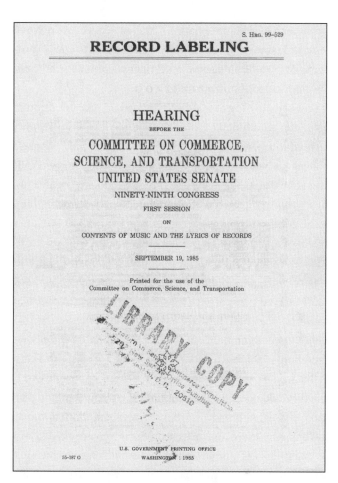

The cover page of the transcripts from the U.S. Senate subcommittee's
"Record Labeling" hearings prompted by the PMRC in September 1985.

And that was only the beginning. Attentive viewers would learn *way* more—thanks to Tipper & Co.—than they'd ever wanted to about songs that detailed pretty much everything the council was trying to protect them from. The media spotlight ultimately highlighted topics raised that included: masturbation (Lauper's "She Bop" and Prince's "Darling Nikki"); slang terms for female anatomy (Easton's "Sugar Walls"); a pageant of sexy female perspectives (Madonna's "Dress You Up" and Vanity's "Pretty Mess"); a salute to marathon screwing (AC/DC's "You Shook Me All Night Long" and "Let Me Put My Love into You"); an invitation to partake in feral copulating (W.A.S.P.'s "Animal [Fuck Like a Beast]"); a primer on satanic death metal (Venom's "Possessed," Mercyful Fate's "Evil," and Mötley Crüe's "Bastard"); possible drug overtones (Def Leppard's "High 'N' Dry [Saturday Night]" and Black Sabbath's "Trashed"); a bit of S&M/B&D fetishism (Mary Jane Girls' "Leather

Queen"); flagrant teenage insubordination (Twisted Sister's "We're Not Gonna Take It"); and sex, sex, and more sex (Mötley Crüe's "Ten Seconds to Love," Van Halen's "Hot for Teacher," Judas Priest's "Eat Me Alive," and Prince's "Soft and Wet," "Irresistible Little Bitch," and the aptly titled "Controversy").

By the time conservative forces realized that *they* had become, through the media, the purveyors of this questionable material it was too late. Even Tipper proclaimed that "I'm a fairly with-it person, but this stuff is *curling* my hair!" Apparently neither she nor her colleagues had given any thought about the public's sensibilities. With Al eyeing a future White House bid, major ass-covering suddenly became necessary, and at some point Tipper mumbled something about how she regretted the whole affair *because* it had all come off *looking* like censorship. For his part, Al Gore would soon try revising history to play down his participation in all of this. Yet the fact remains, he was a ringleader. Author and anti-censorship activist Dave Marsh attended those hearings and later described the central role that the then-senator played at the hearings: "Gore came early, stayed late and led the way in spreading an assortment of lies."

The central lie that the PMRC foisted was that the ratings system they sought would *not* result in censorship. Over time, more of their plans would be revealed and we would learn that in addition to labeling, the PMRC also wanted to establish a citizens' media-watch system that would monitor radio and TV and then organize against broadcasters who aired what they'd deemed "questionable talent." Translation: it oughta be criminal to produce, possess, sell, or broadcast whatever music *we* don't approve of!

The PMRC's hope was to see that musical products were required to be marked with a standardized rating notation/warning sticker that could alert consumers to the presence of objectionable content. Skeptics warned the inquisitors not to take this first step down the path along the proverbial slippery slope. They cautioned that once stickered, those albums were marked for life. They'd have a permanent bulls-eye branded on 'em. And at some later point, the government could simply act to outlaw such material. Others worried that radio stations would censor their own playlists too stringently out of fear of repercussions and that stores would simply be afraid to stock stickered LPs—even though those very stickers were exactly the recommended method of providing proper notification of "questionable content." Another concern was that stores that did elect to continue stocking such products would *still* be held legally accountable if the authorities ever decided to crack down. In short, censorship would result.

Another of the PMRC's accomplishments was to help raise the general state of alarm about music and youth. One result was the wave of repressive measures enacted around the country: in 1985 San Antonio's mayor led the city government in passing an ordinance that outlawed those under 14 from attending rock concerts held in any city-owned venue; that same year Seattle's city attorney dusted off a nearly forgotten blue law (that had been enacted in the '20s as a way to keep predatory sailors from hustling the city's fair maidens) and reshaped it into the Teen Dance Ordinance, which has hobbled dance promoters ever since; in 1989 New Iberia, Louisiana's city council adopted an ordinance designed to keep objectionable music away from *unmarried* people under the age of 17; and in 1990 city leaders in Memphis adopted a policy that barred minors from concerts where they might be exposed to "potentially harmful" music.

Then there were laws designed to intimidate the artists, the record producers, *and* the retailers. In 1988 the music industry got a serious wake-up call when the US Congress passed their Child Protection and Obscenity Enforcement Act—a law that laid a trap for future pornography charges against musical product. That same year, the labels and songwriters—as opposed to the retailers—got a big break when the Pennsylvania House of Representatives joined in by passing a *very* thorough law that required labels on albums with songs that "explicitly describe, advocate, or encourage suicide, incest, bestiality, sadomasochism, rape or involuntary deviant sexual intercourse, [or] advocate or encourage murder, ethnic intimidation, the use of illegal drugs or the excessive or illegal use of alcohol." Whew! The most interesting aspect of this bill, though, was the provision establishing that the artists or record firms would not be responsible for any obscenity infractions—rather it was the *retailers* who would be fully liable for the content of every record they stocked.

Political heat intensified to such a level that on November 1 the RIAA (in cahoots with the National Association of Retail Merchandisers) rolled over for the censors, and its member companies soon began to feel even greater pressure to sticker their products. In short order several dozen record firms were forced to "voluntarily" agree to give in on the matter. But for the next four years these various labels were left to at least in-dependently develop, design, and apply warning labels to albums at their own discretion. By 1990, the censors determined that additional controls were desirable, and that year the RIAA unveiled their "Parental Advisory: Explicit Lyrics" stickers (that we see on certain albums to this day), which were quickly adopted by most major labels—indeed, some 7,500 different album titles were stickered in the first three years alone.

Unfortunately, the sticker solution didn't prove to be the perfect panacea the censors had envisioned, and the rating of albums began to backfire. Just as some predicted, the "Tipper Stickers" were proving the truth of the old Forbidden Fruit Phenomenon. The stickers were accomplishing a lot more than just alerting parents (and kids) who might have been offended. The application of cautionary stickers intended to warn people off actually provided a road map directly to the material the censors were trying to deny them. Some indignant shopkeepers took to segregating all of their stickered LP stock into a special prominent showcase rack placed in a highly accessible location, drawing youths to them like moths to a flame.

And, just as predicted, within a few months of instituting the labeling system, at least 21 state legislatures introduced "explicit lyrics" bills that specified that any albums with Parental Advisory stickers would have to be restricted from sales to minors. The state of Louisiana generated a legislative bill in 1990 that attempted to criminalize sales of recordings that bore warning stickers to any unmarried individuals under 17—a measure that was only halted by a gubernatorial veto. Since 1992 Washington State has had a variety of "erotic music" bills, "harmful to minors" bills, and the like introduced annually, though none has survived judicial review. Then in 1994 (and again in 1995) the Pennsylvania legislature debated a bill that would have outlawed selling *any* stickered records to minors. In 1995 the New York legislature pondered the notion of requiring stickers, and in 1999 considered a bill that would do likewise—as did both North Dakota and Georgia.

And again, as predicted by opponents, once stickered the marked items could be targeted as a class. Thus, by 1992, Guilderland, New York's chief of police announced that he was going to aggressively enforce his state's obscenity laws against any retailer who even *stocked* stickered albums. But there were other problems with the stickering policy as well. Industry insiders derided the fact that, for example, an album by stand-up comedian George Carlin had an "Explicit *Lyrics*" (emphasis added) label slapped on it, as did Frank Zappa's *Jazz from Hell*. The thing is, there's not *one* syllable of vocals on that entire album—it's *instrumental*. Other artists struck back by creating their own customized warnings stickers. Ice-T's *Freedom of Speech* album bore one that read: "X-Rated; Parents Strongly Cautioned; Some material may be X-tra hype and inappropriate for squares and suckers." The sticker made for the Dayglow Abortions' *Feed U.S. A. Fetus* LP—which was confiscated and (unsuccessfully) prosecuted in 1988 on obscenity charges in Canada—promised content containing "poisonous ideas and corrosive concepts." It was no less than a heavy metal band named Reverend whose LP contributed this educational sticker: "The First Amendment of the United States Constitution protects an *artist's* right to make music freely and your right to own the music *you* want. WE SUPPORT BOTH." Interestingly, the sticker that the Dead Kennedys included on their *Frankenchrist* LP—"Warning: The inside fold-out to this record is a work of art by H.R. Giger that some people may find shocking, repulsive, and offensive. Life can be that way sometimes"—apparently wasn't straightforward enough to apprise one obtuse individual who brought legal action against the band after purchasing it.

Another good measure of the minimal high regard with which the PMRC (and other American censors like the Rev. Jerry Falwell and Sen. Jesse Helms) were held by many artists is a quick review of some of the scathing recordings made over the next few years, including "Tipper Gore" (Alice Donut); "Tipper Gore" (The Dread); "Letter to Tipper Gore" (Jello Biafra); "PMRC" (Bouncing Souls); "Dear PMRC" (Karen Finley); "Rapist (Tipper Gore Mix)" (The Flying Medallions); "Tipper Gore" (Fudge Tunnel); "We Love You, Tipper Gore" (Furnaceface); "PMRC Sucks" (Gang Green); "Freedom of Speech" and "KKK Bitch" (Ice-T); "Tipper Gore" (Martin); "Hook in Mouth" (Megadeth); "The PMRC Can Suck on This" (NOFX); "Censorshit" (Ramones); "Tipper Gore for Prozac" (Paul Shanklin); "Jesse" (Todd Rundgren); "God, Jerry & the PMRC" (Victims Family); "Ode to Tipper Gore" (Warrant); "Tipper Gore" (Wolf); and "Porn Wars" (Frank Zappa). Finally, the whole thing came to its ridiculous peak when the Phillips label voluntarily began to sticker their classical and opera recordings in an effort to draw the marketplace's attention to the prolific amounts of sex and violence found in that musical realm. This was *not* the kind of corporate response that the PMRC had hoped for.

Funny? Sure, but the ugly reality of things soon set in because the censors' work had merely begun. Reagan's Department of Justice announced a new National Obscenity Enforcement Unit that began producing and promoting conferences in conjunction with various religious organizations. The president also authorized Attorney General Edwin Meese to launch an investigation of smut in America. The Meese Commission on Pornography set out in 1985 with the agenda of proving a conservative notion that had been consistently debunked by decades' worth of international studies: that pornography *causes* violence and crime. Meese faithfully saw to it that his commission reached the desired conclusions at the end of their inquiry; that more, and harsher, prosecutions of "smut peddlers" should occur.

Record companies continued to feel the heat, and in early 1986 CBS announced a new in-house policy regarding explicit lyrics. It amounted to a crude attempt to intimidate the artists on their roster into producing only material that couldn't be deemed "controversial." Furthermore, despite the PMRC's assurances to the contrary, within a few years of their "voluntary" stickering system being adopted by the record companies, the stickers became a target and numerous major retail chains including Wal-Mart, K-Mart, Sears, J.C. Penney, Camelot, Disc Jockey, and Wax Works simply refused to stock *any* stickered music. The Trans World chain of 400-plus stores went only half way, announcing a new policy of checking customers' ID before a sale of stickered product.

By 1987 record shops in malls were receiving pressure from building management to clean up their acts, and, fearing eviction, began to refuse to stock any albums or singles that contained potentially offensive words. That same year one member of the House of Representatives *secretly* authorized the Congressional Research Service to conduct a study to determine whether or not Congress had the constitutional standing to legally restrict the sale of songs that contain explicit lyrics. The CRS has never been forced to reveal the shy leader's identity, but their affirmative conclusion was soon recognized as nothing but a dead-end battle tactic.

In 1989 the FCC, no doubt with the support of the first President Bush, began cranking up the heat by launching a fresh round of imposing large fines on radio stations that aired "questionable" songs. The incidents included: Miami's WZTA-FM and WIOD-AM both being hit with $2,000 fines over Uncle Bonsai's humorous ditty "Penis Envy";

WIOD paying $2,000 fines for airing "Candy Wrapper" and "Jet Boy, Jet Girl," as well as a comedic remake of the Bangles' hit "Walk Like an Egyptian"—"Walk with an Erection"; Detroit's WLLZ-FM also getting slapped over "Walk with an Erection"; and Las Vegas's KLUC-FM being fined for airing Prince's hit "Erotic City" ("... We can fuck until the dawn ...").

The fact that the FCC was paying attention at all caused many station managers to better realize the increasing risks of broadcasting questionable music. Some failed at that task over the years, and in 1990 Indianapolis's WFBQ-FM paid a $10,000 fine for numerous infractions including the airing of "Stroke Your Dingy," and San Diego's KGB-FM was out a whopping $25,000 for broadcasting "Candy Wrapper" and a bawdy Monty Python comedy piece, "Sit on My Face." And then, over the next few years under President Clinton, the "smut war" continued: Cortland, New York's WSUC-FM was fined for airing a particularly "vulgar" hip-hop song; Dallas's KNON-FM was fined $12,500 over the song "I Want To Be a Homosexual;" and by 1996 the FCC had also levied fines on radio stations in Michigan and Virginia for airing "indecent" material. Meanwhile, San Antonio's KTFM was specifically cited for playing Prince's "Erotic City," and airing various hip-hop tunes also earned fines for stations like Holmes Beach, Florida's WLLD-FM and Madison, Wisconsin's WZEE-FM. Then in 2001 the FCC fined Colorado's KKMG for airing an Eminem song and Portland, Oregon's KBOO for airing Sarah Jones's spicy hip-hop hit, "Your Revolution."

But back in August of 1989, even MTV was running scared and felt the need to announce a new content policy. Their Standards Department would now require (from record labels) an accurate lyric sheet with all newly submitted videos—and videos that seemed to promote violence, drug use, or explicit sex would be rejected. Nice try, but not good enough for the censors. Officials in Texarkana, Texas—in response to what they figured was a widespread disdain of MTV—pressured a local cable firm to make available to their customers a channel-blocking device. When the 22,000 subscribers were informed that they could receive one of the new blockers, a total of 40 households requested them. Then in 1991 Tele-Community Antenna—a major cable firm with 53 systems in six states—cut MTV for all of its 420,000 subscribers. In the face of customer complaints, MTV was restored a mere two weeks later. Within months another cable company (55 systems in 19 states) got cold feet and canned MTV, but after four months gave in and it too reinstated the popular channel.

Both heavy rock bands and hip-hop artists were increasingly under the gun. In 1986 the popular Miami-based rap outfit 2 Live Crew had issued an album, *2 Live Is What We Are* (with songs like "We Want Some Pussy"), that fell afoul of Florida's morality laws. It was in 1987 that some poor part-time record shop employee in Callaway, Florida, was arrested for selling it to a minor. But that was only the beginning of the crew's trouble. In 1988 the owner of a record shop in Alexandria, Alabama, was arrested—based on

The bodacious cover-art graphics (and raunchy lyrics) of 2 Live Crew's '89 hit album (and cassette, as seen here) sparked boycotts, bannings, confiscations, arrests, and harassment from cops and politicians.

a local prosecutor's wishful interpretation of the state's general obscenity codes—for selling a copy of their *Move Somthin'* disc (which included songs like "S&M") to an undercover agent. Feeling the heat, the 130-store Hastings Record Store chain suddenly announced a new policy in 1989 of restricting the sales of certain rock and hip-hop albums to minors. Then in 1990 some county prosecutors in Pennsylvania identified 2 Live Crew's *As Nasty as They Wanna Be* album (which included songs like "If You Believe in Having Sex" and "Me So Horny") as legally obscene and gave local retailers advance warning that they would be prosecuted if they attempted to sell it.

"Me So Horny" brought the crew further trouble when in 1990 a Florida circuit court judge declared the song obscene. After the local sheriff made intimidating "informational" visits to a dozen or so area record shops, 2 Live Crew records became quite scarce in that state. In response, the band chose to file suit. And that case made history when a judge in Tennessee became the first federal court to ever declare a recording legally obscene.

That's just what the Broward County, Florida, sheriff had been waiting to hear. He immediately raced out and busted the last remaining retailer who still stocked the *As Nasty as They Wanna Be* disc—a fellow who was subsequently prosecuted and fined $1,000, thus becoming the first person in American history to ever be convicted of dealing in "obscene" music. In Indianapolis a record shop was threatened by a senatorial candidate for selling the album, as was another by a local sheriff's posse in Hamilton, Ohio. The county solicitor in Columbia, South Carolina, gave area record shops all of ten days notice to junk any additional copies they might have of *As Nasty as They Wanna Be*—or else. For its part, the San Antonio Police Department took it upon themselves to warn by phone 84 record shops, and then tried to make an example out of one by jailing its owner on "obscenity" charges.

A Tennessee judge found, under state law, both the *As Nasty as They Wanna Be* and N.W.A.'s *Straight Outta Compton* albums "obscene" and that retailers could face fines up to $100,000. Duly inspired, state legislatures in Florida, Indiana, Ohio, Pennsylvania, and Wisconsin all moved to tighten their obscenities laws. Ultimately, in response to these attacks, 2 Live Crew recorded "Banned in the USA," a protest song built on the tune to Bruce Springsteen's 1984 hit "Born in the USA."

Meanwhile, Luther Campbell and two other members of 2 Live Crew were arrested on obscenity charges while performing at an *adults*-only club in Florida. [Note: This incident was part of a bigger repressive trend that also affected other artists including the Queens, New York, rapper LL Cool J, who was arrested on charges of "public lewdness" after a live performance in Columbus, Georgia, in 1987. Neo-R&B star Bobby Brown, and Kiss's bassist, Gene Simmons, were each arrested in a message-sending spree by police in that same state in 1989.] But, just as that particular Florida case against 2 Live Crew was summarily rejected by a jury, the original federal verdict against their *As Nasty as They Wanna Be* album was eventually tossed out when reconsidered by a US Court of Appeals. Beyond all that though, the whole matter was permanently resolved in favor of the band—and that little constitutional matter of free speech—when the US Supreme Court passed on its chance to review it and let the court of appeals ruling stand.

Unfortunately, this was way too late for 2 Live Crew. Intimidated record shops from coast to coast had dumped the record in fear that prosecutions—legally justifiable or otherwise—could affect them. Indeed, the large national Record Bar retail chain soon established a policy of not stocking any 2 Live Crew records in its 170-plus shops. In 1992, four shops in Omaha, Nebraska, that dared to stock the next 2 Live Crew disc *Sports Weekend* were entrapped by members of the Omaha for Decency "organization," resulting in criminal charges of distributing materials "harmful to minors." And as late as 1997 three owners of a music venue in Oxford, Mississippi, were arrested and given six-month jail sentences simply for *booking* a concert with 2 Live Crew.

On another front, progress has been made in the realm of gay rights in recent years. Just as our society no longer accepts public declarations of racial bigotry, the general public is now expected to exhibit more tolerance towards sexual minorities. It was not always this way. Consider that as recently as four decades ago—before the Gay Liberation movement had begun sensitizing the general public to their concerns—the radio industry felt little need to withhold support from a string of ostensibly "humorous" records that poked fun at homosexuals. And those tunes—including Phil McLean's 1961 (No. 21) hit "Small Sad Sam" and Steve Greenberg's '69 (No. 97) hit "Big Bruce"—were popular enough to make the national charts.

Times changed however and those cruel days of casual discrimination were

The controversial robot-rapist cover art for Guns N' Roses' hit 1987 album
Appetite for Destruction *was withdrawn by Geffen Records after protests and*
replaced with a generic heavy-metal skull/cross/tattoo–style design.

fading—too bad someone forgot to spread the news to a number of modern-day bigots.
Thus it was in the '80s that the Los Angeles–based heavy-metal band Guns N' Roses
incited outrage with the homophobic (*and* racist, *and* anti-immigrant) lyrical slurs in
their song "One in a Million." Before long the band saw their concerts being picketed
and faced condemnations by various community leaders. Lyricist/singer Axel Rose and
the band even experienced a social banishment of sorts when they were unceremoniously
dumped from the lineup by the producers of a high-profile New York AIDS benefit concert
in 1989. All this occurred without a single congressional inquiry or any governmental
intrusion whatsoever. No records were outlawed. No death threats reported. Yet, the
problem was *dealt* with.

That same year the management at Los Angeles's KDAY radio, deluged with listener
complaints about the homophobic messages in Kool G. Rap and DJ Polo's song "Truly
Yours," yanked it from their playlist. In 2000, complaints by the Gay and Lesbian Alliance
against Defamation prompted MTV to request that the Bloodhound Gang's video for
"The Bad Touch" ("…Baby… we're nothing but mammals / Let's do it like they do on
the Discovery Channel …") be edited. Coming to censorship from another direction
some students at both the University of Wisconsin and University of Maryland petitioned

to have concert dates for the group canceled based on their concern over the lyrical themes of a song that that group hadn't even released commercially yet.

It was in 1999 that music fans first heard about a remarkable new white rapper named Eminem. Though impressively skilled at rhyming, this fellow had a keen knack for being where troubles arose. Touring with several of the reigning hip-hop stars of the day—including Dr. Dre, Snoop Dogg, and Ice Cube—Eminem was part of a concert extravaganza that received a ton of press coverage when Michigan cops took it upon themselves to intervene at two separate shows featuring video snippets with footage of a scantily clad female. As things transpired, only Eminem's mentor and producer, Dre, was charged with "public nudity" violations.

By 2000 Eminem had successfully made himself the lightning rod for gay rights groups. And by unapologetically verbalizing more intolerance per inch of song lyric than anyone this side of Guns N' Roses, he well deserved the negative attention. The rants on Eminem's debut album—while horrific and thoroughly despicable—are nevertheless still difficult to peg legalistically as pure "hate speech." [Personally, I prefer to view them in the same manner as I do Richard Wagner's work: *great* jams / *reprehensible* politics.]

Though some liberals don't want to hear it, Eminem's work *is* absolutely defendable on a First Amendment basis. And just as he has the right to spew his provocatively divisive filth, gay rights and civil rights organizations, and other individuals who are concerned about human dignity, have a *duty* to boycott and/or picket his concerts. That is *not* censorship. It is citizenship in action. It is not an attempt to deprive other folks of the music they prefer—no protesters I heard were demanding that the record be banished from the face of the earth (well, except perhaps one George W. Bush who, in his trademark alarmist way, branded Eminem as "the most dangerous threat to American children since polio")—but rather these actions were methods of taking principled and public stands against what they consider to be offensive ideas. *That* is the "American Way"—and it is exactly what happened when the album was nominated for a Grammy award: protesters mounted a successful Rally Against Hate in response to Eminem's hate-filled expressions.

Less meaningful were the predictable attacks leveled at Eminem by Lynne V. Cheney, the know-it-all wife of the soon-to-be-installed vice president, who testified before a Senate committee in September 2000, characterizing the rapper's work as being about "blood, guts, guns, knives, wives, nuns, sluts. It is despicable. It is horrible." Going well beyond that lyrical critique, our Second Lady has also leveled more generalized threats against the Constitution, saying: "Some in the entertainment industry are consistently failing to act responsibly. They are producing violent, sexually explicit material, and they are peddling it to children. They claim unbridled license to do so under the First Amendment; however, their persistent irresponsibility, ironically, threatens the First Amendment."

While many wondered where Cheney's expertise in constitutional law derived from and what her musicological credentials were, Eminem simply lashed back on a couple of his next tunes like "White America" ("... Fuck You, Miss Cheney! ... Fuck you with the freeness of speech this Divided States of Embarrassment will allow you to have. Fuck you! ..."), and the hit "Without Me," which, in part, addressed political interference in his career ("... I know that you got a job Ms. Cheney... So the FCC won't let me be ... They tried to shut me down on MTV ..."). In a generous bipartisan spirit the rapper also took the time to settle a much older score against earlier censors by also tossing out this barb ("... Fuck you, Tipper Gore! ..."). [Note: By the summer of 2002 Eminem was a prominent-enough target that a British jury heard charges that a sexual attack "may" have been inspired by his song "Ken Kaniff"—yet another instance of music being tarred as the *cause* of criminal behavior. Then in late 2003 the Secret Service—having *somehow* been tipped off to the (anti-money-grubbing) lyrics ("I don't rap for dead presidents / I'd rather see the president dead") of an *unreleased* rap tune called "We as Americans"—made a big news splash by announcing to the press that they would be interrogating Eminem to determine the level of threat he posed President Bush.]

It seems clear that censors like the PMRC, the Rev. Pat Robertson, and Dr. Cheney and their ilk could stand to have a remedial brush-up course on the Constitution's Bill of Rights, democratic civics, and the legal means of dealing with art they object to. Perhaps some Rally Against Hate leaders would be willing to educate them on such matters.

One historical constant in all of this is that good parents naturally hope that their young offspring are not exposed to questionable materials. And while that hope is fully understandable, the simple hard truth is that this big old world has *never* been a perfectly safe place. It's a rough-and-tumble reality out there. "Unregulated" ideas—wild, crazy, sexy, you name it—are regularly touted in the public arena. Crude vocabularies *are* employed at times. People—despite the very best efforts of some "moral guardians" to convince us that sex is bad—will likely continue to show a keen interest in that particular lyrical topic (as well as the physical activity itself) well into the future. It is this way because adults have the right to be adults. The realms of civic and cultural discourse are ones that necessarily address adult topics—this is *not* kid's stuff. Imagine a culture tamed and cleansed to the extent that all its aspects would be perfectly safe for toddlers. The noted Catholic thinker Father Murray once did, and he concluded that "society has an interest in the artist's expression which is not necessarily shared by the family. If adult standards of literature could be dangerous for children, a child's standard is rather appalling for an adult." Truth.

CHAPTER 6

Killing in the Name

Goin' to do like a China man, get some hop,

get myself a gun, and shoot myself a cop...

—Mamie Smith, "Crazy Blues," 1920

Death—though an uneasy topic in most settings—has long been considered fair game in the arts. In fact, it would be difficult to identify ancient societies that did *not* have traditions of singing songs about the matter. And the practice continues today. A couple of prominent musical examples with death as a central theme are a classical masterpiece from 1808, Ludwig van Beethoven's Fifth Symphony, and Ralph Stanley's immortal bluegrass classic from 1950, "O Death."

What we're talking about here, though, are "killin' songs"—or "murder ballads" as they are referred to in academic and folklore circles. While such tunes are part of deep traditions in Anglo-Celtic cultures, they also survive as a mode of expression in modern times. While some may believe that today's music—with the proliferation of hardcore "death-metal" bands and ultra-violent gangsta rap—has pioneered a despicable and indefensible trend, in fact, American killing songs can be traced as far back as our nation itself.

While the most offensive songs often have a celebratory vibe that is troubling, even in the days of old certain songs conveyed plenty of terror and gory detail to their listeners. Such tunes were typically solemn and sentimental, romanticized, or rousing narrative numbers whose purpose was to announce, or recount, dramatic "news" items. Some ballads served to mark deadly natural disasters (major fires, droughts, floods), mythologize accidents (big coal mine disasters, train wrecks, sinking ships), or memorialize wars and their associated victims. Still another category of song were those that documented true tales of contemporary crimes. A brief survey of some of those lovely old chestnuts provides some sense of the extreme violence that has marred every era—along with the tradition of singing about it.

Just consider a few of the many early American songs (from as far back as the 1810s) that dealt with such true-to-life topics as jealous and/or star-crossed lovers, such as "The Tragedy of Henry and Servilla" (jilted dude shoots gal and commits suicide); "Frankie and Johnnie" (jealous gal kills dude [Frankie]); "Banks of the Ohio" (dude beats his gal with a stick and throws her in river); "The Ballad of Polly Williams" (dude tosses marriage-fixated gal off cliff); "The Murdered Wife" (dude poisons new bride); "Down in the Willow Garden" (dude poisons gal's wine, stabs her, and tosses her in the river); "Naomi Wise" (dude, having found new gal, strangles and throws wife in river); "The Ballad of Cooper Milton" (dude discovers and kills wife and her lover); and "The Vance Song" (preacher shoots wealthy dude who had seduced and then rejected his daughter, and is then hung).

Another favored topic was the crime—and occasional punishment—epic: "The Death of Joseph White" (wealthy dude is clubbed and stabbed in inheritance scheme); "The Murdered Peddler" (dude shoots, throws in river, and stones peddler, who survives to finger him); "The Ballad of Josie Langmaid" (schoolgirl beheaded by maniac in 1875); "The Ashland Tragedy" (three maniacs rape and kill three children, then burn their Kentucky home); "The Harry Hayward Song" (dude is hung for shooting, beating, and tossing gal onto a roadway); "Marion Parker" (dude kidnaps schoolgirl, gets ransom, and then tosses a severed body part at her father as he flees).

As horrible as all those historic incidents were, however, none can compare with the disturbing tale recounted in "The Ballad of Pearl Bryan" of 1896, which told how a Greencastle, Indiana, gal died from a cocaine overdose during an abortion and had her decapitated body dumped in an ill-fated attempt to obscure her identity.

Modern examples in the tradition of "killin' songs" would include:

Cole Porter's 1934 classic "Miss Otis Regrets" (spurned gal kills lover, is jailed, then lynched by a mob); the '56 (No. 4) C&W hit "Folsom Prison Blues" (dude shoots dude: "…just to watch him die…") (Johnny Cash); Archibald's '50s version of the old folk tune "Stack-A-Lee" (gambler shoots dude for stealing his Stetson), which became a big (No. 1) R&B hit for Lloyd Price when recut as "Stagger Lee" in '58; the '59 (No. 1) hit "El Paso" (dude gets in a deadly barroom brawl over some gal) (Marty Robbins); "Dixie Fried" (dude captured after a razor fight in a bar and ends up in the electric chair) (Carl Perkins); the '60 R&B classic "Over You" (dude threatens gal if she even *thinks* about dumping him) (Allen Toussaint); the '62 folk standard "Hey Joe" (dude threatens to shoot his gal for cheatin') (Billy Roberts) [Note: After being recorded by Tim Rose in 1966, this song was banned at numerous southern radio stations for "glorifying violence."]; "Ballad of Hollis Brown" (broke and broken dude shoots wife and five kids, then commits suicide) and "Lonesome Death of Hattie Carroll" (angered by poor service, wealthy dude kills a hotel employee with cane at circa '63 high society soiree, and receives short prison sentence) (Bob Dylan); 1969's "Down by the River" (dude shoots his unfaithful gal) (Neil Young); the '94 hit "Independence Day" (gal immolates herself and house along with her abusive spouse) (Martina McBride); the 2000 hit "Goodbye Earl" (gal poisons abusive spouse) (Dixie Chicks); and the 2003 hit "Beer for My Horses" (dudes—and their horses!—celebrate with drinks after lynching evildoers) (Toby Keith and Willie Nelson).

Most relevant here, though, are those songs that recount historical incidents where law enforcement officers have paid the ultimate price of giving their lives in the line of duty. Examples include "The Hennessey Murder" and "Hennessey Avenged"—two ballads that marked the time in 1890 when the chief of police was gunned down on the streets of New Orleans in a Mafia hit.

However, not everyone held the police in such high regard, and the resentment of corrupt cops has long been a theme in songs. The century-old folk classic "Tom Dooley" (dude is hung for stabbing and burying gal in North Carolina in 1866)—which the Kingston Trio scored a massive No. 1 hit with in 1958—was nominally about the crime's perpetrator, but a careful listening reveals that the lyrics also mention the community's suspicions that their sheriff had actually framed poor ol' Dooley. Not exactly a vote of confidence in the local police.

In fact some perfectly law-abiding folks have plenty of reasons to view cops as a threat. One hasn't always needed a criminal record to get on the wrong side of some officers—it often seems that just being the "wrong" color, the "wrong" class, or having the "wrong" opinion is enough to bring on trouble. Consider the case of the labor activist Ella May Wiggins, who wrote the song "Chief Aderholt" as commentary on the murder of the chief of police of Gastonia, North Carolina. It was reported that the tune "particularly riled" Gastonia's officers, and few were surprised when she was mysteriously gunned down by unknown night riders on her way to a union meeting in 1929.

The blues world was another realm where police weren't overly appreciated. Some of the genre's biggest stars were genuinely tough customers who had more than a bit of background with the law. For example, consider those seminal Mississippi Delta giants Son House and Huddie 'Leadbelly' Ledbetter, each of whom served hard time for murder before achieving success in music. Then there was bluesman Pat Hare, who effectively confessed to malice aforethought in his 1954 blues curio "I'm Gonna Murder My Baby"—and a decade later did exactly that and ended up dying in prison for his crime of passion. Beyond that, it was the world's very *first* blues recording—Mamie Smith's 1920 hit "Crazy Blues"—that in making an overt threat to the police provided a blueprint for nearly every anti-authoritarian tune to come down the pike since.

Having reviewed this long background to America's "killin' song" heritage, we are now better prepared to consider more recent songs that explore similar topical terrain.

While overt disrespect for lawmen has clearly been well-trodden lyrical territory for years, it is interesting that a number of such songs actually became commercial winners, including Bobby Fuller Four's 1966 (Top-Ten) hit "I Fought the Law," Eric Clapton's (No. 1) hit version of Bob Marley's classic "I Shot the Sheriff," and John Mellencamp's '84 hit "Authority Song." But in addition to those musical mileposts, ponder a few other anti-police anthems like: 1969's "Today's Pig Is Tomorrow's Bacon" (Floating Bridge); "Police Story" (Black Flag); "Criminal Cop" (Pack of Wolves); "Police Force" (Fartz); "Death to All the Pigs" (Naked Aggression); "Kill the Police" (G.G. Allin); "All the Cops Are Bastards" (Terrorgruppe); "Die Pig Die" (Abscess); "Police Truck" (Dead Kennedys); "All Cops Lie" (F-Minus); "Die U Fuckin' Pigs" (Connected of Darkroom Familia); "Police Crimes" (B.G.K.); "Police on My Back" (The Clash); "Cops Dropping Like Flies" (D8stein); "Police Oppression" (Angelic Upstarts); "Cops for Fertilizer" (The Crucifucks); "Royal Police" (D.O.A.); "Anticop" (TSOL); "Pigs Will Pay" (Propagandhi); "Corrupt Cop" (Mighty Diamonds); "Crooked Cop" (Dove Shack); "Hate the Police" (Dicks); "Fuck the Cops" (White Kaps); "I Hate Cops" (Authorities); "Crime Pays When Pigs Die" (Christ on a Crutch); "Dead Cop" (Area 51); "Abolish Police" (Final Conflict); "Killer Cop" (Capitol Punishment); "No Fan of Cops" (Hellnation); "Pig Until Proven Cop" (One Minute Silence); "Fault the Police" (Corporate Avenger); "Rambo Cop" (Daycare Swindlers); "Police Attack" (Blanks 77); "Police Brutality" (Casuals); "Cop on a Meathook" (AMQA); "Fascist Pig" (Suicidal Tendencies); "Terror Police" (Discharge); "Fuck Police Brutality" and "Police State in the USA" (Anti-Flag); "Don't Call the Police" (Tony Rebel); "New York City Cops" (Strokes)—a song issued on 9/25/01 that was reportedly recalled and disappeared by RCA Records due to perceived post-9/11 sensitivities and some mildly derogatory lyrics ("…they ain't too smart …"); the album *How Do You Call the Cops on the Cops?* (Aspirin Feast); and "Bad Boys" (Inner Circle), a reggae tune made famous as the theme to the popular *Cops* TV show ("…the policeman give you no breaks …"). Finally, even the names of some recent bands—such as Officer Down, Cop Shoot Cop, and Millions of Dead Cops—indicate the uphill challenge facing members of the law enforcement community interested in mending their relationship with a significant portion of the public.

By the late '80s—and having already struck blows against heavy metal bands via the Parents Music Resource Center's senate hearings—conservative Culture Warriors were primed to take on hip-hop culture. And so, under the influence of the PMRC's Tipper Gore and Susan Baker (whose efforts helped confuse the public into thinking that Tone Lōc's 1989 hip-hop hit "Wild Thing" had been *responsible* for the infamous NYC Central Park jogger assault "wilding" incident), it was natural for white, middle-class, suburban-type folks to come to feel generally threatened by hip-hop music, or "rap." And that is because hip-hop—a creation of the ghetto—has to a great extent defined itself as a musical form whose hard-hitting lyrics deal with the harsh realities of urban street life. And just as certain overprivileged white pop stars sing about their reality,

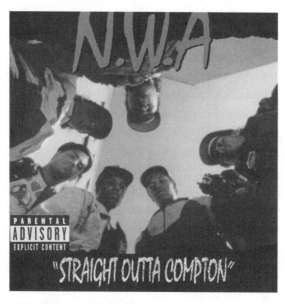

When N.W.A. issued the Straight Outta Compton *CD in '89, their protest against police brutality, "Fuck Tha Police," brought the FBI down on them.*

hip-hop crews likewise respond to their circumstances and surroundings by rapping about the issues relevant to their neighborhoods. It is this fact that accounts for all the raps about poverty, drug addiction, discrimination, unemployment, racism, teen pregnancy, gang warfare, and, yes, police brutality. It is important to keep in mind that a big percentage of rap tunes *condemn* these dismal conditions through the act of simply describing them. But let's not get confused and think the mentioning of—or the protesting of—these conditions *is* the problem.

And it is this matter that brings us to the saga surrounding two of the most infamous songs discussed in this entire book. Both are tunes that fall squarely within the folk, blues, rock, reggae, punk, and hip-hop traditions described above—yet, between the two, they managed to spark firestorms of controversy, boycotts, a warning from the FBI, harassment from various police departments across the land, death threats, and even a bomb scare. The first was N.W.A.'s "Fuck Tha Police" and the second was Ice-T's "Cop Killer."

"Fuck Tha Police" was a tune cut by Compton, California's hardcore rappers N.W.A. (Niggers With Attitude) for Priority Records. The words are a straightforward rap about injustice on the streets ["… police think they have the authority to kill a minority …"] and resistance to police brutality ["… Fuck that shit 'cause I ain't the one for a punk motherfucker with a badge to be beatin' on …"]. A careful reading of the song's words doesn't reveal anything illegal being stated, but nevertheless, in an unprecedented move on August 1, 1989, an assistant director of the FBI (under the first President Bush) sent an ominous note to the band's label. In that correspondence the agency made it known that they had taken note of N.W.A.'s *Straight Outta Compton* album (and "Fuck Tha Police") and were *not* amused: "I wanted you to be aware of the FBI's position relative to this song…." G-Men also reportedly suggested that Priority dump N.W.A., and it was rumored that the FBI also made attempts to intervene in the distribution of the album.

What is certain is that word spread in the law enforcement world and officers (reportedly urged on by the right-wing Focus on the Family group) in towns including Milwaukee, Cincinnati, Washington, DC, and elsewhere worked to get N.W.A.'s concerts banned. In Detroit, N.W.A. was literally rushed off the stage by cops—one of whom bragged to the media (in a statement that had zero legal foundation) that "we just wanted to show the kids that you can't say 'fuck the police' in Detroit." With that series of boycott demonstrations dogging N.W.A.'s entire concert tour that year, the group was ultimately intimidated into dropping the tune from their set list. Then in 1990, a judge in Tennessee declared that *Straight Outta Compton* was "obscene" and that under state law sales to minors would result in fines up to $100,000. But the troubles didn't end there: the following year the British government seized copies of N.W.A.'s new album, *Efil4zaggin',* under the authority of the Obscene Publications Act. Though the authorities later lost in court, their goal was essentially accomplished since the record was effectively made unavailable during the period when it was a hot commodity. Punishment delivered.

Then in 1991 along came the song that holds a special place in history as only one—among the many, many controversial songs noted in this book—that has actually been *banned* in America. It is the *only* one that, due to a tough and successful protest campaign, *you* have been forbidden to purchase and is no longer available at your local record shop. And that song is "Cop Killer" by the Los Angeles–based rap star, Ice-T, and his side-project rock band, Body Count.

The saga of "Cop Killer" becomes most interesting when we pause to consider exactly *why* this song, of all songs, was targeted for enforced extinction. The rationale could not have been based on any notion that "Cop Killer" was the *first* to express animosity towards law enforcement agents—as we know such songs abound. So, why the big fuss when an artist chose to express himself on the same topic that other artists had been exploring for decades? Could simple and raw election-year politics have been the motivating force behind this whole flare-up? In order to examine these and other issues surrounding "Cop Killer," we should first set the historical context to help illustrate how Ice-T managed to hit such a nerve and in doing so, bring down a world of trouble on himself.

Looking back we see that early hip-hop groups were mainly faulted for producing "pornographic" records, but over time the songs that turned out to bring a few rappers serious trouble were those that directly challenged authority. Foremost among them was Public Enemy, from Long Island, New York. The name alone was a brilliant

Rapper Ice-T's part-time rock band, Body Count, sparked a huge backlash with its infamous Cop Killer *CD in 1992. "Cop Killer" was later excised from the album and remains about the only song ever successfully suppressed in America.*

confrontational choice for a hip-hop group who capably expressed their opinions in songs like their defiant hit from 1990 "Fight the Power." It's a no-brainer to see that it was precisely because of such ideas (however valid they may be)—and their massive popularity—that the group received no small amount of grief from cops as they toured America. Main Street America had, of course, little sympathy for the exploits of Public Enemy—but then again, those same folks hadn't really been forced to realize that something was greatly out of whack in the realm of race relations and law enforcement here.

A major wake-up call for the general public came with the notorious videotaped beating of black motorist Rodney King by the Los Angeles Police Department in March 1991. That watershed incident shocked the world and inspired a good number of hip-hop artists to address the injustice in song—yet it was, in particular, the one tune that Ice-T penned that somehow attracted all the unwanted attention of the police. "Cop Killer," Ice-T consistently maintained, was simply an expression of frustration with police brutality in his South Central LA neighborhood. "Cop Killer" was a *fictional* song written from the perspective of a motorist who had been brutalized by a law enforcement officer—not exactly an uncommon occurrence, as the world learned from King's run-in with the LAPD.

Ice-T (and Body Count) began performing "Cop Killer" on their concert tours that year with no direct trouble resulting. But a year later—in the 1992 election cycle—a few Texas cops took note of the song and determined that the political timing was right to send a message. Their actions quickly succeeded in stirring up police unions, hard-line National Rifle Association (NRA) addicts, right-wing militia members, and various anti-democratic politicians, all of whom began raising hell in the media and announced a major boycott of the parent company, Time Warner (formerly WEA), of the label that marketed the CD. The ever-helpful Texas governor, George W. Bush, signed a law directing other state officials to redirect pension funds away from investments in record companies that produce objectionable material. Meanwhile, conservative icons (like convicted felon Lt. Col. Ollie North and the nation's vice president, Dan Quayle) raced to the TV cameras to vilify the song. At least 60 congressmen wrote Time Warner to denounce Ice-T and "Cop Killer." The heat was turned up further when Ice-T's kids were pulled from school for interrogation by government agents and he was notified that his finances would be audited by the IRS.

Not everyone was willing to march in lockstep with the Culture Warriors. While the Combined Law Enforcement Associations of Texas and the Police Benevolent Association led aggressive attacks against the song, the National Black Police Association came out *against* the boycott, noting that: "People have always expressed their feelings and opinions through songs, and they are talking about how African-American people have been victimized by police brutality. And that is very real." Beyond that: "Where were these police groups when the police beat up Rodney King?" Considering that lawmen are, first and foremost, public safety officers, their lack of publicly expressed concern for King's rights is certainly a question worthy of being raised.

From this point, everything escalated, peaking with a campaign of phoned death and bomb threats to the label, Sire Records. Finding themselves in a tight spot, Time Warner must have been horribly torn. Their choices were (a) to gag one of their most promising, bright, and outspoken stars or, (b) to take action and attempt to revive their reputation as a "responsible corporate citizen." Ultimately, Time Warner's president did the honorable thing. He spoke out in defense of Ice-T's legal right to produce the song. But even *that* exasperated Ice-T. In response to people who stepped up in support of his *constitutional* right to make whatever music he chose, Ice-T said: "It was always: 'Well, he has the First Amendment right. I don't agree with him, but ...' *Fuck that!* Back me on the fact that Ice-T has the *grounds* to say: 'Fuck the police.' 'Cause the police have been killing his people. How many black leaders did the police slaughter? They *slaughtered* the [Black] Panthers. The motherfuckers are *savage!* Say: '*That's* why he made the record. He has the *grounds* to make it.' *Not* just the right."

Ice-T is on to something very important here. Beyond the unquestioned fact that he had the constitutional right to create his song, we also ought to acknowledge that his anger is legitimate. "Cop Killer" has undeniably brutal lyrics. They are words, unfortunately, that accurately mirror the violence that African-American citizens, in particular, have received from cops on a regular basis. This is not news. As Ice-T calmly attempted to explain: "The record is *not* a call to murder police. The record is about anger. This is the *end result* of police brutality." While the exceptionally violent message in "Cop Killer" is absolutely *not* to be condoned—it *is*, however, constitutionally viable. We can hate it, condemn it, and even boycott it, but there is *no* legal way to stop it. Author and anti-censorship activist Dave Marsh nailed the situation with his observation that "metaphoric violence in hip-hop records deserves absolute moral condemnation up to the point of banishing an art form." Right on! Hate it. Complain about it. Don't buy it. But going out of your way to force the extinction of something is unacceptable behavior.

In the end, the *Body Count* CD was withdrawn and remarketed after excising "Cop Killer." Now, musically speaking, that may not be the biggest loss in history, however—as measured by the loss of *your* freedom of choice—the impact of the "Cop Killer" ban is incalculable. And then, considering that the song didn't totally disappear, even the censors' victory against Ice-T was limited. It seems that the sentiments behind "Cop Killer" resonated so deeply that numerous other artists, including Thanatos, Jayo Felony, A.N.I.M.A.L., and Hoodlum Priest each chose to cut their own renditions of it. And beyond that, just as police brutality continued, so too did the growing canon of similar hip-hop tunes, including "Fuck These Police" (Jahari), "Damn Police" (Kingpin Skinny Pimp), "Corrupt Cops" (DJ Abstract), "Dirty Cop" (Doun 'N Durdee), "Take 2 Wit Me" (MC Eiht), and "Runnin' from the Police" (C-Murder).

In similar spirit, the politically radical "rap-metal" band Rage Against The Machine stepped up with a rendition of N.W.A.'s "Fuck Tha Police," and The Righteous cut a trio of supportive tributes, "Payback Time," "The Pigs," and "Cop Killer Crew." Meanwhile, a number of labels got skittish and began yanking other recordings by their hip-hop artists, including "Shoot 'Em Down" (Boo-Yaa Tribe), *Live and Let Die* (Kool G Rap and DJ Polo), *Bush Killa* (Paris), "Hoodlum" (Intelligent Hoodlum), and "Bullet" (Tragedy). Already in the hot seat, Time Warner took the precautionary step of forcing another act, the Juvenile Committee, to re-record "Justice for the Head" to delete a cop-killing reference.

In hindsight, it's clear that the targeting of "Cop Killer" as if it were the first or worst-ever song of its kind was completely disingenuous—and the successful campaign to ban it revealed far more about who holds the power in America than anything about our nation's moral state. The whole brouhaha was, at its core, not much more than a cynical revival of the old '50s tactic of trying to tar music as a causal source of crime and violence. Although the theory was—as usual—never substantiated, the conservatives' repressive goal was, in this one instance, attained.

Meanwhile, songs—serving as a cultural mirror—got more rhetorically violent, just as real life on the streets had. Songs with lyrical themes of mindless ultra-violence became more prevalent, with examples such as: "Kill, Kill, Kill" (Blood Duster); "Kill, Kill, Kill, Murder, Murder, Murder" (Gangsta Boo); "I Wanna Kill Somebody Tonight" (Lost Causes); "Intention To Kill" (Children of da Ghetto); "Just Want To Kill Everything" (Registrators); "Gonna Kill U" (GWAR); "Fine Art of Murder" (Malevolent Creation); "Kill for Fun" (Bounty Killer); "Kill Women" (Anal Cunt); "Kill All Humans" (Exit Human); "Kill and Kill Again" (Leatherwolf); "Kill for Pleasure" (Bloodfeast); "Mass Murder Rampage" (Six Feet Under); "I Kill Everything I Fuck" (G.G. Allin); "Awaiting the Kill" (Ritual Carnage); "Kill 4 Thrills" (Spanish Fly); "I Will Kill You" (Cannibal Corpse); "I'll Kill Him" (Treacherous Human Underdogs); "7 Ways to Kill a Man" (Sex Gang Children); "How To Maximize Your Kill Count" (Supersuckers); "Kill Them, Slowly" (Connected of Darkroom Familia); and Eminem's "Kill You" ['...I'm ready to play / I got the machete from O.J....'].

It was a few years after the "Cop Killer" controversy died down that the next major conflict between the law enforcement community and the music world occurred. In August 1999 the national Fraternal Order of Police (FOP) announced a nationwide boycott against a number of prominent musicians who had, in their principled opposition to the death penalty, publicly offered support to Mumia Abu-Jamal. This famous death-row inmate had been seeking a new, hopefully less biased, trial than the one he'd received when charged with killing a police officer way back in 1982. Now, standing up for a fallen brother is an admirable thing—it is, however, quite another for sworn law enforcement officers to intimidate civilians who are actively expressing their constitutionally protected opinions. Yet this boycott was *specifically* launched because, as the president of one FOP lodge explained: "Sting opened his mouth." And because Sting spoke up about an issue he believed in—as did members of R.E.M., the Beastie Boys, Rage Against The Machine, and Harry Belafonte—the FOP declared that its Web site would be posting a list of them and over 300 others with similar sympathies. And if that wasn't bad enough, media accounts reported that the cops took things much further, including phoning in a bomb threat to one New York City event, causing a Belafonte concert to be canceled in Topeka, Kansas, and organizing 400 officers to picket and demand the cancellation of a Rage Against The Machine concert in Massachusetts. The arts community was stunned, and Michael Goldberg (editor of the pioneering music Webzine *Addicted to Noise*) nailed the issue by stating: "What I want to know is, where do the police get off taking a political stance? The police are simply supposed to protect the public."

By the '90s, the public's sense of trust with the police had reached its nadir. Headlines of the era documented egregious violations such as the aforementioned 1991 attack on a black motorist (Rodney King). In 1992 two Detroit policemen beat a black motorist (Malice Green) to death with a flashlight, an incident marked by Seattle grunge band Pearl Jam with their angry ["... Police stopped my brother *again* ..."] song, "W.M.A."

(White Male American). A stream of reports of rampant corruption at Los Angeles' Ramparts precinct followed, along with the case of a Haitian immigrant (Abner Louima) who was beaten and sadistically sodomized by some truly sick NYC cops. Then the world watched massive violations of the civil and human rights of hundreds of peaceful protesters by a newly militarized police force at the 1999 World Trade Organization conference in Seattle. Following that, Cincinnati erupted in a series of full-scale riots triggered by the killing of a black teenager (Timmy Thomas)—and fueled by seething community-wide anger over an apparent pattern of white cops killing blacks.

It was in the spring of 2000 that a few Miami police officers apparently took things a little personally after the hip-hop crew dead prez performed raps like "Cop Shot" and "Police State." Two of its members, Stic Man and M-1, were arrested and reportedly assaulted by the lawmen. That same year, the New York Fraternal Order of Police announced a boycott of Bruce Springsteen after he debuted "American Skin (41 Shots)." This was a heartfelt song dealing with the then-recent slaughter of an unarmed and innocent man (Amadou Diallo) by plainclothes NYC cops, who riddled him with 41 bullets while he was minding his own business in his own home. Instead of accepting the community's need to understand how such an incident could occur, the police seemed bent on shutting down even any discussion of the incident. Whether community dialog is necessary is simply *not* a matter for the police to decide, and their increasing arrogance in such matters is disturbing.

Launching a boycott in an effort to shut up a prominent songwriter may have felt good—the president of the New York state chapter of the FOP certainly got his licks in, saying of Springsteen that "he's turned into some type of fucking dirtbag…he's a floating fag"—but the media blowback merely drew additional public scrutiny to the original crime against Diallo. Another new Springsteen tune, "Code of Silence," was written about the so-called Blue Wall of Silence—reminiscent of the Mafia's code of *omerta*—that corrupt cops have traditionally used to shield each other from having their misdeeds exposed. While there is absolutely *nothing* wrong with private citizens launching a boycott, when one is organized by the public servants who are needed as security for a major concert, like Springsteen's, then the act takes on a very different tone. By refusing to fulfill their expected, and usual, role it begins to smell a lot more like some crude effort to censor an artist. Look, most folks recognize that the vast majority of law enforcement officers are honorable people who deserve our full support, but the problem at hand was perhaps best summed up by Rage Against The Machine's guitarist, Tom Morello: "The issue is not cop killers—it's killer cops."

Another topic worth touching on is the senseless schoolhouse shoot-outs, which began at least as far back as 1979, when a bored female teenager used her new Christmas present (an automatic .22 caliber rifle) on a San Diego grade school, killing two, wounding ten. "I don't like Mondays" was the heartbreakingly callow reason the killer gave for her attack, a phrase that became the title and lyrics for an epic new-wave radio hit hastily written in appalled response by an Irish band, the Boomtown Rats.

It had been a shocking and unheard-of slaughter. By the 1990s such events were widespread. It was in 1996—the same year as the Moses Lake, Washington, school attack—that Sheryl Crow cut a new song, "Love Is a Good Thing," which included the line ["...Watch our children while they kill each other / With a gun they bought at the Wal-Mart discount stores..."]. Amazingly, her record company didn't balk at that lyrical indictment and the disc was released. And so, duly embarrassed, the spotlighted retail chain—the nation's largest—banished her CD from its racks. Unbowed, Crow stuck to her guns and refused to alter the couplet, and, in so doing, paid a steep price personally and professionally. The ban dealt a serious blow to the commercial success of her album—a reported loss of 10% (or *400,000 units*) in overall sales.

Adding to the mounting distress, the mainstream media chose to define the situation—a heartfelt pop tune protesting sloppy gun control vs. corporate image control—by running misleading headlines such as the *Seattle Times*' "Wal-Mart verses smut." Say *what?* "Smut"? Not quite. The only real *obscene* thing here is the reality of kids killing kids—and the media's attempts to scapegoat musicians. While Wal-Mart's policies and actions ought to be debated, it is *not* the media's *right* to distort important public issues.

Today, we are a long way from the times when most record outlets were independent, neighborhood, mom-and-pop businesses. Back then, if some of those shops declined to stock any particular item, a record label had elsewhere to turn. Now we live in a world where the retail outlets have been so tightly consolidated by major corporate mega-chains that a Wal-Mart, or a K-Mart, acting unilaterally can seriously damage the career of any artist they are displeased with. By not stocking a particular item—denying that artist access to the retailer's share of the marketplace—these corporations can negatively impact the bottom line of artists and record companies alike. The loss of freedom of choice for shoppers who may not even have another local retail option is not insignificant either.

The critical issue behind the Crow incident was that the objectionable lyrics directly implicated Wal-Mart Stores, Inc., in America's twisted culture of promiscuous gunplay. The company's sense of self-protection can be understood, but what are we to make of many additional attempts to *shape* the products they stock? Even acknowledging the retailer's right to stock products that they deem appropriate for their customers, it remains troubling to think that retailers—merely the final stop in a creation/production/distribution process—should be dictating matters of content or style to our culture's artists. Yet being pressured into altering their album-cover art, song titles, or lyrics by Wal-Mart (and other chains) is exactly what has occurred in recent years to such top artists as Beck, Catherine Wheel, Ice Cube, Jackyl, John Mellencamp, Nirvana,

OutKast, Primitive Radio Gods, Snoop Doggy Dogg, 311, Type O Negative, White Zombie, and others. This pattern is a rather troubling turn of events for freedom of expression.

In 1997, the Insane Clown Posse made history as the first group ever to get dropped from a major recording contract within mere *hours* of the release of their debut album. All it took for Hollywood Records to toss the controversial Detroit-based "rage rock" act to the wolves was a boycott threat from a Southern Baptist Convention. Actually, the boycott was aimed at Hollywood's parent company, the Disney Corporation—the folks that brought the world such beloved animated characters as Mickey Mouse and Bambi. In spite of this background, the censors were somehow convinced Disney was driven by an "anti-family agenda" that pushed drugs, violence, and homosexuality on kids.

Record labels were coming under such intense pressure from organized conservatives that in 1999 the band Third Eye Blind was forced to alter the lyrics to their song "Slow Motion." Though the tune was clear in its lyrical *condemnation* of violence—school shootings in particular—it did also contain a minor drug reference or two, which gave Elektra Records all the excuse they needed to pull it from the *Blue* album. Elektra could only feebly mutter that "Slow Motion" just "didn't work in the context of the current social climate."

The unfortunate bottom line regarding themes of violence or death is that, like violence in our communities, it exists in our *current social climate*. Exposure to it isn't pleasant, but then again, the arts are merely a reflection of society. Simply put, our country has a deep-seated love affair with guns. America has a stubborn cowboy culture of violence that pollutes many facets of our lives. Given that the ethic of violence is taught to the young by our nation's prime role models (from the president right on down), Hollywood's shoot-'em-up movies, best-selling murder mystery books, and blood-sport video games, it can hardly be considered fair play to isolate music for condemnation without seeking out the deeper sources of our violent impulses. One day soon, hopefully, we will reach a point when the root causes of most violence—poverty, unemployment, educational voids, and other social ills—become our nation's targets, and by tackling those bigger issues, songs of violence will descend into the obscurity they deserve.

CHAPTER 7

Find the Cost of Freedom

I knew a very wise man who believed that if a man were permitted to make all the ballads, he need not care who should make the laws of a nation.

—Andrew Fletcher, 1704

Music—considered as an artistic means of freely expressing ideas—is intrinsically political. Of particular interest here, though, is that much-smaller subset of songs that contain overtly political lyrics. Left, right, liberal, or conservative: regardless of position on the political spectrum, music has long been used to express a wide range of political sentiments, everything from feelings of national pride to those of raw discontent—and at the most extreme, even calls for violent revolution. It is this last-named function, fomenting political upheaval, that most strikes fear in the hearts of the Establishment who, quite understandably, prefer the stability of the status quo to the uncertainties of social, economic, or political change. To the ruling elite (and their supporters) songs that dare to question authority or speak of revolution are, by definition, subversive.

One major exception to this rule is those of us patriotic Americans who recognize that the overthrowing of an oppressor can be a *positive* undertaking. Friends, our own republic is living proof of the joys of righteous revolution. The saga of the United States of America is one of an epic rebellion of the people that resulted in the creation of a new democratic political system anchored by the US Constitution. And the all-important "Congress shall make no law...abridging the freedom of speech" portion of the First Amendment to the Constitution has been invoked in just about every censorship battle over music, the visual arts, literature, or political free speech since the Bill of Rights' ratification in 1791.

In the two centuries since, the country came to accept that the First Amendment protects the expression of almost anything short of (a) falsely hollering "Fire!" in a crowded theater, (b) making an "I've got a bomb" joke at an airport or, (c) e-mailing the White House to say "I'm gonna kill the President." Subsequent case law has also established that certain other forms of communication—such as "false advertising," "slander," "obscenity," and "indecency"—can be restricted and that inflammatory "hate speech" (or fightin' words) can make the speaker liable for whatever subsequent trouble occurs as a result of their expression.

On that, almost everyone agrees. But consensus that those few exceptions just listed are the only constitutionally valid limitations on free expression has been less than steadfast, and the freedom to express dissent has been compromised more times than many will admit. Ironically, dissent is what originally forged, and still defines, this nation. The colonial rebels who launched their insurrection against the forces of the British Empire did not limit themselves to dead-of-night guerilla maneuvers, town square rallies, and petition signing. The whole movement—like battles for freedom in nations far and wide—was bolstered by protest, resistance, and rebellion embodied in song. Music has long been used as a weapon.

One effective tactic was to take songs honored by the British and subvert them by penning new lyrics—a move that irritated the colonial masters and brought humor to the struggling liberation forces. Prominent examples include "God Save the King," which was hijacked and converted to "God Save the Thirteen States"; "The British Grenadiers," which became "Free America"; and most notably "Lucy Locket," which became the famous rallying song "Yankee Doodle."

But the music war had two sides, and the pro-British Tories lashed back with hard-hitting volleys. As early as 1768, songs meant to bolster the courage of the rebels were being penned, including "In Freedom We're Born" and the "Liberty Song." However, this latter tune (which was the "theme song" adopted by the Boston Tea Party guerillas) was used by the Tories to convey a direct threat when they rewrote the lyrics in a sort of fee-fi-fo-fum style to say, "...Ye simple Bostonians, I'll have you beware / Of your Liberty tree I would have you take care / For if that we chance to return to this town / Your houses and stores will come tumbling down...."

Since then, music has been employed in the American political realm for various purposes—often for pure propaganda. To energize an election campaign, there've been songs such as 1800's "Fair and Free Elections," 1864's "Old Abe Lincoln Came out of the Wilderness," 1932's "Row, Row, Row with Roosevelt," 1952's "I Like Ike,"

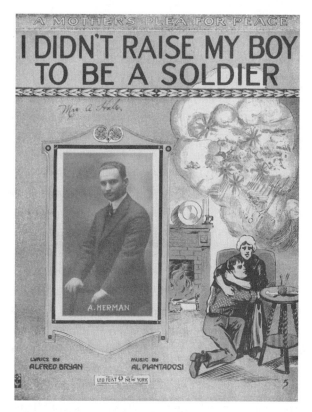

Worries over the USA getting dragged into WWI were expressed in such tunes as 1915's "I Didn't Raise My Boy to Be a Soldier," marketed as a "sensational anti-war song hit."

and JFK's 1960 theme song "High Hopes." Or, to drum up support for military adventures: the Civil War's "Rally 'Round the Cause, Boys" and "When Johnny Comes Marching Home"; World War I's "Over There" and "When the Caissons Go Rolling Along"; World War II's "Remember Pearl Harbor" and "This Is Worth Fighting For"; and the Vietnam War's (No. 1) hit from 1966, "The Ballad of the Green Berets" (Sgt. Barry Sadler). Or, to engage the average citizen, "America the Beautiful," and "This Land Is Your Land"; to fortify militant Christians, "The Battle Hymn of the Republic," "Praise the Lord (And Pass the Ammunition)," and "God Bless America"; and even tunes designed to swell the hearts of symbol-fixated Super-Patriots, "Star Spangled Banner," "You're a Grand Old Flag," and "Stars and Stripes Forever."

Songs have also been used by pacifists and anti-war activists at times of impending—and ongoing—war, including the WWI era's "I Didn't Raise My Boy To Be a Soldier," "Those Draf-tin' Blues," "I've Got the Army Blues," and "I Don't Want To Be a Soldier"; the WWII era's "No More Soldiering for Me," "If They Feel Like a War (Let Them Keep It Over There)," "Stop the War (The Cats Are Killing Themselves)," "Ain't

Gonna Study War No More," and "Santa Claus Is Bringing You Home for Christmas" (which was banned in the UK by the BBC, who deemed it a morale buster for their homesick troops); the Korean War's "Army Blues" (Bobby "Blue" Bland) and "Korea Blues" (Fats Domino); the Vietnam War era's Top-20 hit "Bring the Boys Home" (Freda Payne) (which the US High Command banned on Armed Forces Radio in 1971) and Edwin Starr's (No. 1) hit "War"; and the 1991 Gulf War's (No. 1) hit "High Wire" (Rolling Stones).

But for all the tolerance of dissenting opinion which Americans pride themselves on, history shows that we *do* have our limits. At certain points, steps have been taken by the government to temporarily restrict certain freedoms. And to ban certain songs. Two quick examples: at the Civil War's end in 1865, Union troops were dispatched to oversee the rebuilding of the decimated Confederate states in a program called Reconstruction. Policies were established to contain any lingering resistance by the vanquished rebels, such as a ban on the singing of old Southern chestnuts associated with the Confederacy including "God Save the South," "South, Rise Up and Be Free," and "I'm a Good Old Rebel."

Beyond revolutions, elections, and wars, many other events and sociopolitical movements have generated bodies of music. Just as the anti-alcohol Temperance crowd had songs to rally behind, the activists agitating for the abolition of slavery had theirs, and the women's suffrage struggle was supported in song as far back as the 1850s with tunes like the aptly titled "Let Us All Speak Our Minds If We Dare It."

In fact, daring to communicate freely in opposition to *whatever* has been the risky challenge met by brave artists over the centuries. In recent decades good people and organizations like Amnesty International have successfully exposed governments around the world who have been abusive toward their own citizens. One of the many violations noted in AI reports has been the act of oppressing musicians who dare to perform songs that challenge authority. To be sure, musicians all across the globe have paid dearly and a number of politically aware singers have been assassinated, executed, or mysteriously murdered in various countries—populist folkie Joe Hill (executed by firing squad in the United States), reggae star Peter Tosh (shot by "unknown intruders" in Jamaica), and Chilean folk guitarist Victor Jara (who continued to sing "We Shall Overcome" to his fellow political prisoners after his wrists and fingers were busted one by one, and who was promptly publicly executed in Santiago's stadium).

One area that brings singers trouble no matter where they live is the protesting of poor labor conditions. And America's canon of such tunes is shamefully rich. There are gems from the 1800s like "Down in a Coal Mine," "The Poor Working Girl," and "John Henry"—none of which can really begin to speak of the hell experienced by those laborers through the predations of heartless bosses. In 1905 a glimmer of hope

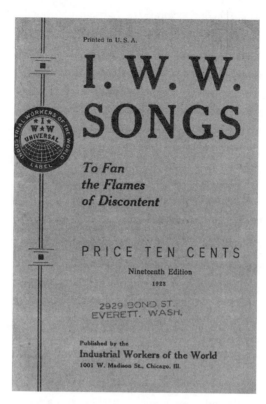

The Industrial Workers of the World distributed their "little red book" of radical labor struggle songs in order "To Fan the Flames of Discontent" in the early 1900s.

for downtrodden workers came when a labor reform movement emerged through the formation of a scruffy organization known as the Industrial Workers of the World (IWW). The IWW—whose members came to be derisively called Wobblies—was instantly attacked by America's industrial and political leaders for espousing "radical" demands such as the establishment of a—gasp!—eight-hour workday and a minimum wage.

President Woodrow Wilson essentially declared open season on the Wobblies, egging-on bloodthirsty vigilantes and private security forces against the IWW, and even unleashing government agents to make roundups. Branch offices were raided, looted, and burned while thousands of union supporters were arrested, many mercilessly beaten and tortured—some shot, and a few castrated and lynched—in fact one was lynched twice for good measure!

In the face of all this state-sanctioned violence, the Wobblies carried on demonstrating, practicing free speech in town squares—and, as they put it themselves, "fanning the flames of discontent" among East Coast textile workers, Northwest loggers, and migrant workers countrywide. The two-decade-long battle was intense, but the movement carried on, their spirits buoyed and bravery roused by a handful of radical songs like Harry McClintock's 1897 classic "Hallelujah, I'm a Bum," E.S. Nelson's 1908 "Workingmen Unite," Joe Hill's "There Is Power in a Union," and Ralph Chaplin's timeless anthem from 1915, "Solidarity Forever."

These songs were no small matters to union supporters. A 1917 issue of the newspaper *The Industrial Worker* defiantly declared to bosses across the land:

> The songs we sing are not the songs of race or creed. They sound the might of a class. We are confined to no country, no flag. Our songs herald your overthrow. This is our day. We are the forgers of revolution—the destroyers of the old and outgrown. We are the nemesis of idlers—the doom of masters—the emancipators of slaves. We are revolt. We are progress. We are revolution.

Even beyond that provocation, the Wobblies' infamous "Little Red Songbook" carried this call to arms: "Sing and fight! Right was the tyrant king who said: 'Beware of a movement that sings.'"

The Powers That Be had heard just about enough from these ragtag revolutionaries. Something had to be done. Unfortunately one Wobbly—musician Joe Hill—would be made to serve as an example. Charged in 1914 in a puzzling in-store murder case (one that he denied participating in till his dying day), Hill was tried and executed by firing squad in an infamous trial in Salt Lake City, Utah. His many supporters were adamant that the government had targeted him not because he had been proven to be some kind of terrorist or traitor, much less a murdering robber, but rather for associating with, and providing inspirational music for, a popular labor reform movement.

If justice was indeed denied him, the consolation prize for Hill is that his memory became a potent symbol for progressive forces. And decades after he was buried, Hill remains the movement's iconic martyr. Indeed, the ballad "Joe Hill" that was penned by a couple of his fellow Wobblies (Earl Robinson and Alfred Hayes) became a countercultural consecration when folk diva Joan Baez sang it as one of the first songs performed at the Woodstock Festival in 1969.

Despite being cast as a critical threat to democracy, the Wobblies in fact embodied the constitutional right to speak freely. But the Wobblies, having been demonized by politicians, community-based "public safety committees," and conservative newspaper editors, never regained their momentum and faded into history. By the Great Depression of the '30s, most folks were happy to have any job at all, regardless of the physical conditions, low pay, long hours, lack of minimal safety precautions, or benefits. Throughout the same period brave union organizers—exemplified by the legendary singing fighter Aunt Molly Jackson, who wrote

1931's "I Am a Union Woman"—used music as a way to draw people together in solidarity.

Throughout the Depression, multitudes of migrants—a number of whom were musicians—rambled back and forth across the country desperately seeking work wherever possible. The most famous of these wandering troubadours was Woody Guthrie, who frequently showed up to sing at dust bowl refugee camps, union halls, and hobo jungles. He also occasionally ran into trouble with strikebreakers, railroad yard bulls, redneck vigilantes, or the law—such as the times he was arrested in Portland, Oregon, and Olympia, Washington, on charges of "vagrancy."

But by 1937 Guthrie had landed his own live daily radio show, and by 1940 he was in New York City making his first recordings and getting his first taste of the big league entertainment industry. The demands the music biz attempted to place on him, though, were enough to cause him to flee. He recalled: "I got disgusted with the whole sissified, and nervous rules of censorship on all my songs and ballads, and drove off down the road." According to Guthrie, even before the US got actively involved in WWII, the Powers That Be were pressuring him to tone down his lyrics in songs like "Hard Times," "Dust Bowl Refugee," and "Vigilante Man." And he wasn't the only artist feeling the heat.

In 1939—two years prior to the country's entry into that war—the performance of a pacifistic song—"The Yanks Are Not Coming"—by a budding jazz diva, Billie Holiday, caught the unwanted attentions of the FBI and earned her a spot on the their Security Index "watch list." [Note: Holiday was in excellent company on the Security Index, joining other artists including Pablo Picasso, Bertolt Brecht, Aaron Copland, and fellow African-American singing stars Paul Robeson and Josephine Baker. Internal FBI documents (circa 1953) reveal that Baker was being spied on for having made "anti–United States statements and her fight for racial equality."] That same troublesome year of 1939, Holiday also got grief over the remarkable song "Strange Fruit." Despite the title, this was no silly exotica number suited for Carmen Miranda. Rather, the lyrics were as risky as anything yet committed to record ("…Black body swinging in the Southern breeze / Strange fruit hanging from the poplar trees…"). And from there the imagery only gets scarier, confronting musically America's habit of lynching black folks for sport. Now, *that* was radical art.

So radical that Holiday's label, Columbia Records, rejected the idea of recording it—claiming it was "too political." And, in an effort not to displease Holiday, who was one of their biggest stars, offered her the freedom to go off and cut it for a different label. She hooked up with New York's small-time leftist label, Commodore Records, and released the song. *Time* magazine eventually took notice, labeling it "a prime piece of musical propaganda." Others better understood the true significance of the piece. The dean of jazz critics, Leonard Feather, identified "Strange Fruit" as "the first significant protest in words and music, the first unmuted cry against racism," and record exec Ahmet Ertegun saw the song as no less than "a declaration of war...the beginning of the civil rights movement."

As public awareness of the song increased, so did Holiday's troubles. Booked at Philadelphia's Earle Theater, she was halted mid-song by house management. Ultimately, after a whole string of New York nightclubs banned her from singing "Strange Fruit," she was forced in future booking contracts to specifically reserve the right to perform whatever songs she pleased. Having the right to perform something doesn't provide one with protection from personal harm, however, and Holiday was accosted verbally on numerous occasions, and at least once physically, by upset audience members.

Noting in an interview with *Down Beat* magazine that she'd "made lots of enemies," Holiday was dogged by police everywhere she went, and the FBI placed her under surveillance as well. Although a musical hot potato that few radio stations opted to air, "Strange Fruit" proved to be remarkably popular, selling a reported 50,000 units within five years. In countries where the government controlled the airwaves, it became an official target for censors, like those at Great Britain's government-owned and near-monopolistic radio network—the BBC—and those within the apartheid regime in South Africa. The song has been acknowledged as one of the half-dozen finest recorded performances of Holiday's entire career and also acclaimed as "one of ten songs that changed the world."

After Allied victories against assorted fascists in WWII, America's own right wing began casting about for domestic enemies to target. This "red scare" era really got underway when President Truman introduced his Loyalty Order of 1947—an act that led to the creation of various loyalty boards to monitor the patriotic commitment of citizens. That same year an ad hoc group of vigilantes—joined by a few FBI veterans—took it upon themselves to hound the folk music scene by launching *Counterattack*, a weekly publication that exposed supposed Communist-inspired songs and listed the names of suspect individuals as well. Around the same time, a number of efforts were made on the state level to expose Communist infiltration, including the formation of the Illinois legislature's Seditious Activities Investigation Committee, and the Joint Legislative Fact-Finding Committee on Un-American Activities in the state of Washington.

It was also in 1947 that some members of Congress decided to target the entertainment industry. Their forum was the House Un-American Activities Committee (HUAC), and while they failed to bring serious charges against very many people, they did successfully destroy the careers, and smear the reputations, of hundreds of individuals in their quest to expose closet Commies and their "fellow travelers."

Though initially rejected by Columbia Records, Billie Holiday's anti-lynching song, "Strange Fruit," became a jazz classic that Commodore marketed as part of their "Starmaker Series."

Among them were musicians like Holiday, who was called in for interrogation, as was Josh White, another black artist who'd begun to perform "Strange Fruit." Similarly, the song's author (schoolteacher Abel Meeropol, a.k.a. Lewis Allen) was dragged before a red-baiting committee seeking to root out potential Commie infiltrators within the New York public school system. Leaned on heavily by the inquisitors, Meeropol nevertheless firmly maintained that he had not been paid to create "Strange Fruit" by the Communist Party.

Another artist called in was perhaps the finest black singer-actor of all time (and the first major concert star to reject performing before segregated audiences), Paul Robeson. Due to his massive international popularity, and willingness to intelligently articulate his dismay with America's endemic racism, he'd become a target of the FBI. It was sadly ironic that this was the very same Paul Robeson who had tirelessly crisscrossed the nation throughout WWII, lending his talents to hundreds of concerts (some in the company of the vice president) in support of the war effort—indeed, the very same Paul Robeson whose records had been banned as "dangerous" by officials in Nazi-occupied territories of Europe.

Unfortunately for Robeson, the Nazis' viewpoint had come to be shared by a number of Americans. Their objections to his eloquent criticisms of racism and economic inequality at home came in the form of lynching threats, canceled concert dates, having his effigy torched, and worse. Examples from 1947: the mayor of Peoria, Illinois, personally interceded and refused to allow Robeson to sing at the city hall (a gig planned after the local Shriners revoked Robeson's booking for an appearance at their hall for April 3). Then the board of education in Albany, New York, tried to cancel his concert scheduled for May 9 at a junior high school auditorium, but when that action was overturned by a judge, the concert was still picketed by angry American Legionnaires. On the opposite coast that fall, Robeson's enemies tried to scare the management of an arena into canceling a booking there. In addition, the Los Angeles city council issued a formal ban on that show. When 16,000 people showed up though, the concert was allowed to go on as planned.

In 1948 another American Legion post made efforts to frighten people from attending one of Robeson's annual outdoor concerts held at a large popular picnic ground just outside of Peekskill, New York. Rather successful at this, the Legionnaires were more than eager the following year when Robeson's concert was announced for August 27. As attendees began arriving a few hours before the concert's start, the veterans started their assault by blocking the entrance with a large truck. From there the 500 misguided patriots proceeded to stone and beat the crowd with clubs, and stabbed at least one concertgoer. In the tumult the thugs also managed to destroy the stage, create a bonfire of chairs and mounds of sheet music, and overturn and destroy numerous automobiles. A few hours later police finally arrived, but alas, no Legionnaires were arrested—either then, or after an FBI investigation.

A local Citizens Committee for Law and Order was organized to confront the "fascist gangs," and Robeson himself announced that having been deterred from performing on the 27th had not intimidated him one whit. A follow-up date was set for September 4 with the venue changed to a theoretically more secure site one mile away. This time 2,500 volunteers and hundreds of law enforcement officers were on hand to protect concertgoers. And thus it was that 25,000 music fans came to be confronted by about 1,000 Legionnaires who tried to disrupt things by yelling epithets, marching around to the loud martial music of a drum and bugle corps, and bellowing insults such as (to the old tune of "Roll Out the Barrel"), "… Roll out the Commies, We've got the reds on the run…." Regardless, the show went on as planned: singer Sylvia Kahn (who had been brutalized at the previous week's riot) began with "The Star Spangled Banner." Next Pete Seeger, the banjo-playing troubadour, offered up a number of American folk songs.

Then Robeson took the stage, enthralling the audience with his commanding and passionate baritone—despite the fact that the stage was buzzed by a helicopter trying to drown him out. But that harassment was merely the prelude. As the large crowd filed out and boarded buses chartered to take them home, they found themselves forced to pass through a gauntlet of crazed Legionnaires and their supporters who lined the exit road for miles and miles. The result wasn't pretty: every single bus

Paul Robeson's rare Victor label recording of the patriotic "Ballad for Americans" was made shortly after he debuted the song in 1939—and about a decade before his career was ruined by paranoid, Commie-hunting Cold Warriors.

and car leaving that day had its windows smashed by stones, bricks, and clubs, with scores of music fans getting seriously injured. And, perhaps most shockingly, it seems that the presence of all those law enforcement officers didn't help a whole lot. Indeed, one press photograph clearly showed a concertgoer being assaulted simultaneously by a sheriff's deputy, a policeman, and several New York state troopers. Another depicted an effigy of Robeson being lynched from a redneck's truck. The so-called Peekskill Riot—which conservatives claimed had all been set up by Communists for anti-American propaganda purposes—received international publicity, and though dismayed, Robeson remained defiant, saying, "I will sing wherever the people want to hear me. I will sing of peace and freedom and life!"

And he did. But having become fixated on the notion of Communist infiltration in America, the Powers That Be pegged Robeson as "a danger and a threat to the U.S. government." Furthermore, his traveling (for concert tours) was deemed "contrary to the best interests of the United States," so Robeson's passport was revoked by the State Department and he was, for eight long years, prohibited from leaving the country. This travel restriction imposed on him—and the resultant

Beleaguered leftist singer Paul Robeson escaped being lynched—but on September 4, 1949, in Peekskill, New York, his effigy wasn't so lucky.

hesitancy American bookers had about hiring an apparent subversive—seriously stunted his career and Robeson never recovered the popular momentum he'd formerly had. As *Ebony* magazine put it: "Whatever the reasons, for all practical purposes Paul Robeson's voice is silent today. The great concert impresarios pretend he no longer exists. City officials padlock public halls at the mere rumor that he is coming.... Autograph seekers who once trailed his every step have dropped by the wayside to make room for FBI agents." One of the nation's finest artists saw his career essentially destroyed because he had dared to voice unpopular thoughts of peace and freedom.

And all that turned out to be just the prelude: President Eisenhower empowered his Subversive Activities Control Board to investigate the political activities of American citizens, and Republican Senator Joseph McCarthy joined in, declaring that the government itself was riddled with Communists. Between 1953 and '54, using his position as chair of the Senate Subcommittee on Investigations, he kicked off a full-scale political inquisition—one that, for a while, scared lots of folks into believing that there were godless reds hiding under everyone's beds. It was McCarthy's hard-nosed take-no-prisoners style that earned him a reputation as the nation's grand inquisitor—a position from which he was toppled only when his fellow senators (with

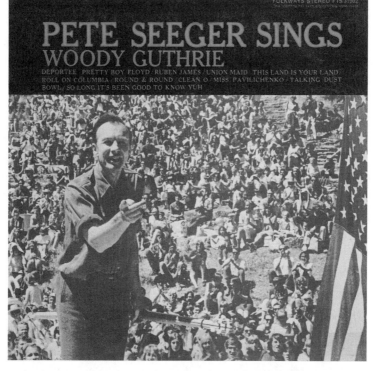

Though blacklisted in the '50s McCarthy era and banned from appearances on the '60s Hootenanny *TV show, banjoist Pete Seeger remained true to his (and his old pal, Woody Guthrie's) ideals and songs — as seen on this 1967 LP.*

even Eisenhower's support) voted to censure him for his autocratic investigative methods and for abusing other senators and committees.

In 1951 Pete Seeger was accused of having Communist affiliations and soon had the FBI hounding him—just as they did his pals Robeson and Guthrie. By 1952 other members of Seeger's group, the Weavers (who had led the folk revival with charting hits like "Goodnight Irene"), were also slandered as Communists during the congressional hearings (leading to blacklisting from concert, radio, and TV opportunities), and by 1953 they were dropped by their skittish label, Decca Records. The Weavers dissolved, but the hearings went on and on. Questioned relentlessly about the lyrics to his songs, Seeger never buckled and was then rewarded with ten counts of contempt of Congress. Convicted on all charges, and sentenced to ten concurrent one-year prison terms, Seeger hoped for vindication on appeal—one that would rest on solid First Amendment issues. Sadly, although Seeger was ultimately freed, the court of appeals chose to make their ruling based on a very narrow technicality—studiously sidestepping key constitutional issues and not taking a stand on the broader free speech matters really at stake.

Another prominent musician, the esteemed composer Aaron Copland—who has been called the dean of American music—also found himself on the wrong side of '50s politics and became the focus of FBI (and when he traveled abroad, CIA) surveillance. Summoned for interrogation by McCarthy, Copland, like Robeson, never gave an inch. But there was a price to pay for this display of integrity: the performance of his music scheduled for President Eisenhower's inaugural ceremonies in 1953 was canceled.

The 1950s were also a time when great civil rights battles began to build steam, and there is no doubt that those brave activists who marched, demonstrated, and held sit-ins found that singing "We Shall Overcome" and other freedom anthems helped them maintain the courage necessary to confront the overwhelming might of the Establishment—not to mention the physical assaults by fringe organizations such as the KKK and John Birch Society.

Billie Holiday's "Strange Fruit" was not the only jazz piece that faced down racial politics in America—and then faced certain consequences. For example, in 1954, when President Eisenhower took the historic step of sending in soldiers to enforce the integration of Little Rock, Arkansas's Central High School, two prominent jazz musicians (Archie Shepp and Max Roach) responded by recording a bitter new song "dedicated" to that state's redneck governor, Orval Faubus. Cowed by the conservative climate, however, their label refused to print the lyrics on the album cover. (Clearly it was still a *long* way away from the day when African-American musicians would be free to respond to racists in-kind with strong declarations like Nina Simone's 1963 "Mississippi Goddam," Sly and the Family Stones' provocative '69 tune "Don't Call Me Nigger, Whitey," James Brown's '68 black pride hit "Say It Loud—I'm Black and I'm Proud," or rapper Willie D's '96 classic "Fuck the KKK." Still, there was a definite sense of "movement" in the air....)

And so, as the 1960s rolled around, new voices began to emerge, picking up right where Joe Hill, Guthrie, and Seeger had left off. Two of the more talented heirs of their legacy were folk/protest singers Bob Dylan and Phil Ochs, who had a talent for creating memorable tunes marking various "news" items, such as Dylan's "Oxford Town" (composed in 1962 in response to the murder of two innocent blacks in Oxford, Mississippi) and Ochs's biting "Here's to the State of Mississippi." Ochs also marked the civil rights struggles with other classics like "Talking Birmingham Jam."

Dylan's second album, *The Freewheelin' Bob Dylan*, was released in 1963—but not without turmoil. At the very last minute the corporate bigwigs at Columbia Records developed weak knees—after reconsidering the content of their singer's new songs. An executive decision was made: the LP was suddenly yanked back by the label and four selections—including "Talkin' John Birch Paranoid Blues"

("…Well, I investigated all the books in the library / Ninety percent of 'em gotta be burned away…")—quietly disappeared and were replaced with other tunes. Ever since that day, there has been speculation that Columbia bowed to unseen right-wing forces and pulled the old middle-of-the-night switcheroo on their young new star. Not coincidentally, "Talkin' John Birch Paranoid Blues" was also the song that CBS told the singer he couldn't perform on his slot on the *Ed Sullivan Show*. In a potentially career-stunting move, Dylan, artistic integrity intact, walked. [Note: It would seem that Dylan and Columbia should have been well aware of the risk in taking on an aggressive organization like the Birchers—just the year prior another folkie act, the Chad Mitchell Trio, had seen their recording of "The John Birch Society" banned at top New York stations like WCBS and WOR, and many other "large stations throughout the country," according to the liner notes of their 1962 LP. Fortunately those intimidated stations "were counter-balanced by exposure on the large independent stations. Threatening calls to WNEW's William B. Williams prompted him on the air to offer a list of names of his sponsors to the threateners."]

Dylan, like the trio, however, successfully won a sizable audience that appreciated the straight talk offered up in his musical indictments such as "Masters of War" and other protest classics. One entity that didn't cotton to Dylan's ideas—or the fact that he had a sizable public platform to disseminate them from—was J. Edgar Hoover's FBI, who began compiling a file on the songwriter.

But the FBI certainly had their hands full, for Dylan was only one of a growing number of discontented folkies playing concerts, political rallies, and recording for major labels during those times. In addition to illegally prying into the private business of civil rights leaders like Martin Luther King Jr., and later the activities of the Black Panthers, the G-Men were also being assigned to monitor the dissidents who were beginning to oppose the undeclared "war" in Vietnam. As Americans began to join that anti-war effort en masse, the challenge the feds faced was immense. Luckily for the forces of repression, a number of ad hoc organizations chipped in to help quash any further pacifistic expressions.

In 1965 Christian Crusade leaders stepped forward to condemn the lyrics ("…you're old enough to kill, but not for votin'…") to Barry McGuire's (No. 1) anti-war folk-rock tune, "Eve of Destruction." They charged that the lyrics were "obviously aimed at instilling fear in our teenagers as well as a sense of hopelessness" with the goal of inducing "the American public to surrender to atheistic international Communism." Well *no*, but the song did contribute to the growing sense that America was pursuing an immoral war in Vietnam. It came as no surprise when the Crusade's leadership also asserted that the negative effects the Beatles were having on the nation's unsuspecting youth was the result of a scientifically designed

Barry McGuire's 1965 hit, "Eve of Destruction," was condemned and widely banned for its trail-blazing anti-war message.

Communist plot: "The Beatles' ability to make teenagers take off their clothes and riot is laboratory tested." Uh, *right*.

Keep in mind that these were the same sorts who thought the Beatles' playfully tossed off tune "Back in the USSR" was intended to promote the Soviet Union over the USA—and that the band's "Revolution" was pure Moscow-directed propaganda. One self-appointed expert, the good Rev. David A. Noebel, thundered in his 1966 book *Rhythm, Riots, and Revolution* that "rock is having a holiday ridiculing religion and morality while at the same time glorifying drugs, sexual promiscuity, and revolution." In this revelation he was joined by one Bob Larson, who also pinpointed exactly where the blame for society's ills should fall in his 1967 screed *Rock and Roll: The Devil's Diversion*—the "lyrics of today's rock songs are a large part of the tidal wave of promiscuity, illegitimate births, and political upheaval that have swept our country." So there you have it, once again we were all being encouraged to believe that art *causes* misbehavior.

Even though the Young Republicans for a Return to Conservatism and the Conservatives for Conservative Action launched letter-writing campaigns to the FCC—and many stations, including the entire ABC network, banned "Eve of Destruction"—the song's resonance with young folks lifted the record into *Billboard*'s No. 1 position. That was about when the prominent radio DJ Bob Eubanks, aggrieved that the song couldn't just simply be rounded up, muttered in frustration:

"How do you think the enemy will feel with a tune like that number one in America?" Well, how about if your question is countered by simply noting that bad war policy is our real enemy, rather than the music that calls attention to it?

By mid-decade America's buildup in Vietnam had become a rallying point among America's youth, and music began to reflect their concerns. Given the conservative bent of corporate leaders in the radio industry, it was a considerable challenge for artists and their record labels to get anti-war songs much airtime. In fact, some of the earliest Vietnam-related songs—like the Fugs' ultra-sarcastic "Kill for Peace" and the quite serious "War Kills Babies" and "Liberty Not War"—never had a chance on mainstream corporate AM radio. It would be the nascent, alternative FM stations that established these songs as "underground" radio classics.

But the managers of commercial radio were hardly the only villains of the day. The Fugs' own producer, objecting to the provocative lyrics ("... I'm not ever gonna go to Vietnam / I'd prefer to stay right here and screw your mom ...") contained in another of their tunes, "Doin' All Right," proceeded to engineer the recording so that that particular vocal snippet was so low in the sound mix as to be nearly inaudible. That aside, the overall message of the song caused the radio industry to shun it en masse. When a handful of daring DJ's lost their jobs for ignoring the bans and airing the song, the Fugs held benefit shows to help support them financially. The governmental response to such songs—such as the Fugs' biting "CIA Man"—included investigations by the FBI, the US Postal Service, the local New York district attorney, and, one can presume, even the Central Intelligence Agency itself. In addition, the Fugs—whose very name marginalized them from the get-go—became targets of the right wing, and subsequently received telephoned bomb threats, a mailed (though fake) bomb, orchestrated boycott pickets, and performance bans from major concert venues like Carnegie Hall and the Santa Monica Civic Auditorium.

Though anti-war/anti-draft sentiments—and the songs that expressed them —were gaining ground at a grassroots level, they were not being given much exposure by the corporate media. The growing ranks of artists who were singing such tunes were essentially nonexistent on the numerous televised variety shows. One exception was CBS-TV's *The Smothers Brothers Comedy Hour* show that debuted in early 1967. The goofy folk music duo performed songs and skits offering up various pointed wisecracks about topics like the military draft, President Johnson, and the escalating Vietnam War. In addition, they provided a forum for old friends and new artists who tended to challenge the Establishment—including, in 1968, a beleaguered pal, Pete Seeger.

Unfortunately, while the Smotherses controlled who performed on their show, their corporate overlords at CBS had their hands on the editing process. When Seeger plunked out his somber anti–Vietnam intervention anthem, "Waist Deep in the Big Muddy," they simply cut him out of the broadcast. While some people were surprised, it was actually just business as usual. In 1969, Tommy Smothers flatly stated to *Look* magazine that "in our case, seventy-five percent of the twenty-six shows we've done this season were censored." In fact, that year was to be their final season as the highly rated show was suddenly axed. Rumors circulated that newly elected President Nixon—fearing that their comedic focus would be transferred from Johnson to him—leaned on CBS to do the dirty deed.

The Smotherses probably never knew that their ultimate fate was actually of some concern in surprising places. A formerly secret FBI memo documenting Elvis Presley's 1970 tour of bureau headquarters noted that the singer advised agents "that the Smothers Brothers, Jane Fonda, and other persons in the entertainment industry of their ilk have a lot to answer for in the hereafter for the way they have poisoned young minds by disparaging the United States in their public statements and unsavory activities." The clean-cut Smothers Brothers were *unsavory?* What a surprise. Tommy, *Look* also noted, pointed out the obvious danger at hand: "And we're mild. Now, if we're thrown off that easily, what will happen to someone who has something really important to say?" Indeed. Even decades later he would muse that "I didn't realize I was important *until* they made me shut up."

It would require a few more years of widening protests—and rising body-bag tallies—before musical statements of dissent were allowed to air by corporate media. One of the first anti–Vietnam War songs ("... each week we lose a hundred fine men...") to be broadcast was Johnny Cash's moving 1971 (No. 3) hit "Man in Black" which he courageously performed on his own CBS-TV show.

Since 1978, the Freedom of Information Act has allowed the public to review many secret government files, and through that process it was revealed that as far back as 1963 the FBI had taken an interest in protest singer Phil Ochs. As a regular at civil rights rallies—and an early and outspoken critic of the undeclared war in Vietnam in tunes like "Draft Dodger Rag," "I Kill Therefore I Am," "What Are You Fighting For?", and the classic "I Ain't Marching Anymore" [of which Ochs quipped, "The fact that you won't be hearing this song over the radio is more than enough justification for the writing of it"]—Ochs had become a real thorn in the Establishment's side. According to agency Director J. Edgar Hoover, it was Ochs's "propensity towards violence and antipathy toward good order and government" that won the singer his place on their dreaded Security Index.

Another mid-'60s singer-songwriter who attracted trouble was Janis Ian. While some individuals resorted to disrupting her concerts by hollering "Kill the Nigger lover!" as she performed "Society's Child," a hit song about interracial dating, the FBI, concerned about her (and her whole family's) liberal political activism, hounded them for years.

It seemed like the government had eyes and ears everywhere. Under Nixon the feds appeared to be monitoring everything—TV, radio, concerts, newspapers, magazines, you name it. As noted in Chapter 4, the Nixon administration pulled out all the stops in order to crush the rising tide of dissent against their war policies, including urging the nominally independent FCC to lean on various radio stations to stop supporting Ochs with airplay. But Nixon's henchmen were not only keeping track of what songs were being played, they also had their ears perked for radical on-air commentary. It's been reported that three Secret Service agents once paid a visit to KSAN—San Francisco's progressive radio station known for airing informational daily Vietnam death count statistics—to have a "chat" with a Black Panther DJ there. The authorities wanted him to know in no uncertain terms how seriously they took the broadcast statements that he would personally defend his own freedom with deadly force (even against the president) if necessary. Furthermore, because he'd also encouraged his listeners to commit to the same idea, he was informed that he'd be charged as an accessory to murder if Nixon should ever be attacked and killed.

Duly upbraided, the DJ wisely moderated his approach in future broadcasts, but Ochs just couldn't resist his enemies. And so it was Ochs who provided the "smoking gun" that convinced the bureau that he might be a genuine threat to Nixon's personal safety. Even if that evidence was merely another smart-ass song. An internal FBI document has surfaced that indicates they investigated "Pretty Smart on My Part," a song from the fatalistically titled 1969 LP *Rehearsals for Retirement*. The lyrics that caught their attention were "...I can see them coming / They are training in the mountains / They talk Chinese and spread disease / They will hurt me—bring me down / Some time later when I feel a little better we will assassinate the President and take over the government. We will fry them...." Now, making heads or tails of those bizarre lines is a big enough challenge that I, for one, must give up trying. And so too apparently did the G-Men who added this disclaimer at the report's end: "This document contains neither recommendations nor conclusions of the FBI."

Meanwhile, campus unrest and anti-war fervor were reaching the point where wild rhetoric about a countercultural revolution became commonplace, and sit-ins and protest marches a way of life. Anti–Vietnam War demonstrations were spreading internationally, and the BBC banned the Rolling Stones' "Street Fighting Man" ("... summer's here *and the time is right* for fighting in the street ..."). So too did various Chicago radio stations rattled by government scares about street violence at the upcoming 1968 National Democratic Convention. (Despite the ban—or perhaps because of it—the single's retail sales established new sales records in that regional market.) Violence did occur in Chicago, and after-the-fact investigative commissions concluded that the worst was instigated by the Chicago cops (whose marching orders from Mayor Daley were "shoot to kill") against largely peaceful marchers—a tragedy decried in Graham Nash's "Chicago" ("…In a land that's known as freedom / how can such a thing be *fair?*…").

Among the artists that joined Ochs in Chicago's Lincoln Park to perform in support of the protesters were the MC5. This was an unusual rock band in that they consciously honed their public image as a "revolution rock" outfit. Their rabble-rousing *git-off-yer-ass* political pieces were later credited by music scholars as a direct predecessor to the punk rock movement, but at the time they were noted for actively promoting countercultural ideas about sex, drugs, and political activism. In hindsight, they were an easy target for conservatives. It was on the release of their debut LP in 1969 that the hammer first came down.

As a Michigan-based group, their core fans were locals, and so it hurt when the top regional department store chain, Hudson's, announced a ban on the record because of the MC5's prominent use of an "indecent" lyrical phrase ("…Kick out the jams, motherfuckers!…"). Rude language to be sure, but fans figured that was merely serving as a convenient excuse to limit the distribution of the other messages that that album contained. When additional stores and radio stations balked, the band agreed, under duress, to have the offending phrase removed from future pressings of the LP.

By this point, the FBI were tracking two radical San Francisco bands, Jefferson Airplane and the Grateful Dead, and internal documents note they were being monitored due to "concerns about domestic security, civil unrest and loyalty of government employees." In other words, the bands' records were becoming popular among young military staff and bureaucrats. With the feds breathing down their necks, the Airplane's label got skittish and held back from releasing 1969's *Volunteers* LP while they tried to force their star act to delete a cop-baiting phrase ("…Up against the wall, *motherfuckers!*…") from the song "We Can Be Together."

By that point the Airplane had such widespread popularity that they resisted the censors at RCA and ultimately the execs relented. Fixated on that one word, no one seemed to notice that the title song on the album was an even more militant blow against the Military-Industrial empire. "Volunteers" was no less than an overt call for revolt: ("… Look what's happening out in the streets / Got a revolution … Who will take it from you? / We will … We are volunteers of America …"). New York's powerful WNEW-FM probably wasn't alone in banning the band's new tunes, but they in particular cited another of that LP's numbers, "Eskimo Blue Day" ("… The human dream / doesn't mean *shit* to a tree…"), for its "obscene" content, and "Volunteers," for, of course, being "seditious." [Note: Another psychedelic group from California, the Electric Prunes, hold a special place in censorship history as a band whose song "You Never Had It Better" was commercially released on LP replete with an actual "beep" tone inserted to block out their lyrical use of that same word.]

With the Airplane's musical call to action also getting massive exposure via the film and recordings of its performance at 1969's Woodstock Festival, the authorities became downright frantic in their efforts to neutralize the influential band. One method was to single the Airplane out and force them to pony up unprecedented cash bonds to discourage any onstage "illegal, indecent, obscene, or immoral" acts. These bonds—think of them as extortion demands—were to be paid in advance of performing at various concert venues. Feeling persecuted, the band—who actually forfeited one such fee after saying "bullshit" during a 1971 Oklahoma show —charged that they'd been unfairly targeted by Nixon's henchmen.

Another key performance at Woodstock was Country Joe and the Fish leading a massive crowd in the rousing introductory chant portion of their sarcastic anti– Vietnam War classic, "Feel-Like-I'm-Fixin'-to-Die-Rag" ("... be the first one on your block / to have your boy come home in a box ..."). Country Joe led the crowd through the highly memorable call-and-response style "Fish" Cheer—("... Gimme an *F*—Gimme a *U*—Gimme a *C*—Gimme a *K*—What's that spell?...")—and with hundreds of thousands of young folks participating, it was something glorious to be-hold. The repeatedly shouted f-word served as shorthand for total rejection of main-stream hang-ups and hypocrisies. And the Powers That Be surely took notice. One of the more politically outspoken of the Haight-Ashbury musicians, Country Joe Mc-Donald was also a target of the authorities. He was arrested and prosecuted on sex-related charges for saying "dirty" words in public, or as the cops put it, "lewd, lascivious, and wanton" (onstage) speech and behavior. That was a typical tactic in the Nixon era: when they couldn't respond to the main issue—in this case the con-tinuation of an *undeclared* and unpopular war—they tried to marginalize the mes-senger. Numerous artists' political ideas have been shrouded by efforts to taint, smear, discredit, and scandalize them over rumored drug or sex matters.

Another leading counterculture band—one that contributed a good share of songs that irked the establishment—also came under surveillance. The Doors had a dramatic flair highlighted in such works as 1968's grim anti-war masterpiece, "Unknown Soldier," which was shunned by mainstream AM radio only to be em-braced by the new underground FM market. The Doors' increasing popularity un-nerved the Powers That Be. Even FBI Director J. Edgar Hoover was familiar with the band, taking the time once to critique their music: "It is repulsive to right-thinking people and can have serious effects on our young people." Various police depart-ments across the country agreed, and the Doors, and Jim Morrison in particular, were targeted for harassment. Whether intended as payback or as a simple lesson in the risks inherent in messing with "the system," Morrison's infamous onstage ar-rests in Connecticut and Florida on obscenity charges (in 1968–69) were enough to make any artist think twice about future lyrical themes—like the Doors' "Five to

One" ("…They got the guns, we got the numbers. We are gonna win, yeah, we are taking over! …")—and stage moves.

In 1970—the same year that a right-wing organization called the Movement to Restore Democracy briefly emerged (with their call for the immediate ban of rock 'n' roll because, well … try hard to connect the dots here … *socialism* was "brainwashing" the minds of American youths)—four young war protesters were cut down by a squad of fired-up National Guardsmen at Ohio's Kent State University and the whole nation took a real deep breath.

After five-plus years of steadily increasing anti-war demonstrations, America now had war-related deaths on the home turf. May 4, 1970, was a turning point in the nation's attitude about its role in Vietnam. Riots erupted from coast to coast, and within days Neil Young lashed out with the blistering—and blame-assigning—classic "Ohio" ("… tin soldiers and Nixon coming …"). Rush-recorded by Crosby, Stills, Nash & Young, the single was shunned by the more conservative radio station chains, and Ohio's Governor James Rhodes actually *ordered* his state's stations to ban it. But the shootings had so stunned middle America that thousands of as-yet-still-independent AM stations joined the new ranks of hip FM stations in giving it airplay—enough to send the radical tune up to No. 14 on the charts. It was a stellar moment both for free speech and the laudable independence of the airwaves—and one that, a few short decades later (after corporate media consolidation became an epidemic), would no longer be possible.

Soon after "Ohio" came the "Jackson-Kent Blues," a bitter lament cut by the Steve Miller Blues Band to mark the same occasion along with the less-publicized incident that occurred only days later on May 15 at Mississippi's Jackson State University when local lawmen went on a rampage ("… Shot some more in Jackson just to show the world what they can do …"). This attack resulted in the death of two and wounding of a dozen African-American students. Stephen Stills provided the requiem for the dead—and for America's devastated innocence: "Find the Cost of Freedom" ("… buried in the ground / Mother Earth will swallow you / Lay your body down …"). Issued as the B-side of "Ohio," the single was released in a sleeve with stark graphics listing the Bill of Rights and including, of course, the various constitutional provisions—the rights to free speech, to protest, and to assemble—that had just been tragically violated by government forces.

Of all the artists who were active in the anti-war effort, it was probably Bob Dylan and John Lennon who irritated the authorities the most. Both were prolific songwriters whose politically tinged tunes captured huge global fan-bases—and both singers were idolized by millions of youths; and that fact troubled government leaders no end. In 1971 Dylan's new tune "George Jackson" (about the murder of that black leader while incarcerated on a two-bit robbery charge at San Quentin

Prison) dealt with a topic white America couldn't yet tolerate a discussion of. The tune was banned by the radio industry on the grounds that the lyrics included one no-no word ("…He wouldn't take *shit* from no one …"). Had Dylan not given them that then-legally legitimate excuse, it might have been interesting to watch the radio industry squirm as they struggled to find some—any—other reason to avoid airing the record.

Then in 1975 Dylan released "Hurricane"—a tune dedicated to bringing greater exposure to the sorry case of Rubin "Hurricane" Carter, a promising African-American professional boxer. Carter was an up-and-comer who maintained that he'd first become a target of the NYPD after a riot in Harlem way back in April 1964. "I said that black people ought to protect themselves against the invasions of white cops in black neighborhoods—cops who were beating little children down in the streets—and that black people ought to have died in the streets right there if it was necessary to protect their children." According to Carter, that tough talk about self-defense—indiscreetly made to a reporter who published it in the *Saturday Evening Post*—earned him a reputation as a cop hater. He was informed that the FBI, Secret Service, and federal marshals were all compiling files on him, and he was arrested more than once on dubious charges. Death threats caused him to decline Martin Luther King's request to join in the 1965 Selma, Alabama, civil rights march. Then in 1966 he was arrested on suspicion of shotgunning three white tavern patrons—and after 17 hours of interrogation, Carter passed a lie detector test and was released. Five months later, however, he was fingered by two white ex-con "witnesses," rearrested, tried before an all-white jury, convicted, and sentenced to triple life sentences. All the while, Carter consistently maintained his innocence and believed that, mainly due to his political beliefs, and "because I will not say that I'm guilty, or act like I'm guilty, I am a threat to the administration, to the politicians." Dylan eventually took up Carter's cause, and although the song was shunned by radio it became a Top-40 hit anyway. Eventually Carter would be set free, but at the time Dylan's tough new songs weren't winning him any new fans among the Establishment.

The FBI's interest in Lennon—the author of the Beatles' song "Revolution"—seems to have begun in the early '70s when he began to attend anti-war rallies and associate publicly with their New Left and Yippie leaders. With the approval of Nixon, the previously obscure Senate Internal Security Subcommittee went to the trouble of preparing and issuing a report in 1972, which recommended that Lennon's visa be terminated. That would have conveniently caused the musician to be deported to England. The justification? Lennon and his wife, Yoko Ono, were both "strong advocates of the program to 'dump Nixon.'"

In subsequent years, information has surfaced that Lennon was actively planning to hold a nationwide series of anti-Nixon fund-raising concerts—his pal Dylan was among those invited to participate—which would have culminated in a show/rally/festival in Miami. This grand finale was to coincide with the Republican National Convention there in August 1972. After a bruising three-year deportation battle—and with Nixon's administration in ruins—Lennon's case was finally dropped. He got to stay in America, but was effectively dissuaded from active dissent and wasn't a public presence at peace rallies again after May 1972.

One year earlier, FBI files reveal, agents were actively monitoring all sorts of public gatherings—and taking notes. In May 1971 some G-Men filed a report noting that a "folk singer" named John Denver had appeared (along with former Sen. Eugene McCarthy and others) at an anti-war rally in Minneapolis. Around this time rock festivals were increasingly being seen as threats to the Establishment, especially as the anti-war movement gained traction. On May Day, 1971, the Washington, DC, police department—with the winking approval of Nixon's attorney general, John Mitchell—attacked a large crowd peaceably awaiting the opening of a festival. The fact that the festival organizers had acquired the required permit—and that the attendees were peaceful—didn't matter to our nation's top legal officer. The ensuing police riot resulted in over 8,000 unconstitutional arrests, few of which survived judicial scrutiny.

During this time, policemen across the nation were making the most of the support that the Nixon administration had been signaling. It was a tough time to be a political dissenter—and occasionally just as risky to attend a musical show. At an Akron, Ohio, concert by Jefferson Airplane in 1972, city police brutally attacked a number of attendees who were dancing in the aisles. The band stopped playing and began criticizing the officers—an act of defiance that led to the arrest of two band members and a big black shiner for singer Grace Slick.

In the spring of 1973, Washington, DC's college station WGTB-FM first felt Nixon's wrath. The fact that the student DJs there regularly spouted anti-establishment opinions over the air had not passed by unnoticed by the Powers That Be. At one point Vice President Spiro Agnew whined to the *New York Times Magazine* that "there is little will to oppose Communism in America anymore." And furthermore, "the voice of third-world communism is pervasive in academia. WGTB … broadcasts what seems to be propaganda for the third world." And so began the blast of warnings from the FCC. The first one was triggered by a complaint from West Virginia Rep. Harley Staggers, who was outraged when his car radio—tuned, for whatever reason, to WGTB—began blaring John Lennon's hard-hitting political ballad "Working Class Hero" ("…Keep you doped with religion and sex and TV / And you think you're so clever and classless and free / But you're still *fucking* peasants as far as I can see / A working class hero is something to be …"). [Note: Upon the song's release in 1971 a number of less-brave radio stations took it upon themselves to excise—in violation of established copyright infringement laws—the (most) offending term from the song and broadcast it in an altered form—that is, until Lennon's lawyers objected.] WGTB's manager—facing a year in prison and a huge $10,000 fine—bravely replied: "The people of Washington are sophisticated enough to accept the occasional four-letter word in context and not become sexually aroused, offended, or upset." Despite that confidence in his audience's maturity—and the FCC eventually backing down a bit on their threats—five additional complaints were sent by the agency to WGTB for other perceived infractions that same year.

At this point, a number of people concluded that it was time to push the "revolution" to its next, more militant, phase and "bring the war home." Flower Power plus Peace and Love just weren't cutting it in the face of direct repression from the Nixon administration. Various cells of radical underground organizations like the Weathermen formed and began garnering headlines with bombings and other anti-establishment actions. In 1974 another faction, the Symbionese Liberation Army (SLA), gained notoriety for kidnapping newspaper heiress Patty Hearst, robbing banks, and submitting lists of political demands. There has long been speculation that the SLA was nothing more than a creation of the FBI meant to discredit genuinely idealistic leftist organizations, but there is absolutely no doubt that the SLA possessed impeccable musical taste. In one of their communiqués, they included the demand that Donny and Marie Osmond desist from producing any more of their trademark saccharine and smarmy pop schlock—and backed it up with a threat to bomb their concerts.

Now—even though we'll need to step away from the main chronology a bit—this seems a good place to address an issue that can fairly be called the Myth of the Liberal Censors. In recent years there has been endless gnashing of teeth amongst conservatives about the censorious goals of "politically correct" liberal "elites." And while it is true that PC leftist intellectuals *have* pushed for greater sensitivity in our public discourse—in other words, asserting that hurtful ethnic slurs, misogynistic crudities, and homophobic epithets are no longer welcome—the task of actually identifying historical examples of them promoting *musical* censorship is a definite challenge. While examples of censorious campaigns from the right wing are abundant enough to, say, fill a book, the most notable incidents that have emanated from the political left can be dealt with in a few short paragraphs.

In 1966 an exceedingly strange record called "They're Coming to Take Me Away, Ha-Haaa!" hit the pop charts. Upon release, and with tons of radio exposure, it instantly vaulted up about 40 slots into the nation's Top Ten and looked to be rocketing towards the top slot when—due to organized protests by liberal do-gooders—it suddenly vanished from radio play lists far and wide. A truly wacky musical monologue about a guy going crazy over a girl and being sent to the loony bin, the recording was credited to one Napoleon XIV. In actuality, the artist was a fellow named Jerry Samuels whose real-life experiences as a patient in a mental ward added just the right touch of authenticity to the comedic piece. That realism, however, also offended a bunch of professional mental healthcare workers. Concerned that Samuels was being taken advantage of, and that fun was being had at the expense of the ill, petitions were drafted, calls were made for investigations, and pressure was placed on the radio industry to withdraw support for the single. In his sixth week of glory, and perched at No. 3, Napoleon XIV's reign was over.

It was a full decade later when the climate was such that women finally felt empowered enough to publicly object to male excesses in rock 'n' roll. In 1976, various women's rights groups—such as Women Against Violence Against Women—rose up in reaction to a giant billboard ad that depicted a bound and bruised woman. Erected by Atlantic Records at a prominent spot in Hollywood, the thing was intended to promote the Rolling Stones' new LP, *Black & Blue*. If nothing else, it certainly succeeded in getting that aging band back in the headlines. The publicity was, however, far from positive as boycotts against the label's parent company —Warner/Elektra/Asylum (WEA)—continued for more than a year. Then, over in England, the BBC banned the Stranglers' "Peaches," in 1977, on the grounds that its lyrics ("…walking on the beaches looking at the peaches …") were of the "women baiting" variety. These were among the first serious strikes against misogynistic tendencies in the rock world, but they would not be the last. In 1978 a Canadian punk band, the ill-named Battered Wives, rightfully earned their status as a target of various feminist organizations. And, if the group's cold moniker and the rather sexist cover art of the debut LP hadn't been enough to spark hostilities, their logo—a clenched fist with lipstick-smeared knuckles—assured that their one-and-only concert tour was ruined by picketing. Then in 1985 an organization called Women Against Pornography began publicly railing against "the sexist and violent content of rock videos" shown on MTV. And in 1982, an awfully cranky NY chapter of the National Organization of Women took Bruce Springsteen to task for his repeated usage of ("…little girl …") as a lyrical device in various tunes by boycotting the songwriter.

Meanwhile, in 1978, another WEA artist, the musical satirist Randy Newman, decided to comment, in his own witty way, on the topic of social discrimination with a biting little number called "Short People." In the song he enumerated the multitude of reasons why people of diminutive stature ought to be abhorred ("…they got no reason to live …"). Because his central point was overlooked by hypersensitive folks who took his lyrics literally, rather than attempting to get at the underlying point of the absurdity of baseless discrimination, the song was banned by many radio stations—some who hid behind the old standby excuse that the song was "disturbing to little children." One suspects that those radio executives simply had no faith in their listeners' sophistication to understand satire. *Whatever.* The song went on to hit the No. 2 chart slot and pull Newman's *Little Criminals* LP up into the Top Ten.

Then in 1979, the Anti-Defamation League (ADL) of the B'nai B'rith—which never hesitates to challenge anything that might be regarded even remotely anti-Semitic—protested Frank Zappa's typically comical song "Jewish Princess" and registered their complaints with the FCC. On the same front, in 1991 the Los Angeles–based Simon Wiesenthal Center objected to a tune—"No Vaseline" ("…You can't be the Nigga for life crew / With a white Jew telling you what to do …") by the former N.W.A. rapper Ice Cube—and successfully pushed several retail chains to drop the (No. 2) hit album *Death Certificate.* Then, in response to complaints in 1995 that his song "They Don't Care About Us" featured anti-Semitic sentiments, that moon-walkin' King of Pop Michael Jackson promptly back-stepped and altered various lyrics: "Jew me" was changed to "do me") and "kike me" to "strike me" in a re-recording of the tune. In 1999 the ADL also issued calls for people to boycott the hip-hop crew Public Enemy because of anti-Semitic lyrics in the song "Swindler's Lust."

A classic example of uninformed misunderstandings involved the 1979 hit "Killing an Arab" by a Brit rock band, the Cure. A dancefloor and new wave radio favorite for years, the tune was belatedly discovered by certain parties—like the Arab-American Anti-Discrimination Committee—who began lodging complaints about it in 1986. Pressure mounted and the controversy eventually forced the band itself to ask the radio industry to desist from airing their song any more. Had those organizations been a bit less reactionary—and maybe even tried listening to the song—perhaps they would have been able to hear the beleaguered band's patient attempts to clarify that the song's message was one of protest *against* the intolerant mentality that had led to the despicable real-life anti-Arab street assault that originally inspired it.

In the late '80s a British concert tour by the American hardcore band Rapeman drew protests by various feminist and student organizations. In addition, various homegrown artists have come under fire from these quarters in the UK, including Blur, whose promotional poster drew scorn for featuring a naked woman riding a giant hippopotamus, and Spinal Tap and Torri B, whose tunes ("Bitch School" and "This Bitch Raps") weren't much appreciated.

Then in 1994, C&W upstart Tim McGraw caused a big stink with his numskulled debut hit, "Indian Outlaw." At a time when liberals were enjoying considerable success in their campaigns to rid various school sport teams of less-than-sensitive names like the Savages, the Braves, and the Redskins, McGraw's song was a thoughtless throwback to times—think of Hank Williams's embarrassing 1952 hit, "Kaw-liga"—when a singer could get away with a lyrical theme that was potentially demeaning to a whole race of people. Despite the pleas from various Native American tribal organizations and airplay bans by a few stations (starting with Minnesota's K102), "Indian Outlaw" became a Top-Ten radio staple, and McGraw stubbornly insisted that the song was not meant in disrespect—even if that's how many folks perceived it.

And so, those examples—and a few others regarding the various boycotts mounted against the hateful homophobic and misogynistic songs already mentioned in Chapter 5—are pretty much the sum total of evidence conservatives can marshal to support their notion that liberals exist to limit *their* freedom of expression. Now, having—through this review of the historical record—dispelled that tired old myth once and for all, let's return to the real action....

In the 1970s—and as a reflection of the times—rock 'n' roll toughened up. That decade saw the increased splintering of the rock 'n' roll audience, and while many folks abandoned hard-driving music to kick back to the easy sounds of weepy singer-songwriters and mellow popsters, or get funky with slick jazz-fusion bands, dedicated rockers headed the other direction. It was then that we saw the first stirrings of new stylistic forms including heavy metal, glitter/glamour rock, reggae ...and the snot-nosed neo-primitivistic movement that would come to be known as—punk rock.

The roots of punk—an energetic if caustic iteration of rock 'n' roll that would frighten mainstream types like nothing since Elvis—can be traced back to a handful of bands who, though dissimilar from each other in many ways, shared a fondness for outraging the squares. Among them were the MC5, Iggy & the Stooges, and the New York Dolls—three bands who sold relatively few records, who attracted trouble everywhere they went, and who would go on to have a *huge* influence on subsequent generations of rock musicians.

If those bands weren't exactly household names, they were known well enough to be on the "watch list" for various law enforcement agencies. On September 21, 1973, the Memphis Board of Review announced that that night's scheduled concert with Iggy opening for the New York Dolls would be under heavy scrutiny. And, they warned, the singer risked arrest if he performed in his usual fashion. The Dolls—whose glittery makeup and girlish hairdos placed them more towards the glam rock side of things—were informed that the impersonation of females was forbidden within the city limits and that the group's performance would be monitored. The concert was disrupted when a member of the audience was beaten by police in full view of the assembled. Then when the Dolls' singer, David Johansen, stopped mid-song in an effort to stem the brutality by rousing the audience in protest, he was arrested and dragged off stage—sparking the riot cops should have known would follow.

Despite the fact that these pioneering punks were less than appreciated by au-

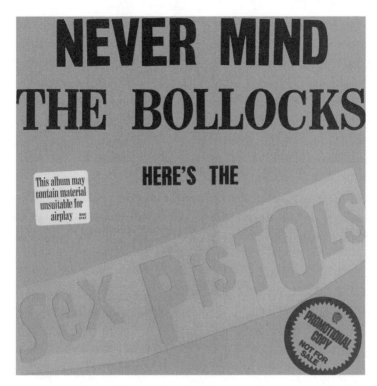

Although the blistering punk-rock politics of the Sex Pistols disturbed British politicians, it was the title *of their 1977 debut LP (seen here in rare USA promotional form replete with a no-airplay warning sticker) that provided the government an avenue of attack via "obscenity" charges.*

thorities in America, they attracted a considerable audience in the United Kingdom. And it was the New York Dolls' UK tour (along with one by another New York punk band, the Ramones) that has been credited with providing the spark that ignited the entire British punk scene. Indeed, the Dolls' own manager played a huge role in launching London's—and the world's—most infamous punk band ever: the Sex Pistols.

In 1976–77, two of the Sex Pistols' ferocious 45s, "Anarchy in the UK" and "God Save the Queen"—each a calculated slap in the face to a nation entranced by preparations for a celebration of Her Majesty Queen Elizabeth II's Silver Jubilee—were released and kicked off a serious firestorm. Unnerved by the band's looks, politics, and cultural impact, one government leader roared: "If pop music is going to be used to destroy our established institutions then it ought to be destroyed first." War was declared against the band: self-appointed royalist vigilantes assaulted various band members and associates on the streets (leading to a whole summer of violent attacks on London's punk community), and bans were immediately imposed by British TV *and* BBC radio as well as a number of retail chains.

Even though reports noted that the "God Save the Queen" single was outselling every other new record, the Establishment kept it from even being listed on various Top-30 charts. In an act that would seem to cast serious doubt on the credibility of all such charts, the managers of those who did choose to list it restricted the song from its rightful place at the No. 1 position. In typical fashion, the government sidestepped the real issue—that a snotty band of scruffy musicians had rubbed their own nation's noses in the fact that history was leaving England behind while citizens clung to their useless "royalty." They instead chose to attack them on a side issue. It was the debut album's title—*Never Mind the Bollocks Here's the Sex Pistols*—that opened the door in late 1977 to a legal prosecution of a London shopkeeper who had mounted a window display of the *Bollocks* LP and was then charged under England's Indecent Advertising Act of 1899. Nice try, chaps, but the case was ultimately tossed out of the courts, and the entire endeavor came off as a case of political persecution.

The British government had much better luck when they took on another political punk band's case in 1982. That's when the Anti-Nowhere League's snotty tune "So What" was prosecuted under the rather-more-updated 1959 Obscene Publications Act. After the police's record-seizing raids on label headquarters, the pressing plant, and distributors' offices, at trial the magistrates concluded that the song—which had already sold a respectable 36,000 units—evinced a "tendency to deprave and corrupt," which resulted in the destruction the confiscated stock and the effective banning of the record. Three years later yet another punk band, Crass—who had dared to criticize Margaret Thatcher's dubious Falklands War in their cynical "How Does It Feel (To Be the Mother of a Thousand Dead)" and "Sheep Farming in the Falklands"—was targeted for prosecution under the same 1959 act. Initially judged obscene, their *Sheep Farming in the Falklands* record was rightfully cleared upon appeal but still, just for good measure, the same obscenity charge was made against the band's "Bata Motel." But in this instance—though once again, not one single word could be considered plainly pornographic—the song's overall lyrical theme was undeniably lewd and the case was upheld by the courts, and the record was banned.

Meanwhile, stateside, Georgia Governor Jimmy Carter successfully challenged the incumbent President Ford in 1976, but three years later, when an Islamic people's revolution in Iran deposed their tyrannical dictator (the CIA-affiliated Shah Pahlavi) and took as hostages a number of American embassy workers and CIA agents, it acutely affected the US's internal politics. American media became thoroughly obsessed with rescuing those hostages—and exacting revenge on Iran and its leader, the Ayatollah Khomeini—all through that year and into the election cycle of 1980. And just as a number of would-be patriot musicians cashed in with belligerent, anti-Arab tunes such as "Bomb Iran" (Vinnie Vincent), "A Message to

In 1982 the Anti-Nowhere League's "So What" single fell victim to England's 1959 Obscene Publications Act. Police raids and a court trial resulted in the destruction of confiscated stock—a rather effective way of imposing a ban.

Khomeini " (Roger Hallmark), "Ayatollah Rocked" (Doc Bart), and "Kick Khadafy's Butt" (Old Glory)—Republican politicians also used the sorry crisis for their own personal gain.

In the face of this crisis, the hapless Carter was tossed out and the Reagan Revolution was ushered in—along with the bleak prospect that the new president's bellicose administration would draw us into any number of wars—a fear subsequently proven valid with his adventures in El Salvador, Nicaragua, Lebanon, et cetera. With inexcusably mindless stunts like his trip to the graves of Nazi soldiers on a visit to a cemetery in Bitburg, Germany, Reagan became phenomenally successful in creating an atmosphere where anti-intellectualism, intolerance, blind nationalism, and personal greed were somehow transformed into virtues.

Right off the bat, Reagan's team set a divisive tone by offering comfort to the hard-line Religious Right, who were emboldened to revive their smoldering hatred toward American pop culture and liberal thought. It was in 1983 that we got one solid indication of the twofold way the Reagan/Bush team regarded music: as a threat—and most usefully, as a weapon. The first time was when Reagan launched a major military invasion of the tiny Caribbean island nation of Grenada. The rationale offered up was that the isle had been threatened by Communist guerrillas, and so the US Army's services were required. While that explanation remains debatable, what is known is that among the first actions our forces took there was to capture and abolish the popular station Radio Free Grenada. Poetically, at the very moment that the power was cut off, the station was airing the 1970 anti-war reggae classic "War" by Bob Marley and the Wailers. Then, the all-new Spice Island Radio that was quickly inserted as a replacement was managed by the Psychological Operations (Psy-Ops) section of the US Army. The kinds of music these mindfuckers approved as safe for airplay? Hall and Oates, Asia, Quiet Riot, and the Beatles.

Initially, the American public was informed that Grenada's democratic government required our assistance in repelling a communist uprising that was poised to threaten the stability of *nearby* nations. That justification was instantly put to lie by a Reagan ally, the Prime Minister of Dominica, who screwed up a bit by getting "off message" and candidly stating: "We weren't worried about military intervention coming out of Grenada, we were worried about *the spread of ideas.*" As the weeks unfolded, we learned that the main thing "rescued" by the invasion—other than the island's radio airwaves—had been a handful of overprivileged American "students" whose mommies and daddies had gotten worried about their safety on that sunny and sandy Caribbean "college" campus. It didn't take long for the observant among us to connect the dots and realize that the whole Grenada escapade had likely been nothing but a PR sham intended to draw the public's attention away from the embarrassing loss of 241 US Marines who had just been slaughtered in a barracks bombing in Beirut, Lebanon, a mere 48 hours earlier.

Another incident during that first term in office shed even more light on the administration's view of rock music. In 1983 Reagan's Secretary of the Interior, James Watt, in a remarkable display of his political tin ear, suddenly announced that America's least-controversial good-time band, the Beach Boys, would be banned from mounting their annual Independence Day concert on the mall in Washington, DC. The uproar was so strong that damage control became necessary. Desperately seeking a way out of the PR brouhaha, First Lady Nancy Reagan was trotted out to sing a different tune. Expressing her fondness for that sun-and-fun-lovin' band, she tendered a "heartfelt" personal invitation for them to return. They accepted, and the 1984 concert drew a crowd of 100,000 fans to a stage near the Washington Monument.

A whole different strata of rock 'n' rollers—the underground punk rock community—were the ones to recognize the threat that the Reagan Revolution posed, and many artists spared no fury in denouncing him, blasting out such blistering tunes as: "Reagan's In" (Wasted Youth); "Reagan Country" (Shattered Faith); "Who We

Hatin' Now, Mr. Reagan?" (CDC Boys); "Battle Hymn of Ronald Reagan" (Fartz); "Reagan at Bitburg" (Frank Zappa); "Fucked Up Ronnie" (D.O.A.); "Bonzo Goes to Bitburg" (Ramones); "Reagan der Fuhrer" (D.I.); "Impeach Reagan" (A.P.P.L.E.); "We Don't Need This Fascist Groove Thing" (Heaven 17); and "Irritable Bowel Disorder: Project Reagan" (Scrotum Grinder). There were countless additional punk songs that lambasted Reagan, along with bands who expressed their horror at his rise to power in their very *names*: Reagan Youth, the Cancerous Reagans, and the Reagan Squad (who contributed "Mindless Violence" as commentary on the times). All this was an unintended consequence of the Republicans' policy initiatives, but the Reagan Era provided plenty of inspiration to dissenting artists and, in fact, sparked a remarkable musical watershed that re-energized the rather dormant tradition of protest songs.

Meanwhile, San Francisco's Dead Kennedys formed and immediately became America's highest profile political punk band. If detractors could get over the band's defiant look, mocking moniker, and purposefully grating sound, they'd hear that the band was serving up a tough, intelligent, and blisteringly anti-establishment critique of society's follies. The DKs impressed young fans and simultaneously earned the ire of the right by railing against warmongers ("Holiday in Cambodia"), main-

The Dead Kennedys' '82 anti-Nazi single, "Nazi Punks Fuck Off," denounced the emergence of fascist thugs within the punk-rock movement during the Reagan Era.

stream society's alcohol-centric culture ("Too Drunk to Fuck"), police brutality ("Police Truck"), and many other issues, most notably the neo-Nazi resurgence that was smoldering on the fringes of the hardcore punk rock scene. In 1982 the band responded to the increasing presence of Nazis at their gigs with a clear musical rebuke—"Nazi Punks Fuck Off"—a bold rejection that was answered when several thugs savagely attacked singer Jello Biafra. Throughout the band's existence they also attracted the unwanted attention of various police departments, who began a regular practice of showing up at DK shows and harassing the audiences, the band, and the venues.

George Orwell's classic police-state novel *1984* had targeted its temporal setting fairly accurately, and that very year seemed to usher in a new era where political expressions were no longer countered with opposing ideas, but instead slandered (and thus marginalized) as "obscene." Re-elected in a landslide, Reagan's momentum guaranteed that the conservatives' war against pop culture would accelerate. The state of California got into the spirit of things by prosecuting Biafra for violating the Distribution of Harmful Materials to Minors section of the state penal code in 1986. The item at issue was a bonus poster included in the Dead Kennedys' *Frankenchrist* album. In the end, that obscenity charge disintegrated under judicial scrutiny and the case was tossed out of court—the process, though, seemed to effectively expose the whole effort as an abusive ruse meant to disguise the matter of true concern to the Powers That Be: the uncompromisingly anti-corporate, anti-conformist *ideas* expounded in Biafra's lyrics. A concern that may have been a motivation behind the passage of the Child Protection Act of 1988—a law that (among other provisions) handed the federal government the ability to jail both the makers and promoters of "offensive" music.

The rightward drift on the political front was not confined to the United States. Great Britain got so distracted worrying about a few popular leftist punk bands that they had little time to recognize the serious threat posed by the rise of violent right-wing "skinhead" rock bands like Skrewdriver, No Remorse, and Brutal Attack. Inspired by these fascist-right acts, American racist rock bands soon formed. First there was Chicago's Final Solution, who built up a small following of like-minded neo-Nazis, who were joined by New Glory and Arresting Officers, and followed by Tulsa, Oklahoma's Midtown Boot Boys, Minnesota's Bound for Glory, Detroit's Hacken Kreutz, and Dallas's Bully Boys.

Splinter movements emerged over time, including the self-described "national socialist black metal underground" of White Power bands like Absurd, Burzum, and Graveland. There was also a so-called experimental wing represented by racist bands like Blood Axis, Blut Kampf, and NON. By the '90s, a number of governments saw the threat posed by these new and even-more-virulent neo-Nazi groups. Among those monitored were Britain's No Remorse, whose song "Blood-sucker" attacked both Jews and Asians, and Hungary's CPG (for Gypsy Destroyers Guard Regiment) whose agenda was made clear by their song "Gypsy Free Zone." Germany, in their trademarked manner of efficiency, banned outright the music of such bands as Endstufe ("Final Stage"), Noie Werte ("New Values"), and Sperrzone ("Prohibited Area"). Various kindred "white noise" groups also arose in Sweden (Svastica, Vit Aggression, and Division S), in Wales (Celtic Warriors), and in Finland, where one band, Mistreat, was ultimately prosecuted for inciting racial hatred.

In America, various racist entities—think the White Aryan Resistance, American Front, the Aryan Nations, and the KKK—came to recognize the value of music in recruiting youthful members. Their organizational skills gave rise to the emergence of many supremacist record companies, such as Virginia's Holycaust Records, West Virginia's Resistance Records, Illinois's Death To Peace, Ohio's Hate Rock, Minnesota's White Terror, and Washington's Total War Records.

In 1989 Vice President George H.W. Bush took over as president, and the following year Iraq's Saddam Hussein ignited the Persian Gulf War by invading his southerly neighbor, Kuwait. One of the "first responders" was C&W singer Hank Williams Jr. who—in the tradition of WWI's "I'd Like to See the Kaiser with a Lily in His Hand," "With a Yankee Noose Around the Kaiser's Neck," and "What'll We Do with Him Boys? (The Yanks Made a Monkey Out of You)," and WWII's "Der Führer's Face," "The Jap and the Wop and the Hun," "We're Gonna Have to Slap the Dirty Little Jap," "We'll Knock the Japs Right into the Laps of the Nazis," and "You're a Sap, Mr. Jap"—issued the highly personalized taunting ode, "Don't Give Us a Reason (An Open Letter to Saddam Hussein)," a small gesture of support that led the president to quip, "When I need a little free advice about Saddam Hussein, I turn to country music." Bush's other response was even more direct: he launched Operation Desert Storm, a high-tech blitzkrieg that he and his team crowed would bring about a whole "New World Order" and even an "End to the Vietnam Syndrome." [Translation: an end to the citizenry ever being in the least bit squeamish about further military adventures abroad, and, in Bush's everlasting dreams, a halt to any further questioning—and, most certainly the protesting—of their leaders' questionable policies.] More than one artist struck back with musical critiques of Bush—think Neil Young's "Rockin' in the Free World"—but it was a Seattle Grunge Era group, Coffin Break, whose wildly reckless 1991 protest single "Kill the President" gained news coverage when it drew the predictable visit by Secret Service agents. Another artist sickened by the manipulated patriotism of the day was Irish singer Sinead O'Connor, who, in 1990, had simply refused to go on if the American anthem was played at her show in New Jersey. Well, that was just too much for New York Sen. Nicholas

Spano, who demanded that she be banned from performing in his state—a position backed by that ol' lady killer, Mr. "New York, New York" himself, Frank Sinatra, "who said for O'Connor's sake that 'we'd better never meet.'" Then came the protesters who rallied to urge arriving fans to boycott her concert...all told, an object lesson for us that "free speech" may be free, but at times it certainly doesn't come without cost.

Meanwhile, the international allies that Bush corralled for his war also did their part to try and squelch dissent—or even the *discussion* of alternatives to war. The United Kingdom's Radio One (the BBC's pop channel) produced a list of 67 songs that had the potential to undermine public support for the military effort to protect the West's oil supplies. Some of the tunes listed as unfit for broadcast were obvious anti-war songs—"Give Peace a Chance" (John Lennon) and "War Baby" (Tom Robinson)—but others seemed to be victims of grasping censors: "Walk Like an Egyptian" (Bangles); "Fools Rush In" (Ricky Nelson); "We Gotta Get Out of this Place" (Animals); "Killing Me Softly" (Roberta Flack); "I'm on Fire" (Bruce Springsteen); "In the Air Tonight" (Phil Collins); and "I Just Died in Your Arms Tonight" (Cutting Crew). Interestingly, no equivalent "blacklist" surfaced here in America—that eventuality would require a different decade, a different Bush administration, and another war in Iraq.

In 1992 Bush was rejected for re-election in favor of Arkansas Gov. Bill Clinton. Part of Clinton's initial appeal was a somewhat hipper, younger, baby-boomer image that was successfully showcased in his TV appearance honking out rusty R&B sax chops (while wearing Blues Brother–style shades) on the *Arsenio Hall Show*. While it was refreshing to have a new leader who seemed to have at least some clue about pop culture, any hopes that a grand new progressive era was dawning after 12 years of conservative rule were quickly dashed. An early sign came during the campaign itself when candidate Clinton (in an obvious attempt to create a greater sense of political distance between himself and black America) chose to publicly condemn the words of New York rapper Sister Souljah. Denouncing her as "a propagator of hate," Clinton's symbolic sop to the Democrats' conservative wing did the job; he was elected.

Once in office, Clinton regularly betrayed Democratic ideals by supporting disastrous pro-big-biz policies including: signing the Telecommunications Act of 1996, which (like Reagan's Child Protection Act of 1988) made it a felony to distribute objectionable music, and also authorized the FCC to step up efforts to punish radio stations on obscenity and indecency charges. In addition, that bill removed hard-won and worthwhile restrictions on media ownership—a change that allowed the dramatic consolidation of formerly independent and locally accountable radio stations into just a few huge, generic, faceless, and generally conservative, chains. The most dramatic example being San Antonio, Texas's little ol' Clear Channel Communications, Inc., which expanded from a modest 43-station chain before this deregulation into a merger-crazed, mega-powerful entertainment industry that as of this writing holds a market-domineering total of 1,233—enough to control ten percent of the total (and 60 percent of the rock portion) of America's commercial radio business. This monopoly game was a *major* change of the playing field that was purposely slipped under most folks' radar, but one that—coupled with the Republican-led, and unjustified, dismantling in 1987 of the FCC's perfectly sound Fairness Doctrine, which for decades had simply required broadcasters to air *balanced* views regarding controversial topics—would in due time prove to have lasting negative implications for the free flow of information in the media.

Meanwhile, in 1994, the Speaker of the House of Representatives, Newt Gingrich, demanded that advertisers yank all contracts with radio stations that featured rap music. The House Subcommittee on Commerce, Consumer Protection, and Competitiveness set about exploring the potential need for the enforced stickering of hip-hop records. That same spring, the Senate Juvenile Justice Subcommittee opened two different series of hearings on "gangsta rap" music. Having served the intended purpose of bringing media attention to the politicians themselves—and burnishing their tough-on-crime bona fides along the way—these inquisitions ultimately concluded without resulting in any new legislation.

In 1995 two prominent conservative busybodies, William J. Bennett and C. Delores Tucker, launched a new public initiative to challenge hip-hop culture. Bennett (the failed former Bush drug czar) justified their anti-music crusade with the grandiose premise that "nothing less is at stake than *civilization*" (emphasis added). For her part, Tucker (chair of the National Political Congress of Black Women) remains a hardcore zealot—and an individual who will go down in history for mindlessly advocating that "anything offensive to anyone should be removed." And so, two of America's highest-profile (though self-appointed) scolds proceeded to identify targets both musical and corporate. Their goal was to try and publicly shame the five main entertainment conglomerates (Bertlesmann Music Group, Polygram, Thorn EMI, Time Warner, and Sony) that market gangsta rap. Among the popular artists who most displeased them were: Bone Thugs-n-Harmony, 2pac Shakur, Gravediggaz, Tha Dogg Pound, Notorious B.I.G., and Ol' Dirty Bastard. Tucker was her usual histrionic self, asserting that "these companies have the blood of children on their hands."

The farce continued: in 1997 the Senate Commerce Committee launched a new round of hearings—to investigate whether or not the less-than-decade-old "Parental Advisory" labeling system was functioning adequately, the presumption being that it was not. In the process, no significant new information was uncovered—but *all* the old canards about music and Satan, music and drugs, music and sex, and music and violence were systematically recycled. By the following year, these cultural warriors—now working with conservative Democrats like Senators Joe Lieberman and Sam Nunn—re-energized their campaign by updating the hit list with a few more hip-hop targets: Cypress Hill, the Geto Boys, and the Wu-Tang Clan—and for good measure tossed in a dance/club music act (Lords of Acid), as well as a couple of bluesy pot-smoking rock bands, the Black Crowes and Blues Traveler.

It was Lieberman who, in 1999, stooped so low as to threaten the entertainment industry: "If you don't use your rights with some sense of responsibility, there is a danger that those very rights will be endangered." That same year, Clinton felt it politically necessary to try and counter the Democrats' reputation for a more liberal attitude towards culture by suddenly getting tough on pop culture. He prodded Congress into authorizing both the Justice Department and the Federal Trade Commission (FTC) to launch investigations into whether or not the entertainment industry aimed its advertising campaigns at kids in an effort to sell violent material. Having yet another governmental inquisition was unappealing, but some folks welcomed the examination of an issue more serious than just another "dirty" lyric scare. Then, Senators Lieberman and John McCain (R) submitted their 21st Century Media Responsibility Act that same year—a bill that, if enacted, promised to closely regulate music. And videos. And music magazines. In his 2000 State of the Union speech, Clinton demanded that the entertainment industry devise a universal ratings system to cover all realms of media. Later that election year, the US Senate hosted hearings that resulted in recommendations that laws be enacted to "regulate" the industry.

After the bitter 2000 Presidential "selection," George W. Bush's new regime had only been settled in for a brief nine months when the morning of September 11, 2001—now universally known as 9/11—dawned and America awoke to learn of heinous acts of terrorism by jet-crashing al-Qaeda terrorists. Jolted out of our lingering election-related malaise, a new survival-driven spirit of national unity emerged—along with a consensus promulgated by the mainstream media that, suddenly, "Everything has changed."

That alone was a heady thought, but before it could even really sink in, the reality that *some* things, in fact, *never* change became all too clear. Indeed, while the nation was instantly ready and willing to unite and face new threats head-on, some of our political leaders just couldn't let go of old battles. And so, in a time of an officially declared state of emergency—when all energies should have been strictly focused on the nation's great challenge of a massive war against terrorism—conservatives (both political and corporate) instead saw the anti-terrorism imperative as a perfect cover for renewing their beloved culture war against liberals at home.

Dissent—or even the expression of diverse opinion—was suddenly under attack in America and the right wing's anti-democratic tendencies had reemerged in an ugly way. The first evidence of this came within mere *hours* of the attack. That's when reports surfaced that the Clear Channel network had issued a memo to their stations blacklisting 158 songs from further airplay. Some things *never* change.

Censorship issues aside, public speculation immediately focused on the rapidity with which that list was prepared and disseminated. Well, it did seem awful likely that it *must* have been drawn up in advance of 9/11. Setting aside those admittedly disquieting timeline issues, let's consider here that in a time of calamity, perhaps it is a fully reasonable reaction for a responsible media entity to review the content of their broadcasts with a greater degree of care than usual. Even if we accept that premise, however, questions necessarily arise when we examine Clear Channel's selections: does the radio industry have the moral right to try and shield listeners from certain thoughts? And if such songs do indeed have the potential to trigger negative emotions in listeners, perhaps they should *never* be aired out of concern for anyone who might be upset. While Clear Channel's list included songs that bore titles—or lyrical themes—that perhaps did seem at least momentarily inappropriate given the specific nature of the terrorists' tactics, others were a bit far-fetched and might just have easily applied to *any* type of disaster—including a common fender bender, a house fire, or even a tumble off a stepladder.

Regardless, Clear Channel personnel had compiled a list of songs they feared might remind listeners of such touchy topics as:

- Airplanes: "Leavin' on a Jet Plane" (Peter, Paul & Mary)," "Jet Airliner" (Steve Miller), and "Fly Away" (Lenny Kravitz)
- The World Trade Center: "New York, New York" (Frank Sinatra), "Crumbling Down" (John Mellencamp), "Jump" (Van Halen), and "Free Fallin'" (Tom Petty)
- Terrorism: "Sabotage" (Beastie Boys) and "Hey Man, Nice Shot" (Filter)
- Accidents: "Wipeout" (Surfaris), "Crash and Burn" (Savage Garden), and "Crash into Me" (Dave Matthews Band)
- Explosions: "TNT" (AC/DC), "Blow Up the Outside World" (Soundgarden), and "You Dropped a Bomb on Me" (Gap Band)
- Fire: "Burning Down the House" (Talking Heads), "Disco Inferno" (Trammps), and "I'm on Fire" (Bruce Springsteen)
- Death: "Spirit in the Sky" (Norman Greenbaum), "Dust in the Wind" (Kansas), and "Knockin' on Heaven's Door" (Bob Dylan)
- Bummers in General: "End of the World" (Skeeter Davis), "Worst That Could Happen" (Brooklyn Bridge), and "It's the End of the World as We Know It" (R.E.M.)

While it can be debated whether or not the airing of any particular song could actually undermine America's war readiness in some serious way—people can, after all, wage a war and still *hope* for peace—Clear Channel also instinctively banned a number of popular anti-war songs like "Blowin' in the Wind" (Bob Dylan), "Eve of

Destruction" (Barry McGuire), "War" (Edwin Starr), and "War Pigs" (Black Sabbath), as well as peace movement anthems like "Peace Train" (Cat Stevens), "Get Together" (Youngbloods), and "Imagine" (John Lennon). Beyond that, the firm went so far as to scotch a few war-neutral songs that, over time, have come to be associated in the public's mind with the sorry spectacle of Vietnam, such as "Hey Joe" (Jimi Hendrix), "We Gotta Get Out of This Place" (Animals), "Rescue Me" (Fontella Bass), and "The End" (Doors).

Taking things an inexplicable step further, Clear Channel also blacklisted songs that might very well have served the purpose of soothing, comforting, and calming a grieving and panicked nation: uplifting and unifying tunes like "Bridge over Troubled Water" (Simon and Garfunkel) or "He Ain't Heavy, He's My Brother" (Hollies). Worse yet, some inclusions on the list simply defied reasonable explanation. For example, what would merit banishment for popular favorites like "What a Wonderful World" (Louis Armstrong), "Wonderful World" (Herman's Hermits), "Morning Has Broken" (Cat Stevens), "American Pie" (Don McLean), "A Day in the Life" (Beatles), "Daniel" (Elton John), and "America" (Neil Diamond)?

Most revealingly of all, Clear Channel had singled out the *entire* body of recorded works by one, and only one, band, Rage Against The Machine. Given the anti-authoritarian and anti-war messages in that Grammy-winning group's songs—like "Know Your Enemy," "Take the Power Back," "Freedom," and the hit "Killing In the Name" with its defiant lyrical hook ("... *Fuck you,* I won't do what you tell me! ...")—it's quite understandable that a conservative corporation would resent them. But that's a far cry from accepting the fact that the discussion boards of the band's Web site were shut down by their service provider after the Secret Service contacted that company inquiring about anti-Bush statements allegedly posted there by fans.

Witnessing the government of "the world's only superpower" lashing out in fear of a song—or a mere *rock band*—only highlights its internal sense of domestic insecurity. But also disturbing is the specter of major corporations trying to limit the ideas that American audiences can be exposed to. Within weeks of 9/11 Clear Channel sacked their popular hip-hop expert Davey D from his long-held slot at KMEL radio in San Francisco—seemingly in punitive response to his raising questions about troubling issues surrounding 9/11 that the government didn't appreciate. Then, Greenville, South Carolina's WMYI-FM radio personality Roxanne Walker was fired by Clear Channel after being cajoled into airing her anti-war views by a couple of pro-war peers. Finally there was the curious case of the disappearance of a new hit song, "Chop Suey!", by the then *top-selling* band in the country, System of a Down. Though the Clear Channel chain had initially been supportive of the tune, that backing instantly evaporated after the band's vocalist posted on the Internet a quite incisive essay, "Understanding Oil," which calmly synopsized US foreign policy as it related to Middle Eastern energy sources. Touchy topic? Perhaps. But hardly an incendiary *anti*-American polemic. Still, the band's weak-kneed label, Sony Music, quickly yanked the essay—described by its author as a "plea for peace"—off the Web site, and the song faded into undeserved oblivion. Considered together, these actions cast considerable doubt on Clear Channel's defensive claim on September 18 to "strongly" believe in "the freedom of speech" and that the blacklist was not an act of censorship but merely an advisory memo.

Then, word began spreading that people were suddenly having their service cut by the nation's largest Internet provider, America Online (AOL)—apparently as punishment for having contributed to on-line discussion board chats about the political aspects of Bruce Springsteen's lyrics. Not discussions about favorite bomb-making recipes, preferred plane hijacking techniques, or the fine points of weapon smuggling, mind you—but, rather, simple dialog about pop songs. For its part, AOL maintained that this was really just all a matter of inappropriate language having been used—specifically the vulgarity of posted lyrics to about a dozen Springsteen songs including, "Spirit in the Night" ("... Jenny's fingers were in the cake ..."), "Pink Cadillac" ("... My love is bigger than a Honda, yeah it's bigger than a Subaru ..."), and "Spare Parts" ("... Bobby said he'd pull out, Bobby stayed in ..."). Well, if those examples were intended to serve as a justification for the firm's heavy-handed actions, they not only seem to fall a bit short of even the legal obscenity threshold, but they also indicate the presence of an AOL monitor who has a really dirty mind. Some things *never* change.

The media's business mission is to entertain, inform—and hopefully educate—their audience. In doing so, radio stations clearly have the right to carefully select music for broadcast. It is, however, very disconcerting when a company —through those choices—attempts to narrow our national dialogue by censoring songs (as well as news coverage) for political purposes. In an era when the consolidation craze of corporate mergers has left Americans with far fewer locally owned, community-minded, independent media outlets, an increasingly few media conglomerates are in fact deciding which ideas are acceptable. Which sentiments can be publicly expressed. In effect, what notions become the accepted "truth."

Now, it is one thing for the US military to have a list of songs perpetually banned from Armed Forces Radio, but absolutely quite another for similar constrictions to be placed on the civilian citizenry's access to any particular music. Even during wartime Americans have the right, and the maturity, to handle messages more complex than canned, Pentagon-approved, patriotic drivel. We've successfully made it this far in history as an informed people, and now is no time to abandon our capability to absorb and weigh challenging new information. Music that brings a different, perhaps underrepresented view to the table—even songs with messages of *dissent*—cannot weaken this great nation.

That conclusion, however, would seemingly be news to George W. Bush and his crew, who after 9/11 began chanting their simplistic "good vs. evil" mantra—along with blithe assertions about America forging a "new domestic order" (in their daydreams, no doubt, a more socially conservative one) and broad and barely veiled threats like "You are either with *us*, or with the *terrorists*." Jamming on the same repressive riff, Bush's then chief spokesman, Ari Fleischer, was unleashed to intimidate a frightened citizenry into silent acquiescence with the ominous assertion that: "There are reminders to all Americans that they need to watch what they say—[and] watch what they do." Finally, in an unmistakable attempt to squash any sort of traditional national policy debate, Bush asserted that "America speaks with one voice"—his. And *that* singular voice was focused on war. According to his team, war that may last "for generations." Even perhaps "war without end." In particular there would turn out to be a war on the al-Qaeda terrorists; a war on Afghanistan; a war on Iraq. And maybe, they hinted, wars against North Korea, Syria, and Iran. The White House's hit list seemed to expand daily, and before long the first tentative murmurings of protest began rising from the people. It was then that a top Pentagon advisor, Richard Perle, made a preemptive strike against anyone who might dare to question the White House's game plan—or who would (in his demented terms) dare attempt to "incite pacifism" at a time when the Bush regime was seemingly gung-ho on, well, to quote another Perle-of-wisdom: "total war."

Setting aside such grandiose goals for global conflagration, the first step (that most of our citizenry came to agree upon) was to crush Afghanistan's fundamentalist theocratic Taliban government—the entity which, we'd been told, had harbored some of the al-Qaeda terrorists. But even having *that* giant task on his plate was not enough to keep Bush fully occupied. And thus on December 5, 2001, the FTC issued a report to Congress condemning—*surprise!*—the music industry. Even though the record labels had long-ago submitted to slapping "Parental Advisory" stickers on albums, the crusaders were still preoccupied with concerns that the firms continued "to advertise explicit content recordings"—well, why not? After all, such items (that are not obscene) remain *legal*—and so, of course, additional governmental "efforts will be needed to achieve widespread compliance." Joining the fray, Sen. Lieberman then came forth to promise that lawmakers would soon be contacting the major record companies to demand that they shape up and amend their evil ways. And then for their part, the shameless music industry—as represented by the RIAA—tried to profit from the post-9/11 panic by having their lobbyists push politicians to sneak (into the pending USA-PATRIOT Act) a provision that would allow them to hack private citizens' computers to delete what *they* consider to be illegal MP3 song files. So, America, nevermind all the anthrax scares, Homeland Security's periodic Code Orange declarations, the draconian aspects of the Patriot Act, the heartland spying by the proposed Total Information Awareness office, and the new Amber Alerts—it is the internal threat posed by *music* that remains a priority for certain "leaders." Some things *never* change.

And thus, with America in a benumbed state of national trauma, some of our leaders took craven advantage of our fearful post-9/11 state by taking up old unsettled battles against liberals. That is why—at a critical time when all energies should have been united in appropriating maximum federal funding for domestic security—we instead saw conservative congressmen sneak into an emergency budget bill numerous questionable pork-barrel projects perhaps best epitomized by the line item that earmarked $237,000 towards Missouri's Blue Springs Youth Orchestra Outreach Unit. The purpose? To fund "educational training to combat Goth culture." *Oh, my.* In other words, a program aiming to brainwash kids into preferring Mozart over Marilyn Manson, and Rachmaninov over Trent Reznor. Some things *never* change.

This sort of right-wing tomfoolery is hardly the sort of "combat" that most citizens expected their taxes to be directed towards in the midst of a purportedly serious War on Terrorism—not to mention the serial attacks on Afghanistan, Iraq, Iran, or Syria that Bush's team was beating the war drums or testing the water for. Then, in February 2003 just as anti-war protesters by the millions marched globally in opposition to Bush's war plans, GOP Senate Judiciary Committee chairman Orrin Hatch somehow found it timely to announce that he would soon be launching (yet another!) governmental investigation into what was possibly the most *irrelevant* issue of the day: payola in the radio business! Some things *never* change.

Meanwhile, amidst all that divisive activity—and even before the cinder pile of the World Trade Center had stopped smoldering—conservative cable-TV host Bill O'Reilly launched yet another front against musicians. Not impressed with the united and patriotic stand shown by the numerous artists who appeared on the "A Tribute to Heroes" televised benefit concert that had been hastily organized for September 21, O'Reilly chose to broadly attack those artists (including Bruce Springsteen, Sting, Eddie Vedder, Dave Matthews, and Neil Young,) as being "phonies" and further denigrated them by asserting that "most of these stars are selfish people." Perhaps O'Reilly and his ilk were actually miffed that Young had shown the temerity to perform one of Clear Channel's *verboten* tunes: Lennon's "Imagine." He couched his gripe, though, as a concern that the fund-raising sales of that concert's resultant CD had been slow (*only* 600,000 units sold), and so, *of course*, it was somehow the participating artists' fault: they hadn't promoted it well. In sum, O'Reilly's attack was a transparent ploy to find some, any, reason to condemn the musicians, many of whom have admirable track records of lending generous support to good causes. Some things *never* change.

One inspiring example of musicians publicly rejecting Bush's radical vision of a hyper-militaristic American empire was the founding of a new nonprofit organization, Musicians United to Win Without War. Created by such stars as David Byrne, Sheryl Crow, Dave Matthews, Missy Elliott, OutKast, and Jay-Z, the group began promoting alternatives to the Iraq War well before any missiles were ever launched. Then—with Bush continuing to studiously ignore several long months of massive worldwide street protests that had overwhelmingly rejected his obsessive crusade against Iraq—an innovative new online Internet "label," Protest Records, was launched in order to disseminate exactly such songs. By the Grammy Awards weekend in February 2003, CBS television network executives went so far as to warn nominated musicians to refrain from expressing themselves on current political matters or face having their microphones unplugged, declaring: "There is a time for political commentary. This is not one of them." For the record: Sheryl Crow, Fred Durst, and Bonnie Raitt were among the musicians who rebelled and found ways to make anti-war statements or gestures that were in line with the international consensus that Bush had offered zero proof that Iraq was tied to the 9/11 attacks. Bravely dissenting from the positions of the Powers That Be, these artists were faithfully fulfilling their historically customary role by questioning the authorities. Some things we hope will *never* change.

Meanwhile—like at any other time of war (and because some things *never* change)—flag-waving Hyper-Patriotism was expressed by musicians as well. A whole string of country songs, which ranged from the sentimentally patriotic to the belligerently jingoistic, came forth: from Aaron Tippin's "Where the Stars and Stripes and the Eagle Fly" to Charlie Daniels's "This Ain't No Rag, It's a Flag," and from Clint Black's "I Raq and Roll" to the Warren Brothers' "Hey Mr. President." Probably the most touching contribution though, was a tune offered up by America's best-selling country group, the Dixie Chicks. Indeed, in the months leading up to war their tender hit "Traveling Soldier" had plenty of folks—both pro-war and otherwise—a little misty-eyed.

The war season's *biggest* chart busters, though, were of the crudest ilk of chest-thumping, Arab-bashing variety: Toby Keith's award-winning "Courtesy of the Red, White and Blue (The Angry American)" ("... you'll be sorry that you messed with the U.S. of A. / 'Cause we'll put in a boot in your ass / It's the American way...") and Darryl Worley's No. 1 hit "Have You Forgotten?" ("... Some say this country's just out looking for a fight / Well after 9/11 man, I'd have to say that's right ..."). It was the Dixie Chicks' singer Natalie Maines who stepped up to take a swat at Keith's hit, describing it as "ignorant... and [it] makes country music sound ignorant"—a reasonable point that I would only suggest actually applies better to *Worley's* hit. Keith's song is merely one in a long line of macho war songs—Worley's accusatory lyrics ("...And *you* say we shouldn't worry about bin Laden ...") on the other hand seem to suggest that the patriots who earnestly opposed Bush's Iraq invasion plans were merely treasonous appeasers of the fellow who was initially fingered as our actual enemy: the 9/11 terrorist "mastermind," Osama bin Laden. The thought that the *anti*-war movement was *pro*–bin Laden is a big and unhelpful red herring, but such notions *do* at least offer some evidence the Bush regime's unrelenting disinformation campaign had successfully—at least in the hearts and minds of a few probably well-meaning but misinformed cowboy singers—bridged the lingering (albeit righteous) anger about the 9/11 terrorist attacks directly on over to long-standing, if unrelated, plans to settle old Bush dynasty scores with Saddam Hussein in Iraq.

Among those folks around the world who remained skeptical about Bush's true motives (and bullying style) were the Dixie Chicks, who stated that they were "embarrassed" that Bush hailed from their home state of Texas. Though hardly an act of treason (or even something that could conceivably undermine the morale of our well-disciplined, battle-ready soldiers), their flip comment was plenty enough to reveal that America's thin-skinned Super-Patriots were in no mood to tolerate *any* criticism of the president—including his daddy George H.W. Bush, who said of the Dixie Chicks, "they're on my shit list."

And thus, the Dixie Chicks—whose single "Traveling Soldier" had in previous months made them the absolute darlings of the pro-war, military-oriented crowd—were suddenly the targets of a seething campaign of reactionary hate mail, death threats, residential vandalism, retail boycotts, and right-wing talk-radio *fatwas*. The fracas began when KRMD, a Shreveport, Louisiana, radio station, organized a revenge rally highlighted by having a gigantic tractor crush mounds of CDs and cassettes—an event that one syndicated columnist rightly noted "rather smacks of Germany circa 1933" (not to mention the 1966 Beatle bonfires or the 1992 anti–Sinead O'Connor rallies) before, also correctly reaffirming that "a consumer has a right to boycott what offends him." Perfectly true—it's just the violent undercurrent of such "family-friendly" rallies that some of us find unsettling. For the Dixie Chicks the little silver lining in all of this was perhaps, as George Harrison pragmatically quipped about the album-burners back in 1966, that at least "they've got to *buy* them before they can burn them." Some things *never* change.

But an airplay ban snowballed big-time when various radio chains yanked the group's hits from further rotation and gleeful conservative pundits, music critics, and even a few fellow country stars all piled on—especially the hotheaded Toby

Keith, who was likely still smarting over Natalie Maines's rebuke of his song—even going so far as to wishfully predict (if a bit prematurely) the demise of the band.

As the brouhaha escalated—published reports of CD sales skidding by 40 percent; Lipton Tea (the corporate sponsor for the band's upcoming tour) getting skittish and withdrawing most of their endorsement deal; a hastily arranged "alternative concert" (featuring the faded ol' Marshall Tucker Band) announced in South Carolina to "compete" with the opening night of that tour; and that state's legislature passing a resolution denouncing the shell-shocked musicians—a number of brave souls (including country stars Vince Gill and Faith Hill) stepped forward in the Dixie Chicks' defense. Bruce Springsteen lent support via his Web site, saying of the Dixie Chicks:

> To me, they're terrific American artists expressing American values by using their American right to free speech. For them to be banished wholesale from radio stations, and even entire radio networks, for speaking out is un-American. The pressure coming from the government and big business to enforce conformity of thought concerning the war and politics goes against everything that this country is about—namely freedom. Right now, we are supposedly fighting to create freedom in Iraq, at the same time that some are trying to intimidate and punish people for using that same freedom here at home."

The sort of punishment perhaps that for two rebellious C&W radio DJs who defied the ban imposed at Colorado's KKCS came in the form of job suspensions. Some things *never* change.

That's about the point in time when the sham unraveled, revealing that the flare-up against the Dixie Chicks was in fact a "carefully orchestrated uproar" that was sparked "after an e-mail and telephone campaign reportedly originating with the Republican National Committee" in Washington, DC. On a local level, calls urging people to attend the Marshall Tucker show were traced (using Caller ID—*duh!*) straight back to South Carolina's Republican Party headquarters. Hardly the spontaneous grassroots uprising by aggrieved fans that it was initially touted as—indeed, the entire "backlash" was as one news source put it "a political maneuver no less calculated than the Watergate break-in." But like that famous earlier Republican dirty trick—do some things *ever* change?—the anti-Dixie Chicks Operation was, once similarly exposed, doomed to failure. And thus, within weeks the Dixie Chicks album was back at No. 1 and their entire 2003 concert tour had sold out.

Meanwhile, just days before the Iraq War was launched, and while Bush busily hyped the Iraqi threat, plainclothed army officers paid a visit to the home of a member of the band Spearhead and interrogated his *mother*. In response to being shown a photo of him onstage at an anti-war rally wearing a T-shirt emblazoned with the slogan "Dethrone the Bushes" (incorrectly characterized by them as an "un-American" sentiment) she responded, "Well, that's free speech"—a comment that met with this ominous riposte: "Well, things are changing these days."

Then—in a manner similar to the radical anti-choice organizations that have infamously targeted doctors who provided women with legal abortion services by posting their names, photographs, and addresses online—another right-wing Web site (www.probush.com) that asserts "if you do not support our President's decisions you are a traitor" began posting its "Traitor List™," which features various dissenting artists and includes musicians like Laurie Anderson, Sheryl Crow, Barbara Dane, Zach de la Rocha, Ani DiFranco, Dixie Chicks, Fred Durst, Steve Earle, Michael Franti, Bill Frisell, Rakaa Iriscience, Phil Lesh, Madonna, Tom Morello, Mos Def, Ozomatli, Tom Petty, Bonnie Raitt, Amy Ray, Barbra Streisand, and Eddie Vedder. Let's now hope that said artists never meet the same violent fate that some of those doctors subsequently have.

It was mid-March when Bush finally triggered his invasion of Iraq and the flag-bedecked corporate media clicked their heels, saluted, and fell right in line. That's when the entertainment division of the radio behemoth Clear Channel suddenly began promoting a nationwide series of effectively *pro*-war "Rally for America" events—a political step that one major newspaper noted was "unique among major media companies, which have confined their activities in the war to reporting and occasionally commenting on the news." The BBC contributed to the war fever by having Radio One ban the hit song "Bandages" (Hot Hot Heat) over concern that the title/chorus hook might cause upset amongst some listeners. It was also reported that MTV was refusing to air anti-war public service messages taped by various musicians. The sister company, MTV Europe, went so far as to issue a memo recommending that music videos depicting "war, soldiers, war planes, bombs, missiles, riots and social unrest, executions" and "other obviously sensitive material" not be shown on MTV in Britain and elsewhere. Specifically called out were videos for such songs as "You, Me, and World War Three" (Gavin Friday), "Boom!" (System of a Down), "B.O.B. (Bombs Over Baghdad)" (Outkast), "Lucky" (Radiohead), "Hot in the City" (Billy Idol), "Don't Want to Miss a Thing" (Aerosmith), and, humorously enough, "anything by the B-52's."

But faster than even the most dedicated censors could ever hope to ban them, a roaring flood of fresh anti-war songs flowed forth, including: "We Want Peace" (Lenny Kravitz with Kadim Al Sahir); "A Song of Peace" (Harmonious Combustion); "Peacekeeper" (Fleetwood Mac); "I Am Not at War with Anyone" (Luka Bloom); "Final Straw" (R.E.M.); "Jacob's Ladder (Not in My Name)" (Chumbawamba); "The Grave" (George Michael); "Angel of War" (Yusef Islam [formerly Cat Stevens]); "Love and Forgiveness" (Meshell Ndegeocello); "The Price of Oil" (Billy Bragg); "March of

Death" (Zack de la Rocha); "The Pledge to Resist" (DJ Spooky); "Life During Wartime" (Green Day); "Youth Against Fascism" (Sonic Youth); "Big Blue Ball of War" (Nanci Griffith); "Bomb the World" (Michael Franti and Spearhead); "This Is Total War" (Total War); and "War After War" (Abstractions).

Beyond those tunes, others—reflecting the worldwide notion that (absent Bush's personal obsession with revenge) this *particular* war had been avoidable—have emerged, such as "Hardon for War" (Mudhoney), "Let's Start a War" (Soylent Gringo), "Revenge" (Bitter, Bitter Weeks), and the Beastie Boys' "In a World Gone Mad." Then there are the songs more generally critical of Bush's overall performance, such as "Bushleaguer" (Pearl Jam), "To Washington" (John Mellencamp), "Son of a Bush" (Public Enemy), "George Bush Is a Stupid Asshole" (Wesley Willis), and "STOP (Stop The Oppressive Politics)," by an all-star lineup of West Coast hip-hoppers produced by DJ Fredwreck.

Mind you, these modern songs of dissent have basically received a uniformly cold shoulder from America's corporate radio—a naturally risk-aversive industry. Perhaps this is not coincidental, given current fretting about some major business and regulatory matters still pending in a Washington, DC, run by vengeful Republicans. With no desire to try and spin a conspiracy theory here, it seems fair to ponder whether the series of seemingly ill-timed threats that conservative politicians lobbed towards the music industry—and just in the months *since* 9/11—might have had ulterior purposes. Could it be possible that, taken collectively, those announcements—Sen. Hatch's eve-of-war promise to investigate radio practices; the FTC's December 2001 report damning the music industry for underusing "Parental Advisory" stickers; Sen. Lieberman's bullying demand that record companies straighten up; and finally, the slowly dragged-out process inevitably leading to the FCC's June 2003 shit-canning of the long-standing regulatory limitations on further media consolidation—were *all* stage-managed in order to place unprecedented pressure on the big chains like Clear Channel, Infinity Broadcasting (Viacom), Cumulus Media, Cox Radio, and Entercom Communications to play ball with the Bush regime? Could that sort of political equation account for the ongoing flood of pro-Bush propaganda and near-universal banishment of oppositional ideas and songs from corporate radio and TV?

Given the growing concentration of the media in fewer and fewer (and more and more conservative) hands, we are left to wonder who now—or in the future—will offer airtime to minority opinions and to songs conveying unpopular messages? And, has the political (and economic) risk of giving refuge to liberal thought *already* gotten too great? Even a huge corporation like the *New York Times* can see an emerging problem when that paper reports "there are plenty of angry people, many with prime music-buying demographics. But independent radio stations that once

Public Enemy continued to "Fight the Power" with their 2003 slam on the war-mongering Bush dynasty, Son of a Bush.

would have played edgy, political music have been gobbled up by corporations that control hundreds of stations and have no wish to rock the boat. Corporate ownership has changed what gets played—and who plays it."

This increasing overlap between our (formerly) "mainstream" news and entertainment media and brazenly right-wing ideology is quite troubling. Because of this imbalance the ideals of free expression (and unintimidated music-making) clearly face major challenges in the days ahead. At a time when a majority of the information industries have chosen to play it safe, any hope of fair representation being given to ideas or music that go against the current conservative flow is apparently just expecting too much. One promising factor though, is that: some things *never* change. And so, now as ever, it remains a truism that if an idea (or song) is deemed by the Powers That Be to be a target worthy of censorship, then it is also, by definition, too significant for the people to allow its banishment. Meaningful music can help us weather rocky times such as we find ourselves in today—but history informs us that we can rest assured that for every "controversial" idea to be expressed in the songs of the future, repressive forces will emerge in attempts to ban those bands and censor those songs—because in the realm of "taboo tunes," well, *some things never change.*

Notes and Sources

Notes

The sources used for *Taboo Tunes* cited below include quotes or material from various author interviews, books, government documents, news clippings, periodicals, and Web sites. Due to space limitations this is a necessarily selective listing that attempts to focus on the more obscure and/or classic sources. Any omissions are inadvertent and subject to update at tabootunes.com. Details of references listed in the Notes can be found in the Sources section that follows.

CHAPTER 1: Fear of Music

• **Anatomie of Abuses** [Stubbes] • **"pertinent question"** [Grade] • **Thoreau** [Thoreau] • **1413 & 1543 laws** [Cloonan]• **Beatles "alien ideology"** [*Seattle Times*, 5/25/03] • **Malawi** [the fileroom.org] • **Iran** [nytimes.com] • **Israel** [Katzenell] • **Egypt** [allstarmag.com, amnesty.org] • **France, mocking anthem** [*Seattle Times*, 1/26/03] • **Jordan** [amnesty.org] • **India** [amnesty.org] • **Indonesia** [Larson] • **"sex crimes"** [Brummitt] • **West Africa** [Wallis] • **Iraq** [Barkho] • **Nigeria** [Block] • **Japan** [Sadin] • **guitar ban** [The Ventures] • **Italy** [*Seattle P-I*, 11/30/01] • **China** [Jones] • **Poland, Czechoslovakia, Hungary, Yugoslavia** [Ramet] • **Chile** [Kornbluh] • **Jara quote** [Petley] • **Afghanistan** [amnesty.org] • **Beatle haircuts** [Gerlin] • **women singing** [Knickmeyer] • **music on radio** [*Times of India*] • **Madonna and Pepsi** [*No More Censorship*] • **100% Americans and Johnny Rebel** [Russell] • **"BROWN BAGGED"** [Shapiro] • ***The New Yorker*** [Kiley] • **DeMent lyrics** [Cantwell]

CHAPTER 2: Beat Crazy

• ***Daily Mail*** [Baddeley] • **Godwin quote** [Godwin] • **1322 decree** [Bargreen] • **"dulls taste" and "avaunt"** [Berlin] • **WMCA "degrading"** [Delong] • **"polite society"** [Pfeffer] • **1899 newspaper** [Frohnmayer] • **"Musical Impurity"** [Berlin] • **"cross rhythm" and "recklessness"** [*Seattle Daily Times*, 6/14/21] • **Cleveland ordinances** [NBEA.com] • **"'boll weevil wiggle!'"** [Adams] • **"Victims of the dancing craze"** [Cloonan] • **"'strange' rhythms"** [Owen, Korpe, Reitov]

• dance instructors and *Musical America* [Berlin] • **regulating dancehalls** [Hills] • **Portland headlines** [Hills] • **Hoover and Coolidge headlines** [UK Cannabis Internet Activists] • **Morrison trial** [Morrison interview] • **Curtis Publishing** [Hills] • **"dancing was waning"** and **"narcotic menace"** and **"succumb to jazz,"** [*Seattle Daily Times* 6/13/21] • **"hell-soaked institution"** [Clark] • **"jungle standards"** [Ewan, 1980] • **"hysteria, incites idleness"** [Solomon] • **"Watch Your Step"** [Solomon] • **"moral degradation"** [*Seattle Daily Times*, 6/16/21] • **Congressman Allen** [*Seattle Times*, 12/22/33] • **Ordinance Against Negro Culture** [Petley] • **"jazz inebriates"** [Solomon] • *Radio Guide* "Musical Garbage" [Thompson] • **"degenerate sax players"** [leede-forest.org] • **Archbishop of Dubuque** [prorev.com] • **"screaming savage"** [Denisoff] • **"plot to mongrelize"** [Satzmary] • **"devil worshippers"** [Martin & Segrave] • **Cardinal Stritch** [Bronson, Martin & Segrave] • **Rev. Riblett "devil's diversion"** [Denisoff] • **"leer-ic garbage"** [Martin & Segrave] • **"violence and mayhem"** [Heins] • **"Rumble" banned** [Roeser, Bronson] • *Melody Maker* "terrifying" [Martin & Segrave] • **"cannibalistic"** [*New York Times*] • **Pablo Casals** *Music Journal* [Casals] • **Casals and *Time*** [Martin & Segrave] • **Sinnott quotes** [*Seattle Times*, 5/4/03] • **Alan Freed quotes** [White, C.W.] • **Hoover "corrupting"** [Jackson, J. A.] • **Biondi @ WKBW** [Martin & Segrave] • **Coasters** [Nicholl] • **Bobby Darin** [Taylor] • **stations drop rock** [Pat O'Day, and others] • **KEX and KMPC** [Martin & Segrave] • **Network "salacious"** [Martin & Segrave] • **Jim French** [French] • **"The Twist"** [Dawson, and others] • **"sexual atrocities"** and **"bodily motion"** [Larson] • **"succumb to message"** [Della Valle] • **"foaming at the mouth"** [Cloonan] • **crAP Sucks Page** [slrkull.tripod.com]

CHAPTER 3: The Devil in Disguise

• *New York Times Magazine*, 1958 [Bertrand] • **"Devil's masterpiece"** [Garlock] • **1712 law** [Ernst & Schwartz] • **Diabolus en Musica** [Hanford, and others] • **"jew's harp"** [Ernst & Schwartz] • **1714 organ** and **"reproach"** and **"diabolical art"** [Fisher] • **"devil's boxes"** [Wolfe] • **"Satan knows what organs"** [White, E.G.] • **1953 jukebox ban** [Nuzum] • **"Devil Send Elvis?"** (Betrock) • **Jimmy Dean** [O'Day] • **WAYX** [*Waycross Journal-Herald*] • **KLUE and Beatles** [newsoftheodd.com] • **Grand Dragon and Lennon "I apologized"** [beatles-discography.com] • **WAQY DJs** [AP Wide World] • **WAQY and WSAG and Imperial Wizard** and **"Restore Christianity"** [Hinterberger] • **Sinead quote "through fear"** [Ross] • **"syncopated beat"** [Royko] • ***"Why Knock Rock?"*** [Peters] • **Des Moines and Keokuk church** [Nuzum] • **Chapel of Peace** [*Seattle P-I*, 5/3/82] • **"one-eyed church of Satan."** [Wolfe] • **experts disagree** [Nuzum] • ['... ***Turn me on, dead man ...***'] and ['... ***I live with satan ...***'] [*Seattle P-I*, 5/3/82] • **"Rain,"** *Kilroy* LP, 'Annuit coeptis,' J. Geils, 'Welcome to the big show,' "Ya Hozna," Prince, Stones [Poundstone] • **Rev. Farrar** [*Seattle P-I*, 5/3/82] • **Mr. Ed** [Poundstone, and others] • **brainwashing centers** [RRC] • **Jordan** [amnesty.org] • **forced hospitalization** [*Rock & Rap Confidential*, 12/98] • **Mayor of Warsaw** [Yahoo! News] • **Cradle of Filth** [nme.com] • **"Korn is indecent"** [*Tower/Pulse*] • **Pat Boone** [*DISCoveries*]

CHAPTER 4: Token Drug Song

• *Hammurabi* [King] • **absinthe use** [Conrad] • **Berlioz** [Cairn, and others] • **Mozart** [wowessays.com] • **Schumann and Schubert** [Solbrekken] • **Paganini and Mussorgsky** [eh.mit.edu/tengo] • **Brit drinking songs** [Palmer, and others] • **American Temperance** and drinking songs [Wenzell & Binkowski, and others] • **Anslinger's "darkie" quote** [reefer-madness.org] • **"Puff, the Magic Dragon"** [Bailey, and others] • **"author's intended meaning"** and "Hey Jude" [Bailey] • **Association @ Disneyland** [Taylor] • **"Stairway" lyrics** [Gladwell] • **Crome Syrcus' name** [Anderson] • **"Lucy in the Sky with Diamonds"** [Bailey] • **BBC "A Day in the Life" and "He blew his mind" and "had a smoke"** [Taylor] • **"an ode to pot"** [ukcia.org] • **Jefferson Airplane "Runnin'"** [Braitman] • **Linkletter "murder"** [Urban Legends Reference Pages] • **Denver's FBI file** [Romano, Sheheri] • **'no perfume'** [GOLUBLOG] • **FCC warns radio** [FCC Notice 71-205, Denisoff, Kane] • **Brewer and Shipley** [Simon, Denisoff, and others] • **Elvis letter** [NARA] • **Elvis @ FBI** [Smoking Gun] • **Nixon re: drinks vs. drugs** [Lardner] • **Illinois Crime Commission** [Kane] • **"orgiastic aspects…"** [*Seattle P-I*, 9/7/69] • **Anslinger's "brainwashing"** [reefermadness.org] • **Beach Boys FBI file** [Venezia] • **Beach Boys' manager** [dotmusic.com] • **New Orleans Rave law** [aclu.org, ga1.org] • **FDA tests Ecstasy** [Newton]

CHAPTER 5: Let's Talk About Sex

• **"Love For Sale"** [Brooks] • **'bridal suite' and 'favorite doggy'** [GOLUBLOG] • **"The Pill"** [Emory] • **"a fine of 40S."** [Armitage] • **WQQK-FM** [*Tennessean News Services*] • **blue laws re: entertaining and flirting** [Ernst & Schwartz] • **"waste of beer"** [Fisher] • **1815, 1821, 1842, and 1865 laws** [Ernst & Schwartz] • **Comstock** [Ernst & Schwartz, and others] • **Ben Light** [Matos] • **Party Records** [Blue Pages, Matos, and others] • **"Sweater Girl"** [Miller] • **1931** *Variety* [Nuzum] • **Tait's Café** [Riddle] • **NBC 147 songs** [Winfield] • **Maddox Bros.** [Whiteside] • **Dean Martin and O'Brien** [Fore] • **"Control the Dim-Wits"** [Martin & Segrave] • **1948 raid** [Nuzum, gettyimagesnews.com] • **WDIA** [Bronson] • **WABB and Crusade For Better Disks** [Martin & Segrave] • **San Antonio** [Nuzum] • **"jumpy hot stuff"** [Martin & Segrave] • **Ruth Thompson** [Bronson] • **Richard's "Tutti Frutti"** [White, C.] • **Hank Ballard** [Ballard, Alexander interviews] • **James Brown riot** [nighthawk.co.nz] • **"Light's Out"** [Carpenter] • **"Raunchy"** [O'Day interview] • **"What'd I Say" rejected** [Lydon] • **"Louie Louie" R&B tune** [Berry interview, and others] • **"Louie Louie"and FBI** [U.S. Dept. of Justice, 5/25/65 document] • **Sinnott quote** [*Seattle Times*, 5/4/03] • **Ind. Governor** [*Seattle-P-I*, 1/24/64] • **"head in shame"** [Larson] • **"a naughty girl"** [Taylor] • **Pretty Things** [Taylor] • **Nightcrawlers** [Cooper] • **Standells** [Cafarelli] • **"Brown Eyed Girl"** [leoslyrics.com] • **Rationals** [Unterberger] • **"Rhapsody in the Rain"** [Urban Legends Reference Pages] • **"corrupting the youth"** [Mervis & Masley] • **"Double Shot"** [Downey] • **Hendrix "too suggestive"** [Cloonan] • **Stones in China** [Oleson] • **Jethro Tull 'bastard'** [Currie] • **Carlin "Explicit Lyrics"** [Chastagner] • **Zappa lyrics** [Simmons interview] • **"parallels to Nazi Germany"** [Wilson-McLeish] • **"swift acquiescence"** [Goldstein] • **Ling quotes Mentors** [Senate Hearing 99-529] • **"publicize the excesses"** [Gore] • **"Gore came early…"** [Marsh, 10/13/99] • **"Me So Horny"** [Page] • **"Relax"** [Taylor] • **"polio"** [Henderson] • **Father Murray** [Ernst & Schwartz]

CHAPTER 6: Killing in the Name

• **American murder ballads** [Burt, and others] • **"glorifying violence"** [Brend] • **Aderholt** [Burt] • **"Wild Thing"** [Howell] • **"the FBI's position"** [FBI letter, 8/1/89] • **FBI and N.W.A.** [*Rock & Rap Confidential*, 5/96] • **cops and Focus on the Family** [Nuzum] • **"'fuck the police'** in Detroit" [Pollack] • **Pension funds** [Nelson] • **National Black Police Assoc.** [Landis] • **Ice-T calmly attempted** [*Seattle P-I*, 7/29/92] • **"metaphoric violence"** [Marsh, 9/14/98] • **In-telligent Hoodlum** [Cloonan] • **"Sting opened mouth" and bomb threat and Topeka concert** [Redwing] • **FOP and Goldberg quote** [Goldberg, 9/3/99] • **dead prez** [*Rock & Rap Confidential*, 5/00] • **Diallo incident** [Barnes, *Rock & Rap Confidential*, 7/00] • **"fucking dirtbag"** [ear-pollution.com] • **Morello quote** [Redwing] • **Sheryl Crow** [Strauss, and others] • **"smut"** [*Seattle Times*, 12/20/96] • **Elektra** [*Rock & Rap Confidential*, 2/00] • **White Supremacist and Nazi bands** [Burghart, and others]

CHAPTER 7: Find the Cost of Freedom

• **Fletcher** [Noebel, 1974] • **early American songs** [G. S. Jackson, Ewan] • **"Ye simple Bosto-nians"** [Ewan] • **"Yanks Are Not Coming"** [Goldsmith] • *Industrial Worker* [McClelland] • **"I got disgusted"** [Guthrie] • **Feather and Ertegan quotes, Holiday and FBI** [Margolick] • **Santa Claus** [Cloonan] • **Peekskill Riot** [Sylvester, Goldsmith, Hamilton] • *Ebony* magazine [Hamilton] • **Copland banned** [Superville] • **"Threatening calls"** [Noonan] • **Christian Crusade, Citizens for Conservative Action, Young Republicans** [Denisoff] • **"laboratory tested"** [Noebel, 1965] • **Bob Eubanks** [Denisoff] • **Elvis re: Smothers** [U.S. Government Memo, 1/4/71] • **Smothers "shut up"** [tvparty.com] • **Janis Ian** [Taylor, Raab] • **KSAN** [Neer] • **Ochs and FBI** [U.S. Dept. of Justice document, 10/22/69] • **MC5 vs. Hudson's** [Fines] • **WNEW** [Neer] • **Electric Prunes "beep"** [Unterberger] • **Hoover re: the Doors** [angelfire.com] • **'Hurricane' Carter quotes** [Steinberg.] • **FBI re: Lennon** [foia.fbi.gov] • **anti-war…Minneapolis** [Romano] • **FCC Notice 71-205** [Denisoff] • **Agnew WGTB quote** [Raz] • **NY Dolls in Memphis** [Cagle] • **SLA bomb threats** [NewsMax.com] • **Napoleon XIV petitions** [Collins] • **"Short People" ban** [Marcus] • **Battered Wives picketed** [www.canoe.ca] • **Rapeman Blur** [Cloonan] • **Anti-Nowhere League & Crass** [Cloonan] • **Radio Free Grenada** [Marsh, 1985] • *Frankenchrist* [*No More Censorship*, and others] • **neo-Nazi bands** [Pitts, Burghart] • **Bennett "nothing less"** [Goldberg] • **Sinatra quote "better never meet"** [Ross] • **Tucker "anything offensive"** [massmic.com] • **AOL** [*New York Daily News*, RRC] • **CCC blacklist** [Armstrong, Wolk, RRC, and others] • **CCC ban denial** [CCC] • **AOL and Springsteen lyrics** [Marsh, 10/22/01] • **Perle's "total war"** [Pilger] • **"widespread compliance"** [FTC] • **"pork barrel"** [nytimes.com, 4/9/02] • **Maines "ignorant" quote** [RRC, 5/03] • **"Germany circa 1933"** [Pitts, 5/4/03] • **Harrison quote** [beatles-discography.com] • **Springsteen quote** [brucespringsteen.net] • **"carefully orchestrated uproar"** [Lyons] • **"shit list"** [Texas Monthly] • **"That's free speech"** [Strickman]• **"political maneuver" and "Caller ID"** [RRC, 5/03] • **KKCS DJs** [washingtonpost.com] • **CBS warns Grammys** [Drudge Report, 2/21/03] • **"gobbled up"** [Staples]

SOURCES
Books

Armitage, Gilbert. *Banned In England*. Great Britain: Wishart & Co., 1932.

Aranza, Jacob. *Backward Masking Unmasked: Backward Satanic Messages of Rock and Roll Exposed*. Shreveport, La.: Huntington House, 1983.

Baddeley, Gavin. *Lucifer Rising: Sin, Devil Worship, and Rock 'n' Roll*. London: Plexus, 1999.

Berlin, Edward A. *King of Ragtime: Scott Joplin and His Era.* New York: Oxford University Press, 1994. Quoting 9/21/12 *Musical America*, 9/1914 *Musical Observer*, and 1/1900 *Etude* magazines.

Bertrand, Michael T. *Race, Rock, and Elvis.* Champaign: University of Illinois Press, 2000. Quoting Gertrude Samuel's "Why They Rock 'n' Roll—and Should They?" essay, *New York Times Magazine*, 1/12/58.

Betrock, Alan. *Unseen America: The Greatest Cult Exploitation Magazines 1950–1966.* Brooklyn: Shake Books, 1990.

Brend, Mark. *American Troubadours.* San Francisco: Backbeat Books, 2001.

Burghart, Devin, editor. *Soundtracks to the White Revolution: White Supremacist Assaults on Youth Music Subcultures.* Chicago: Center for New Community, 1999.

Burt, O.W. *American Murder Ballads—And Their Stories.* New York: The Citadel Press, 1958.

Cairns, David. *Berlioz: Servitude and Greatness 1832–1869.* Vol. 2. London: Viking UK, 2001.

Clark, Norman H. *The Dry Years: Prohibition and Social Change in Washington.* Seattle: University of Washington Press, 1965 (revised 1988).

Cloonan, Martin. *Banned! Censorship of Popular Music in Britain: 1967-92.* Arena, England, 1996

Cloonan, Martin, and Reebee Garofalo, editors. *Policing Pop.* Philadelphia: Temple University Press, 2003.

Collins, Ace. *Disco Duck and Other Adventures in Novelty Music.* New York: Berkeley Boulevard, 1998.

Conrad, Barnaby, III. *Absinthe: History in a Bottle.* San Francisco: Chronicle Books, 1988.

Cray, Ed. *The Erotic Muse: American Bawdy Songs.* Champaign: University of Illinois Press, 1992.

Cushman, Thomas. *Notes from Underground: Rock Music Counterculture in Russia.* Albany: State University of New York Press, 1995.

Dawson, Jim. *The Twist: The Story of the Song and Dance That Changed the World.* Boston: Faber and Faber, 1995.

Delong, Thomas E. *The Mighty Music Box.* Los Angeles: Amber Crest, 1980.

Denisoff, R. Serge. *Solid Gold: The Popular Record Industry.* New Brunswick, N.J.: Transaction, 1975.

Emery, Ralph. *The View from Nashville.* New York: William Morrow, 1998. Quote from Lynn interview with *Penthouse*, 1980.

Ernst, M.L., and A.U. Schwartz. *Censorship: The Search for the Obscene.* New York: McMillan, 1964.

Ewen, David. *Songs of America.* Chicago: Ziff-Davis, 1947.

Ewen, David. "Popular Music of the Decade." Essay. *Ain't We Got Fun? – Essays, Lyrics, and Stories of the Twenties*, Solomon, Barbara H., editor, New York: Mentor, 1980.

Fisher, W.A. *One Hundred and Fifty Years of Music Publishing in the United States.* Boston: Oliver Ditson, 1933.

Frohnmayer, John. *Out of Tune—Listening to the First Amendment.* Golden, Colo.: Fulcrum Publishing, 1995.

Garlock, Frank. *The Big Beat: A Rock Blast.* Greenville, S.C.: Bob Jones University, 1971.

Garofalo, Reebee, editor. *Rockin' the Boat: Mass Music and Mass Movements.* Boston: South End Press, 1992.

Godwin, Jeff. *Dancing with Demons: The Music's Real Master.* Chino, Calif.: Chick Publications, 1988.

Goldsmith, Peter D. *Making People's Music: Moe Asch and Folkways Records.* Washington, DC: Smithsonian Institute Press, 1998.

Gore, Tipper. *Raising PG Kids in an X-Rated Society.* Nashville: Abingdon Press, 1987.

Hamilton, Virginia. *Paul Robeson: The Life and Times of a Free Black Man.* New York: Harper and Row, 1974.

Heins, M. *Sex, Sin, and Blasphemy: A Guide to America's Censorship Wars.* New York: The New Press, 1993.

Hills, Tim. *The Many Lives of the Crystal Ballroom.* Portland, Ore.: McMenamins Pubs and Breweries, 1997.

Jackson, G.S. *Early Songs of Uncle Sam.* Boston: Bruce Humphries, 1933.

Jackson, J.A. *Big Beat Heat: Alan Freed and the Early Years of Rock and Roll.* New York: Schirmer, 1991.

Jones, A.F. *Like a Knife: Ideology and Genre in Contemporary Chinese Popular Music.* Ithaca, N.Y.: East Asia Program, Cornell University, 1992.

Larson, Bob. *Rock & Roll: The Devil's Diversion.* Rev. ed. McCook, Neb.: Privately published, 1970.

Lydon, Michael. *Ray Charles: Man and Music* (uncorrected proof copy). New York: Riverhead Books, 1998.

Marcus, Greil. *Mystery Train.* Revised 3d ed. New York: Plume, 1990.

Margolick, David. *Strange Fruit: Billie Holiday, Café Society, and an Early Cry for Civil Rights.* Philadelphia: Running Press, 2000.

Marsh, Dave, et al., editors. *The First Rock & Roll Confidential Report.* New York: Pantheon, 1985.

Martin, L., and K. Segrave. *Anti-Rock: The Opposition to Rock 'n' Roll.* New York: Da Capo, 1993.

McClelland, John, Jr. *Wobbly War: The Centralia Story.* WSHS, 1987. Quoting 5/1/17 *The Industrial Worker* newspaper.

Neer, Richard. *FM: The Rise and Fall of Rock Radio* (advance uncorrected proof). New York: Villard, 2001.

Noebel, David A. *Rhythm, Riots, and Revolution: Communist Use of Music.* Tulsa, Okla.: Christian Crusade Publications, 1966.

——. *The Marxist Minstrels: A Handbook on Communist Subversion of Music.* Tulsa, Okla.: American Christian College Press, 1974.

Nuzum, Eric. *Parental Advisory—Music Censorship in America.* New York: Perennial, 2001.

Owen, Ursula & Korpe, Marie & Reitov, Ole., editors. *Smashed Hits: The Book of Banned Music.* Index On Censorship, London, 1998.

Palmer, Roy, editor. *A Touch on the Times: Songs of Social Change 1770 to 1914.* London: Penguin Education, 1974.

Peters, Dan and Steve. *Why Knock Rock?* Minneapolis: Bethany House Publishers, 1984.

Ramet, S.P., editor. *Rocking the State: Rock Music and Politics in Eastern Europe and Russia.* Boulder, Colo.: Westview Press, 1994.

Russell, Tony. *Blacks, Whites and Blues.* New York: Stein and Day, 1970.

Satzmary, David P. *Rockin' in Time: A Social History of Rock and Roll.* Englewood Cliffs, N.J.: Prentice-Hall, 1991.

Shapiro, Harry, and Caesar Glebbeek. *Jimi Hendrix: Electric Gypsy.* New York: St. Martin's Press, 1990.

Solomon, Barbara H. "Smoking and Dancing as Symbols of Liberation." Essay. *Ain't We Got Fun? – Essays, Lyrics, and Stories of the Twenties,* New York: Mentor, 1980

Starr, S. Frederick. *Red & Hot: The Fate of Jazz in the Soviet Union.* New York: Limelight Editions, 1985.

Stubbes, Philip. *The Anatomie of Abuses.* Medieval and Renaissance texts and studies, 245. Tempe, Ariz.: Arizona Center for Medieval and Renaissance Studies, 2002.

Thoreau, Henry David. *Walden and Other Writings.* New York: Random House/The Modern Library, 1937/1950.

Unterberger, Richie. *Urban Spacemen and Wayfaring Strangers.* San Francisco: Miller Freeman, 2000.

Wenzel, Lynn, and Carol J. Binkowski. *I Hear America Singing.* New York: Crown, 1989.

White, Charles. *The Life and Times of Little Richard.* New York: Pocket Books, 1984.

Whiteside, Jonny. *Ramblin' Rose: The Life and Career of Rose Maddox.* Nashville: CMF Press and Vanderbilt University Press, 1997.

Winfield, B.H., and S. Davidson. *Bleep! Censoring Rock and Rap Music.* Boulder, Colo.: Greenwood Press, 1999.

Wolfe, Charles. *The Devil's Box: Masters of Southern Fiddling.* Nashville: Vanderbilt University Press, 1997.

Periodicals, Newspaper and Magazine Articles, Press Releases, Web Pages, Photos, and Miscellenea

aclu.org. "Censorship Is Latest Drug War Tactic as Government Seeks to Put 'Rave' Dance Music Promoters in Prison." Press release, 3/7/01.

Anderson, Rick. "What Is Rock Lyric 'Message'?." *Seattle P-I,* 11/26/70.

angelfire.com. "The Doors." *Celebrity Files.*

AP Wide World Photos. Caption to "Beatle Ban" photo (TR#APHS181), 8/8/66.

Armstrong, Mark. "'Imagine' All the Inappropriate Songs." *E! Online News* [eonline.com].

Bailey, William J. "Society's Mixed Messages: Countering the Influence of Popular Music on Creating an Environment Conducive to Alcohol, Tobacco, and Other Drug Use." Adapted from a paper presented at the 1995 PRIDE World Drug Conference. drugs.indiana.edu, 1998.

Bargreen, Melinda. "Obscenity—An Old Story." *Seattle Times,* 11/4/90.

Barnes, Julian E. "Springsteen Song about Diallo Prompts Anger from Police." nytimes.com, 6/12/00.

beatles-discography.com. "Beatles History—1966."

Block, Robert. "'Soldier Go, Soldier Come' Is the Refrain for Jaded Nigerians." *Wall Street Journal*, 2/24/99.

Braitman, Stephan M.H. Letter to the Editor. *Goldmine*, 5/24/96.

Bronson, Fred. "A Selected Chronology of Musical Controversy." *Billboard*, 3/26/94.

Brooks, Michael. *Songs of the Depression: Boom, Bust, and the New Deal* (4 CDs). Bear Family, 1999.

brucespringsteen.net. Essay. *News*, 4/23/03.

Brummitt, Chris. "Indonesians Argue over Pop Star's Dance." *Seattle P-I*, 5/5/03.

Cafarelli, Carl. "An Informal History of Bubblegum Music." *Goldmine*, 4/25/97.

Cagle, Van M. "The Contextual Limitations of Marginality in 1970s Glitter Rock: The Case of the New York Dolls." Paper, c.1996.

Cantwell, David. "Homespun of the Brave." *No Depression*, 11/96.

Carpenter, Bil. "Dr. John's Shady Past." *Goldmine*, 4/10/98.

Casals, Pablo. "A Disgrace to Music." *Music Journal*, 1/61.

CCC. "Clear Channel Says National 'Banned Playlist' Does Not Exist." Press release. clearchannel.com, 9/18/01.

Chastagner, Claude. "Parents Music Resource Center from information to censorship," www.philagora.org, 4/98.

Chicago Tribune. "'Obscene' Lyrics Cause Records To Be Seized," 10/14/84.

Cooper, Kim. "The Nightcrawlers." *Scram* no. 24, 1998.

Currie, Christopher. *Live: Bursting Out* LP review. alt.music.yes, 1998.

Della Valle, Paul. "Reformed Rocker Preaches the Evils of the Backbeat," *Lancaster [Mass.] Times*, 11/5/97.

DISCoveries. "Pat Boone's Heavy Metal 'Joke' Backfires," 4/97.

dotmusic.com. "Snortin' USA." Quoting Beach Boys' manager, Elliott Loss. 5/11/00.

Downey, Pat. Review of *Dick Bartley Presents Collector's Essentials Vols. 3 and 4 CDs*. discol.com, 11/20/98.

Drudge Report. "CBS Executives Want No 'Anti-War Statements' during Grammys." drudgereport.com, 2/21/03.

earpollution.com. "Cops Pissed at the Boss," 7/00.

eh.mit.edu/tengo. "Niccolo Paganini (1782–1840): His Life."

eh.mit.edu/tengo. "Modest Mussorgsky (1839–1881): His Life."

Fines, Ian. "The Rise and Fall of the MC5." furious.com.

Fore, Lindsay R. "*Rolling Stone's* Response to Attempted Censorship of Rock 'n' Roll," in Winfield and Davidson, *Bleep! Censoring Rock and Rap Music*.

French, Jim. "The Land of Fifth Rate Entertainment." *Advent*, 6/59.

ga1.org. "What's at Stake! Property Rights and Right to Dance under Attack, Drug Policy Alliance Action Center."

Gerlin, Andrea. "In Herat, Broken Dolls and Shattered Lives." *Seattle Times*, 12/9/01.

gettyimagesnews.com. Caption to "Obscene Mess" photo, image JM6831.

Gladwell, Malcolm. "Rock Lyrics: Parents Worry But the Young Aren't Listening." *Seattle Times*, 5/19/91.

Goldberg, Michael. "Elvis Fan Bill Bennett Attacks Rap, Marilyn Manson." 6/1/96, addict.com.

Goldberg, Michael. "Land of the Double Standard." addict.com, 9/3/99.

Goldstein, Patrick. "Parents Warn: Take the Sex and Shock Out of Rock." *Los Angeles Times*, 8/25/85.

GOLOBLOG. "Too Darn Hot (9th of Av)." Essay by Alex. lancelot.uchicago.edu, 7/16/02.

Grade, Michael. "Two Exceptions and Proof for Rules," in *Index On Censorship*. indexonline.org/news, 2/3/03.

Guthrie, Woody. "My Life," in *American Folksong*. 1947; reprint, New York: Oak Publications, 1961.

Hanford, Jon. "The Mysteries of the 'Purple Haze' Chord Revealed." Lecture presentation, 12/00.

Henderson, Damien. "Eminem's balcony scene-stealer," www.theherald.co.uk, 6/25/03.

Hinterberger, John. "John Lennon, Literary Beatle, May Have Had Some Reasons." *Seattle Times*, 8/7/66.

Howell, Debi A. "PMRC Update," in *No More Censorship*, Fact Sheet (#3), Summer/89.

Kane, Joe. "Dope Lyrics: The Secret Language of Rock." *High Times*, c.1978.

Katszenell, Jack. "Despite Protest, Wagner Work Performed for First Time in Israel." *Boston Globe*, 10/28/00.

Kerrang! "'Satanists' White Zombie Banned by American Town," 2/10/96.

Kiley, Brendan. "Shut Up Yourself." *Resonance*, c.2000.

King, L.W., translator. *Code of Hammurabi*. Avalon Project at Yale Law School [yale.edu].

Knickmeyer, Ellen. "Alliance's Laws Less Harsh, But Still Severe." *Seattle Times*, 11/18/01.

Kornbluh, Peter. "CIA Acknowledges Ties to Pinochet's Repression." 09/19/2000 [http://www.gwu.edu/~nsarchiv/news/20000919].

Landis, David. "Record Protest." *USA Today*, 6/18/92.

Lardner Jr., George. "Nixon Defended Envoy's Groping 1972 Tapes Also Reveal Talk of a Justice Dept. 'Full of Jews.'" *Washington Post*, 3/1/02.

leedeforest.org [leedeforest.org/broadcaster]

leoslyrics.com. "Van Morrison: Brown Eyed Girl."

Lyons, Gene. "Republican Patriot Police Protect Bush from Critics." smirkingchimp.com, 4/16/03.

Marr, John. "Rock 'n' Roll Will Steal Your Soul: A History of Anti-Rock Books: 1966–1988." *Chemical Imbalance* (Chattanooga, Tenn.), no. 8, c.1990.

Marsh, Dave. "An Insult To Uncle Tom." addict.com, 9/14/98.

——. "Pro Choice Politics." addict.com, 10/13/99.

——. "AOL Keyword: Censorship." starpolish.com, 10/22/01.

Marsh, Dave, and Lee Ballinger, editors. *Rock & Rap Confidential*, 1983.

massmic.com. Quoting 11/20/96 CNBC debate.

Matos, Michaelangelo. "Second Chances." *Seattle Weekly*, 1/11/01.

Mervis, Scott, and Ed Masley. "Hitsburgh: Battling the British Invasion." post-gazette.com, 2/1/01.

Miller, Chuck. "That Saucy Blonde!" *Goldmine*, 5/9/97.

Mire, Beverly. "The 'Tipper Sticker:' Is It Censorship or Not?" *Gavin Report*, 5/18/90.

NBEA.com. "Rules and Regulations." National Ballroom and Entertainment Association.

Nelson, Chris. "Limit Set on Texas Ban of Music Investments." sonicnet.com/news, 4/16/98.

New York Daily News. "AOL Names Itself Boss over Lyrics." nydailynews.com, 10/25/01.

New York Times. "Rock-and-Roll called Communicable Disease," 3/28/56.

NewsMax.com. "Osmonds Bare the Truth," 2/6/01.

newsoftheodd.com. "John Lennon Proclaims Beatles 'More Popular than Jesus' (March 4, 1966)."

Newton, Christopher. "FDA OKs Clinical Testing of Ecstasy." washingtonpost.com, 11/7/01.

Nicholl, Don. "The Disc Banned by the BBC." *Disc*, 3/21/59.

nighthawk.co.nz. Online list, "Banned!"

No More Censorship, Fact Sheet (#3), Summer/89.

Noonan, Tom. *Chad Mitchell Trio at the Bitter End*. LP liner notes. Kapp Records, 1962.

nytimes.com. "Watchdog Group Cites Congressional 'Pork,'" 4/9/02.

Olesen, Alexa. "China Orders Rolling Stones to Ax Songs." *Seattle P-I*, 3/12/03.

Page, Clarence. "Lyric Police Don't Seem to Realize It's Only Rock 'n' Roll." *Seattle P-I*, 3/5/90.

Peifer, Redge. *The Rock and Roll Nightmare*. 4-page handbill. Thunder and Lightning Street
Ministries (Ramsay, Mich.), 1991.

Petley, Julian. "Smashed Hits." *Seattle Weekly*, 3/19/99.

Pfeffer, Murray L. "Roots of 'Jazz.'" The Great American Big Bands Database [mlp@info.net].

Pilger, John. "Two Years Ago...." in *Pilger in Print*. pilger.carlton.com, 12/12/02.

Pitts Jr., Leonard. "Rock Lyrics of Hatred Sweep through Europe, America." *Miami Herald*
(via *Seattle Times*), 2/7/93.

——. "Plucky Chicks Victims of Southern Conservatism." *Miami Herald* (via *Seattle Times)*,
5/4/03.

Pollack, Phyllis. *Straight Outta Compton*. Liner-note essay. Priority Records reissue CD, 2002.

Poundstone, William. (c.1983), public.planetmirror.com.

prorev.com. "Recovered History." *The Progressive Review*.

Raab, Barbara. "Singer-Songwriter Janis Ian Faces Controversy Because Her Songs Deal
with Society's Issues." freedomforum.org, 6/20/00.

Raz, Guy. "WGTB Tribute." *Washington City Paper* (via dcrtv.com), 1/29/99.

Redwing. "Rage and Sting: The Show Must Go On. Notes on Defeating the Concert Police."
Revolutionary Worker no. 1030, 11/14/99 [rwor.org].

Ressner, Jeffrey. "To Sticker or Not to Sticker..." *Rolling Stone*, 2/7/91.

Reuters. "Cambodia Has New Weapon in War on Karaoke—Tanks," 12/26/01.

Riddle, Randy A. "Ray Bourbon's Story: Nightclub Scene." coolcatdaddy.com.

Roeser, Steve. "Link Wray: Guitar Godhead." *Goldmine*, 2/13/98.

Romano, Michael. "FBI Had 33-page File on John Denver." *Denver Rocky Mountain News*
(via Media Awareness Project [mapinc.org]), 1/15/00.

Ross, Mike. "O'Connor? Oh My! Singer's No Stranger to Controversy." Express Writer [www.ca-
noe.ca], 8/8/97.

Royko, Mike. "Music To Get Pregnant By." *Stereo Review*, 5/76.

RRC. *Rock & Rap Confidential,* newsletter issues no. 133 (5/96), no. 158 (12/98), no. 169
(2/00), no. 172 (5/00), no. 173 (7/00), no. 198 (5/03), etc.

Russell, Charles. "Lyric Evangel Warns Of 'Filth in Music.'" *Seattle P-I*, 1/3/55.

Sadin, Glenn. "Nihon no Pops: Japanese Pop from the 1950s to the 1990s." home.earth-
link.net/~glenn_mariko/rokabiri.htm.

Seattle Daily Times. "Is Jazz Menace to Civilization? Worse than Booze, Say Club Women," 6/13/21.

——. "Jazz, Like Music of the Savage, Harms Nervous System, Says Doctor," 6/14/21.

——. "Jazz Music All Right; Fault Lies With Dancers, Says Woman Musician," 6/16/21.

Seattle P-I. "Ind. Gov. Hears Obscene Words On Record," 1/24/64.

——. "The Rock Fest," editorial, 9/7/69.

——. "$2,000 Worth of Rock Records Set Afire by Church," 5/3/82.

——. "Rapper to Pull 'Cop Killer' from Album," 7/29/92.

——. "Mob Rap: Mafia Folk Songs," 11/30/01.

Seattle Times. "Hot Cha! Jazz Intoxication Study Asked in Legislature," 12/22/33.

——. "Wal-Mart Versus Smut," editorial, 12/20/96.

——."Tough Anti-Crime Proposals Bring Out Protesters in Paris," 1/26/03.

——. "Richard Sinnott Was Behind Boston Bans," obituary (Associated Press), 5/4/03.

——. "People," 5/25/03.

Sheheri, Tami. "Rocky Mountain High: Was It Cocaine?" APBnews.com, 4/20/99.

Simon, Jeremy. "'55-Year-Old Hippie' Tom Shipley Still Laughing About 'One Toke.' *Knight-Ridder*, 7/96.

slrkull.tripod.com. "Why Rap Sucks," slrkull.tripod.com/rap/why.

Solbrekken, Max. "Addictions," mswm.org.

Staples, Brent. "The Trouble with Corporate Radio: The Day the Protest Music Died." *New York Times*, 2/20/03.

Steinberg, Josh. "Rubin 'Hurricane' Carter." Quoting 1975 *Penthouse* interview. www.angelfire.com/ma3/SteinDawg18/main.

Strauss, Neil. "Wal-Mart CD Policy Results in Passive Form of Censorship." *NY Times* (via *Seattle P-I*), 12/2/96.

Strickman, Andrew. "Army Questions Spearhead Mom—Band's protest ways draws military inquiries," RollingStone.com /news, 4/3/03.

Superville, Darlene. "FBI Probed Composer Copland in 1950s." AP, *Seattle P-I*, 5/11/03.

Sylvester, Bruce. "American Dreamer: The Life of a 'Modern Day Johnny Appleseed.'" *Goldmine*, 4/11/97.

Taylor, Sam. "Banned! The Records 'They' Didn't Want You to Hear." *Q*, 3/96.

Tennessean News Services (Nashville). "Station Drops Song Following Reaction," 5/3/97.

Texas Monthly, 6/03 [via democraticunderground.com, 6/19/03].

Thomas, Karen. "Wal-Mart Bans Sheryl Crow Album over Lyric." *USA Today*, 9/11/96.

Thompson, Stephen. "Collectormania." Quoting E.J. Solomon's letter to *Radio Guide* editor, 3/9/35. *Goldmine*, 5/10/96.

The Times of India. "Music Heard on Kabul Radio after Five Years," 11/13/01.

Tower/Pulse. "Smells Like Teen Censorship," 6/98.

tvparty.com. "The Smothers Brothers Show."

ukcia.org (UK Cannabis Internet Activists). "Reefer Madness Rears Its Ugly Head."

Venezia, Todd. "FBI Just Said No to Beach Boys." APBnews.com, 5/9/00.

Wallis, William. "'Dirty Dancing' Generates Indignation in West Africa." *Seattle Times*, 8/2/98.

washingtonpost.com. "DJs Suspended for Playing Dixie Chicks," 5/6/03.

Waycross Journal-Herald. "WAYX Bans the Beatles, Listeners Back Action: For Religious Slur" (8/8/66); and "Beatle Bonfire in Waycross" (8/9/66).

White, C.W. "The History of Boston Rock & Roll." Orig. 1985; dirtywater.com.

White, Ellen G. "Address to the Young," in *Testimonies from the Church No. 12.* Essay compilation, 1867, [egwestate.andrews.edu].

Wilson-McLeish, David. "'Work It': How Disco Got Down," www.ePeak.sfu, 4/8/02.

Winfield, B.H. "Because of the Children: Decades of Attempted Controls of Rock 'n' Rap Music," in Winfield and Davidson, *Bleep! Censoring Rock and Rap Music.*

Wolfe, L. "MTV Is the Church of Satan," www.alternativescentral.com/turnoffyourtelevision.

Wolk, Douglas. "Widespread Panic Hits the Radio: And the Banned Play On." *Village Voice,* 9/26/01.

Woods, Karen. "Police On My Back." *Spin,* 9/92.

wowessays.com. "Death of a Great Composer."

Yahoo! News. "Keep Your Children Away from Marilyn Manson—Mayor." uk.yahoo-inc.com, 2/13/01.

Authors's Interviews

Alexander, Pernell. Seattle, 1988.

Ballard, Hank. Seattle, 1989.

Berry, Richard (song composer). Tacoma, 1983.

Dennon, Jerry (President, Jerden Records). 1986–98.

Kingsmen, The (Jack Ely, Mike Mitchell, Dick Peterson). By telephone, 1984–2000.

Morrison, H.O. "Morrie" (dance instructor). Seattle, 1983.

O'Day, Pat (Seattle radio DJ). Seattle, 1987–2000.

Paul Revere and the Raiders (Paul Revere, Mike Smith, Jim Valley, Phil Volk). Seattle and Reno, 1985–2000.

Simmons, Jeff (member of Frank Zappa band). Seattle, 1985–2000.

Ventures, The (Don Wilson, Bob Bogle, Nokie Edwards). Los Angeles and Seattle, 1988–95.

United States Government Documents

Department of Justice / FBI. 1951–53 documents, File # 62-95834: "Josephine Baker Special Inquiry," foia.fbi.gov.

——. 5/25/65 document: "Recording 'Louie Louie.'" Acquired by author via FOIA, 1998.

——. 10/22/69 document: "Phonograph Record Entitled 'Rehearsals for Retirement' by Phil Ochs Threat against The President," Rhino.com.

——. 1972 documents: "John Winston Lennon," foia.fbi.gov.

——. 8/1/89 document: Letter from Assist. Dir. Milt Ahlerich to Priority Records re: N.W.A. Via *Straight Outta Compton* CD booklet, 2002.

——. "FTC Releases Second Follow-Up Report on the Marketing of Violent Entertainment to Children." Press release, 12/5/01 [ftc.gov].

FCC. 3/5/71 document, Notice 71-205: "Licensee Responsibility to Review Records Before Their [sic] Broadcast."

NARA (National Archives and Records Administration)."When Nixon Met Elvis," http://www.nara.gov/exhall/nixon.

U.S. Government Memorandum. "Bureau Tour 12-31-70," 1/4/71, thesmokinggun.com.

U.S. Senate. Senate Hearing 99-529: "On Contents of Music and the Lyrics of Records," 9/19/85. Courtesy of U.S. Senate Committee on Commerce, Science, and Transportation.

Web Sites of Interest

Amnesty International—www.amnesty.org

Blue Pages: The Encyclopedic Guide to 78 R.P.M. Party Records—www.hensteeth.com

Fileroom, (The)—www.thefileroom.org

The Freedom Forum Online—www.freedomforum.com

Freedom of Information Act—www.foia.fbi.gov

Free Expression Clearinghouse—www.freeexpression.org

FREEMUSE—www.freemuse.org

Index On Censorship—www.indexonline.org

Massachusetts Music Industry Coalition—www.massmic.com

Media Awareness Project—www.mapinc.org

The Memory Hole—www.blancmange.net

National Coalition against Censorship—www.ncac.org

Peacefire—www.peacefire.org

Protest Records—www.protest-records.com

Reefermadness.org—www.reefermadness.org

Rock & Rap Confidential—www.rockrap.com

Rock Out Censorship—www.theroc.org

The Rumor Mill News Agency—www.rumormillnews.com

SAFE (MIT Students Assoc. for Freedom of Expression)—www.mit.edu/activities/safe/home

The Smoking Gun—www.thesmokinggun.com

Tabootunes.com—www.tabootunes.com

Urban Legends Archive—www.urbanlegends.com

Urban Legends Reference Pages—www.snopes.com

Acknowledgments

Taboo Tunes is the result of more than two decades of research, and in its creation I was aided and abetted by countless kind folks: authors, cyber-pals, DJs, historians, librarians, media archivists, musicians, musicologists, record collectors, and reporters. It would require a book-length list to acknowledge them all individually, but a few that I must salute include the crews at the Index on Censorship and FREEMUSE organizations, along with Dave Marsh and his comrades at *Rock & Rap Confidential,* whose pioneering (and ongoing) anti-censorship work have been particularly inspiring. Additionally, I'd like to offer a tip of the hat to a couple of friends who showed a keen interest in this work, but just couldn't stick around long enough to see its publication: writer and musicologist Robert Palmer (RIP), and Park Avenue Records' Bob Jeniker (RIP). I have also benefited from the general encouragement and/or sage advice received from friends including Adam, Angel, Charley, Jeff, Joe, Judy, Kay, Keith, Ken, Larry, Michael, Rob, Steve, and Walt. Also appreciated are all my friends at the Smithsonian Institution, the Association for Recorded Sound Collections (ARSC), the ARChive of Contemporary Music, the Rock and Roll Hall of Fame, the Country Music Foundation, and the Experience Music Project. Friends at Alternative Tentacles Records, Bop Street Records, Fallout Records, Golden Oldies Records, Park Avenue Records, Rockaway Records, and Sub Pop have also been most helpful. Extra-special kudos must go out to Laurie McEachron who—dig this!—actually *volunteered* to edit my original manuscript —an axing that was a pivotal advance in the book's qualitative evolution. Another giant leap was the final edit done by my copyeditor, Joseph Newland...thanks for watching my back as usual—great to work with you once again! It should also be confessed here that I honestly assumed that it would require an epic struggle to find a publisher willing to take this book on. And so, it was a major surprise when Richard

Johnston (my executive editor at Backbeat Books) recognized the merits of *Taboo Tunes* and then made our negotiation process both fun and easy. From there he, along with managing editor Nancy Tabor, marketing manager Nina Lesowitz, and their fine team, made heroic efforts to see that this book was published with an eye to timeliness. Then too, I appreciate David Beck's contribution of the hilarious cover illustration. Thanks again to all who helped! Most importantly, I thank my sweet wife Kate who willingly agreed to slog through my first unreadable draft—and also provided unfailing support within the peaceful cat-nest we call home, that *really* made the writing of *Taboo Tunes* possible.

About the Author

Peter Blecha is a woefully rusty garageband drummer who served hard time in Seattle's used record shops for untold years. Then, after stints as a radio DJ and a columnist for *The Rocket* magazine, he spent nearly a decade as a senior curator with Seattle's rock 'n' roll museum, the Experience Music Project (EMP). Blecha was a member of the Washington Music Industry Coalition (WMIC) and has served as an executive board member with JAMPAC (Joint Artists and Music Promotions Political Action Committee), which contributed to the successful battles against various proposed Washington State legislature music censorship bills and to overturn Seattle's onerous teen-dance ban and anti-postering law. The author of *Wired Wood: The Origins of the Electric Guitar*, Blecha's writings have also appeared in such periodicals as *Life* magazine, *Vintage Guitar*, *DISCoveries*, *Seattle Weekly*, *Radio Guide*, *Feedback*, and *The Monthly*, as liner notes on many LPs and CDs, and via the Pacific Northwest's online regional history Web site www.historylink.org—not to mention his own new anti-censorship Web site tabootunes.com.

Index